T0358458

Business in Post-Communist Russia

It is a widely held idea that Russia has completed its revolution, which brought down the Soviet economy, and that many companies after privatisation work as typical Western companies. Another belief is that Russia has adopted a market economy but then reverted to authoritarianism. With these two ideas in mind, this book discusses the suggestion that the key element of post-Soviet economic and political reforms in the last two decades was the redistribution of assets from the state to oligarchs and the new elite. It looks at why most Russian companies could not achieve strong long-run corporate performance by analysing in detail a range of different Russian companies. The book is a useful tool for understanding the future prospects for Russian business.

Mikhail Glazunov has a PhD from the Business School at the University of Hertfordshire, UK.

Routledge Contemporary Russia and Eastern Europe Series

Business in Post-Communist Russia

Privatisation and the limits of transformation

Mikhail Glazunov

Routledge
Taylor & Francis Group

LONDON AND NEW YORK

First published 2013
by Routledge
2 Park Square, Milton Park, Abingdon, Oxon OX14 4RN

Simultaneously published in the USA and Canada
by Routledge
711 Third Avenue, New York, NY 10017

Routledge is an imprint of the Taylor & Francis Group, an informa business

British Library Cataloguing in Publication Data
A catalogue record for this book is available from the British Library

Library of Congress Cataloging in Publication Data
Glazunov, Mikhail.
    Business in post-Communist Russia : privatisation and the limits of
transformation / Mikhail Glazunov.
        pages ; cm. – (Routledge contemporary Russia and Eastern Europe
series ; 46)
    Includes bibliographical references and index.
    1. Privatization–Russia (Federation) 2. Business enterprises–Russia
(Federation) 3. Mixed economy–Russia (Federation) 4. Russia (Federation)–
Economic conditions–1991- 5. Post-communism–Economic aspects–Russia
(Federation) I. Title. II. Series: Routledge contemporary Russia and Eastern
Europe series ; 46.
    HD4215.15.G53 2013
    338.947'05–dc23
                        2012050413

ISBN: 978-0-415-63661-2 (hbk)
ISBN: 978-0-203-76678-1 (ebk)

Typeset in Times New Roman
by Taylor & Francis Books

MIX
Paper from
responsible sources
FSC
www.fsc.org   FSC® C013604

Printed and bound in Great Britain by
CPI Group (UK) Ltd, Croydon, CR0 4YY

Contents

Illustrations

Figures

Tables

About the author

Mikhail Glazunov is an independent consultant, writer and a visiting university lecturer. He graduated from Moscow State University in BSc (Hons) Psychology and studied business at the Russian Presidential Academy of National Economy (MBA) and then went on to develop his academic career at the University of Hertfordshire (PhD Economics).

He began his career as a social psychologist in industrial companies and after was appointed as a researcher for the State University of Management (Moscow). Since 1991, he was an active participant of the privatisation process in Russia. The prime focus of his career has included seven years as Chief Executive Officer of a paper company and many years of experience as a consultant in the gas, paper, car, consumer goods and financial service sectors. He is a highly experienced expert in Russian business practice.

His main research interest is the investigation of corporate performance in Russia. He has dedicated special attention towards how to deliver strategic ideas, having understood the financial implications, and in how financial decisions are made in the context of corporate strategy.

Mikhail is 50 years old and divides his time between Moscow and Bedfordshire, UK.

Acknowledgements

I want to thank Sowden Peter, my editor at Routledge. Peter's positive editorial experience has proven invaluable in enabling a Russian researcher to write for readers beyond the limitations of the traditional approach. Many thanks to the staff at Routledge, in particular, Jillian Morrison. I would like to thank my collaborators Elena Zhukova, Nicolas Anderson and the rest of the supportive team, who have been my daily intellectual colleagues for the last few years.

For the duration of putting my book together, I have benefited from intellectual discourse with Professor Colin Haslam from the University of Hertfordshire, who inspired me with many ideas for my writing. I am thankful for the substantial advice that he provided, and for his aid in configuring and adjusting the chapters in order for the book to take its final shape and reach completion.

The University of Hertfordshire is my intellectual home and for the duration of writing this book I was surrounded by a wonderful scientific atmosphere. I am grateful to everyone at the University of Hertfordshire Business School that has made this book possible. My colleagues at the University of Hertfordshire merit particular acknowledgement too. Ya Ping Yin, Edward Lee and Nick Tsitsianis have my gratitude for their moral support and constructive criticism. I would like to make special note to Professor Jane Hardy and Professor Mike Haynes, who read my words with admirable care and attention, making some especially valuable suggestions that I have incorporated.

I would like to especially show appreciation to my old friend Andre Perchan, chairman of Avtoelektronika, my business partner Mikhail Galchenko, director of Kondrovo Paper Company, Vladimir Krupchak, former chairman of Arkhangelsk Paper Mill, Vladimir Kadannikov, former president of Avtovaz and Mikhail Prokhorov from Norilsk Nickel who helped me in the collection of information for my research. I have learned a lot from many other executives whose names I omit, out of discretion.

I am also deeply grateful to the people who took many hours to talk with me about their practice in Russian business and government organisation; their ideas contributed to the creation of my vision of Russia: Demidov Boris, Victor Ten and Igor Kolesnikov.

I would like to express my particular appreciation to Jane Chappell, Igor Podkovko and Philip Cox for helping me in understanding English words and idioms that frequently puzzled me. Last, but certainly not least, I want to thank my family. Most of all, of course, I must thank my wife, Maria. She surrounded me with love and support. I greatly appreciate her tolerance as she endured all stages of my research preparation with admirable patience.

Mikhail Glazunov
Bedfordshire, England
June 2012

Abbreviations

AE	Avtoelektronika
AFC	Automobile Financial Corporation (Russia)
AFH	away from home
APPM	Arkhangelsk Pulp and Paper Mill
AVVA	All-Russian Automobile Alliance
BHP	Billiton Ltd.
CAGR	compound annual growth rate
CEO	chief executive officer
CIS	Commonwealth of Independent States
EBITDA	earnings before interest, taxes, depreciation and amortisation
FDI	foreign direct investment
GDP	gross domestic product
GKI	Russian State Property Committee
GM	General Motors
HR	human resources
IAS	International Accounting Standards
IMF	International Monetary Fund
IP	International Paper
IPO	initial public offering
ISO	International Organization for Standardization
JSC	Joint-Stock Company
KGB	Committee for State Security, Soviet Union
KPC	Kondrovo Paper Company
LME	London Metal Exchange
LTD	long-term debt
M&A	mergers and acquisitions
MICEX	Moscow Interbank Currency Exchange
MVD	Ministry of Internal Affairs (Russia)
NMMP	Nornickel Norilsk Mining and Metallurgical Plant
Nornickel	Norilsk Nickel
OJS	open joint stock
P&G	Procter and Gamble
PGM	platinum group metal

R&D	research and development
RAS	Russian Accounting Standards
ROCE	return on capital employed
ROE	return on equity
ROS	return on sales
ROTA	return on total assets
RTS	Russian Trading System
SCC	Southern Copper Corp
SOE	state-owned enterprises
Stora	Stora Enso
UPM	UPM-Kymmene
USSR	Union of Soviet Socialist Republics
VEB	Vnesheconombank (Bank of Foreign Economic Activity)
WGC-3	Third Generation Company of the Wholesale Electricity Market
ZAZ	Zaporizhia Automobile Building Plant

Preface

The book reveals that Russia has completed its pseudo-revolution that brought down the Soviet system, adopted some elements of market economy, changed the pattern of ownership, however, the underlying support factors are not sufficiently robust and therefore privatisation may not deliver sustainable development of business. The Russian economic and political systems could not dramatically change the inept market institutions. After 20 years of transformation, Russia has elements of both a quasi-market economy and authoritarianism.

The outcomes of privatisation and transformation are analysed by investigating corporate performance of Russian companies in a broad economic and social context. A wide range of primary and secondary evidence has been collected and corroborated, interpreted and analysed on the basis of relevant (institutional) economic and accounting frameworks. The main question addressed by the book is why most Russian companies could not achieve a strong long-run corporate performance. The post-reform quality of the business (from both operational management and strategic perspectives) is comparable to the pre-reform level.

The book shows that the key element of post-Soviet economic and political reforms in the last two decades was the redistribution of assets from the state to oligarchs and the new elite. The Russian economic and political reforms become more comprehensible only if we understand that they are an instrument of redistribution of property rights.

Introduction

It is a widely held opinion that Russia has completed its revolution that brought down the Soviet economy and that many companies after privatisation work as typical Western companies. Another belief is that Russia has adopted a market economy but then reverted to authoritarianism.

Contrary to that first position, there was not total Russian revolution in the early 1990s but merely replacement of one group with another. The dissolution of the Soviet Union was determined by centrifugal forces of the national republics and the inability of President Gorbachev, the central government and the KGB to protect the imperial construction. Modern Russia is a feudal society, where many Russian companies depend upon an autocratic regime and continue to employ old-fashioned models of management despite some modernisation lustre.

These two approaches describe these and other aspects of the Russian existence. Not denying the importance of these approaches, this book rests upon the idea that the key element of post-Soviet economic and political reforms in the last two decades was the redistribution of assets from the state to oligarchs and the new elite. Moreover, the Russian economic and political reforms in the last two decades become more comprehensible only if we understand that Russian reforms are an instrument of redistribution of property rights.

Privatisation has changed the economic business environment in Russia and caused managers to bring about dramatic change in corporate governance, strategic priorities and performance. There is a transient process of adjustment of the company to work as an independent manufacturer. This transient process affects different corporate functions: finance, human resources, operations, marketing and logistics.

Two central issues are relevant: first, there are many empirical studies on the effect of divestment on the operating performance of former state-owned enterprises and a large proportion of these studies employ the traditional econometric methodology that does not serve as an adequate instrument for in-depth case studies of post-privatisation performance. As a result, they rarely give adequate detailed explanations as to why corporate performance changed after divestment.

Second, despite the considerable privatisation experience of Russia this phenomenon is still a black box as there is little empirical understanding of the critical issues involved, namely: (1) Why has privatisation succeeded in many countries of Eastern Europe but was relatively unsuccessful in Russia? (2) How has privatisation changed Russian companies? (3) What impact has privatisation had on the financial and operating performance of divested firms?

The main question addressed by the book is why most Russian companies could not achieve strong long-run corporate performance. The author's investigation of the privatisation process in Russia reveals that company-level case analysis should be a valuable investigative object. As a result, we have employed two possible research strategies: an investigation of the determinants of privatisation outcomes by focusing on business environment, corporate governance and strategy, institutional development and economic reforms. The second strategy is an explanation of how the transfer of ownership to private investors can affect corporate performance. This book attempts to answer these questions by analysing a comprehensive database of different Russian companies.

A broad investigation of the Russian economy gives many examples of both success and failure of privatised companies and this prompts a number of questions: Why is one company successful and yet others fail? Why have some firms managed to reorganise and adapt to new conditions, taking advantage of the opportunities created by economic reform, whereas other managers have experienced the opposite? How have strategic objectives changed after privatisation of the company? How can we assess achievements and corporate performance? Privatisation has changed the economic business environment in Russia and caused managers to bring about dramatic change in corporate governance, strategic priorities and performance. Moreover, the transition of a company from state to private ownership results in changes in objectives, in corporate decision-making structures and in monitoring systems that impact on post-privatisation corporate performance.

This book explores Russian business post-communist transformation and the companies and managers that generated these changes, from the viewpoint of corporate level analysis. A central idea is that management could not dramatically overhaul corporate performance. Despite an attractive corporate portrait, the post-reform quality of the business (from both operational management and strategic perspectives) is comparable to the pre-reform level.

This book is academic but nontechnical, designed to be understandable to a wide range of readers: investors, businessman, students and people who are interested in Russian politics and the economy. The author expects that his research will provide a better understanding of what happened in the Russian economy from 1991 to 2011. In addition, the book will be a very useful tool for understanding Russian prospects today, allowing the reader to form an opinion of the prospects of future Russian business.

The structure of the book

This book is structured into 11 chapters. In the first chapter, I reveal that privatisation was central to Russian reform and the driver of transition. The chapter discloses the different perspectives on both the process of privatisation and the outcomes of Russian privatisation. This process of transition is understood from a neoclassical and institutional standpoint. The first approach argued that privatisation should be carried out and completed as quickly as possible and that quick privatisation would generate the political force necessary to support economic reforms. The second approach notes that the largest mistake of the past decade was the tendency to privatise as soon as possible without understanding the corresponding institutional infrastructure requirements. As a result, the Russian reforms created conditions for illegal activity, lobbying, corruption and growth of criminality.

Chapter 2 shows that the Russian reforms established a small number of oligarchs and concentrated enormous riches in the hands of a few but did not contribute to effective management of capital and did not make the enterprises attractive to foreign investors. Oligarchs, by virtue of the sheer scale of their accumulated wealth, stand outside of management and control of state institutions. The ability of Russian state institutions to regulate the behaviour of oligarchs is further diluted the more financially powerful the business elite becomes.

Significantly, Russian privatising concentrated on ownership and control in a few of the largest business groups that control a substantial part of Russian industry. The largest private owners and their financial–industrial groups control enterprises in a number of strategic sectors such as oil, gas, mining, metallurgy, automobiles and chemicals. Large business groups have an opportunity for arbitrage in different segments of the national economy and between the economies of the Russian regions.

However, the process of accumulation has become conjoined to capital market conditions because it is often dependent upon stock market growth, commodity price inflation and leverage. This sets up the possibility that the process of privatisation in Russia is not so much about financial transformation as the instability that can be engendered by the decisions of a few members of the business elite.

Chapter 3 reveals that there are different factors affecting corporate performance: internal to the enterprise and external to the enterprise. The internal environment comprises internal stakeholders such as the management and personnel while external factors affect firm performance in many large-scale ways, both directly and indirectly.

We add a number of additional elements that help support an understanding of the performance outcomes of Russian firms after privatisation such as being overly embedded, the nature of power relations and rent-seeking behaviour of individuals for wealth accumulation.

We establish that conditions within the country, a deficit of modern economic and political institutions, regulatory policy framework and non-transparency were paramount factors in determining the strategy and influencing outcomes from privatisation in relation to economic productivity and welfare in Russia.

Chapter 4 shows that there are many empirical studies on the effect of divestment on the operating performance of former state-owned enterprises and a large proportion of these studies employ traditional econometric methodology, which argues that there is a correlation between privatisation and corporate performance. However, these researchers tend to analyse a relatively short period of corporate life and the majority use macro-economic theories, which do not serve as an adequate instrument for in-depth case studies of post-privatisation performance. As a result, they rarely give adequate detailed explanations as to why corporate performance changed after divestment.

In this book, the research method will focus of the construction of firm-level case studies that will in turn be the product of both narratives and numbers. The narratives used in the case studies are to be collected and summarised from semi-structured interviews carried out with managers and executives of the various privatised Russian companies selected.

In addition to the collection and interpretation of narratives, this book collects financial information from the case study firms covering the period 1994 to 2008. This financial information will be structured into key performance ratios employing a nature of expenses approach with a view to also triangulating the interview material. The objective is to employ a rich financial dataset and utilise this information to make visible corporate performance in the case study firms.

Chapters 5 to 9 bring together a collection of cases about the most significant challenges that Russia's companies faced during the 15 years of transition. Step by step, this part of the book analyses the major corporate changes starting from the first years of privatisation to the financial crisis of 2008–9. Throughout the chapter, we show five case studies for Russian companies, which included Arkhangelsk Pulp and Paper Mill (pulp and wood), Norilsk Nickel (non-ferrous metal), Kondrovo Paper Company (consumer goods and packaging), Avtoelektronika (electronic components) and Avtovaz (car). These companies are different sizes, from relatively small to global, producing different types of products. These firms also have a variable impact on the national economy from insubstantial to significant; where each firm also operates with different types of operation, strategy, geographical and regional conditions. The objective is to investigate the post-privatisation performance and the factors that determine performance.

In this book, the objective has been to show that the process of connecting privatisation, changes in ownership, governance, strategy and financial outcomes is not straightforward. At the firm level, we find that ambiguity and contradiction(s) are present, which can at times promote positive outcomes or frustrate achievement.

Chapter 10 presents the conclusion and the issues arising out of the cases analysed. Specifically it reveals how ownership and control is concentrated in the hands of a few owner-managers. The analysis that has been undertaken suggests some key success factors of corporate performance. There were many external and internal factors, which determined the corporate performance of

Russian companies, and these factors were grouped in different patterns, which determined success or failure of the companies.

To summarise, all successful companies had similar patterns of internal factors such as the successfully selected sector, efficient employment of manufacturing capacity, reduced expenditure, optimisation of taxes, the absent threat of acquisition and a strong lobby; whereas, unproductive companies did not have the same adequate pattern of internal factors.

Corporate wealth of the four companies became concentrated in the hands of a few business oligarchs. Oligarchs operating in commodity industry sectors benefited from inflated commodity prices and favourable global market demand, which in turn helped to increase company cash earnings and inflate stock market valuation.

Chapter 11 considers the impact that the global financial crisis is having on the Russian economy and Russian oligarchs' business. The financial collapse has harmed Russian markets because of the weakness of the national financial system and its institutions. The Russian economy has been seriously affected by the economic crisis, because when commodity prices were at their zenith it did not diversify its economic base and launch any structural economic reforms.

The conclusion presents the authors' judgment on the transformation of Russian business and the economy for the last 25 years, and the fate of Russian business. In the conclusion, the author tries to evaluate the main approaches to the Russian renovation and find options for the sustainable development of business in Russia.

1 Russian revolution or redistribution of rights

Chapter 1 reviews the literature on privatisation from a Russian economic perspective and the justification for the wholesale privatisation of Russian state enterprise. The chapter reveals that privatisation was the central element of Russian reforms and the driver of transition, and it discloses the different perspectives of the outcomes of Russian privatisation.

The process of privatisation is understood from two standpoints. The first approach states that privatisation should be carried out and completed as quickly as possible. The supporters of shock therapy consider that this programme would guarantee economic growth with low inflation and stability. The second approach notes that the largest mistake was the tendency to privatise hastily without understanding the related institutional infrastructure requirements. As a result, transplantation of the most advanced Western institutions in the Russian environment was a failure; quick privatisation did not generate the wide political force necessary to support reforms and created conditions for corruption and growth of criminality.

The privatisation phenomena

The Depression of the 1930s, the Second World War and its aftermath and the disintegration of colonial empires forced national governments to take a more active role in the economy, including ownership of production and provision of all types of goods and services. In Western Europe, governments debated how deeply involved they should be in the regulation of the economy and which industrial sectors should be reserved specifically for state ownership. Recent privatisation programmes have significantly reduced the role of state-owned enterprises (SOEs) in the economies of most of these countries. In the case of developing and transition countries, this retreat in state ownership took place rapidly during the 1990s. In these countries, SOE share of gross domestic product (GDP) declined from more than 10 per cent in 1979 to less than 6 per cent by 2003 (Megginson 2005).

According to Vickers and Yarrow (1988), privatisation, essentially a change in the allocation of property rights, leads to a different structure of incentives for management and results in changes in both managerial behaviour and company functioning.

Privatisation now appears to be accepted as a legitimate (often a core) tool of statecraft employed by the governments of more than 100 countries. One of the most significant elements of this continuing worldwide phenomenon is the increasing reliance on markets for the efficient allocation and distribution of resources. The term privatisation is at times used narrowly to mean the transfer of previously state-owned businesses to the private sector. However, it can also be employed to describe a range of activities on the path to privatisation. A public sector organisation may go through many stages on the path to privatisation (Shleifer and Vishny 1996).

In practice, the meaning of privatisation frequently depends on a nation's position in the global economy. In non-transition economies, it is easy to deal with privatisation singularly as a question of domestic policy. Nevertheless, where the likely buyers are foreign, as in transition countries (i.e. Russia), privatisation of state-owned enterprises often means denationalisation – a transfer of control to foreign investors.

Arguments for privatisation

The set of objectives, which privatisation programmes are anticipated to achieve, are much broader and involve, as a fundamental component, the improvement of microeconomic efficiency. Although different countries have a variety of reasons for embarking upon privatisation programmes, there are some general objectives or results, which they have in common (Shleifer and Vishny 1996):

- to raise revenue for the state;
- to promote economic efficiency;
- to reduce government interference in the economy;
- to promote wider share-ownership;
- to increase competition and the role of the private sector in the economy.

Governments often undertake privatisation programmes in response to economic crises as a means of reducing their deficits from loss-making SOEs. The sale also provides immediate funds to reduce public debt and consequently generate resources, which can be allocated to other areas of government activity (Megginson 2005).

Microeconomic level of analyses

At a microeconomic level the justifications for privatisation provide a platform for the efficient utilisation of resources and optimal technical productivity and efficiency, because incentives are present. There are different perspectives on the causes of poorly performing public sector organisations and the lack of incentives. For example, the 'managerial perspective', which takes the position that incentives are absent in publicly owned firms and therefore efficient resource allocation is compromised (Vickers and Yarrow 1988).

It is argued that the managers of state-owned enterprises are poorly monitored because in these firms share capital is not traded in the capital market unlike in the private sector. This fact eliminates the threat of takeover when the company performs poorly. Because shareholders are absent, they cannot observe and influence the performance of enterprises by forcing a change in management or ownership to increase returns on capital invested (Martin and Parker 1997). Likewise, debt markets cannot play a role in disciplining managers because an SOE's debt is a public debt that is both perceived and traded under different conditions (Vickers and Yarrow 1988).

State-owned enterprises, whilst not exposed to the demands of the capital market, are exposed to political interference and this, it is argued, distorts the objectives of state enterprise (Shapiro and Willig 1990). They argue that a combination of political interference and access to soft government funding distorts the priorities of managers. According to Kornai (1988), a major source of inefficiency in public firms is the 'soft' budget of the government where the state is unlikely to allow a large SOE into bankruptcy. Thus, the discipline enforced on private firms by capital markets and the threat of financial distress is less significant for state-owned firms, and this impacts on how resources are managed and organised. It is generally argued that state enterprises operating in a competitive environment do not deliver the same profit rate of return as private businesses operating in similar product markets.

The microeconomic evidence employed to support this argument, for example, using cross-country data Shleifer and Vishny (1996) show that privatised firms improve their profitability after their sale, even allowing for macroeconomic and industry specific factors, but that part privatisation reduces profit rates compared to full privatisation.

Private investors have a particular goal to maximise the value from invested resources. In contrast, governments can have a number of aims and objectives other than just wealth maximisation and these objectives can change over time. Furthermore, Megginson and Netter (2001) argue that if a government cannot commit to a state policy framework then the efficiency of an SOE's operations will be significantly reduced. In addition, government aims regarding maximisation of social welfare are often at odds with private sector managerial priorities for profit and cash extraction. For example, reducing labour costs to extract additional profit may compromise a government's objective to maintain employment.

Macroeconomic level of analyses

It is difficult to separate the policy of privatisation from the government's need to maintain both macroeconomic stability and aggregate measures of national output and finances. The relationship between privatisation and macroeconomics comes from the fact that macroeconomic instability, particularly large budget deficits, results in accelerated privatisation. Sheshinski and López-Calva (1999) argue that there is a strong relation between higher public budget deficits and faster public sector restructuring due to poor public sector financial health having a bearing on government willingness to reform. On the one hand, poor performing state enterprise is a drain on government funding because cash and employment levels need to be underwritten, but this worsens state finances and puts pressure on tax rates and maintenance of sound monetary policies. On the other hand, privatisation can improve the public sector's financial health where state assets can be sold thereby augmenting government funds and circumventing traditional monetary policy measures.

Where privatisation is aggressively pursued, López-De-Silanes (1993) argue that, in general, privatisation reduces a government's net transfer to SOEs in the aggregate. It is argued that privatisation will generally have a negative effect on unemployment in the short run but a positive effect in the medium and long run. In addition, a distinct growth in the financial sector can be seen in countries that privatise companies through IPOs because this creates a greater opportunity for financial intermediation.

One central motivation for privatisation is to help develop liberal free markets with the general presumption, in welfare economics, that efficiency is achieved through competitive markets. Thus, to the extent that privatisation promotes competition, privatisation can have central efficiency effects. It has been clear in transition economies that the success of privatisation depends on the strength of the financial markets within the country, and vice versa. Thus, the impact of privatisation will differ across countries depending on the strength of the existing private sector. Similarly, the evidence suggests that the effectiveness of privatisation depends on institutional factors, such as the protection of investors (Megginson 2005).

The transition process

Generally, the label 'transition economy' is used to refer to the countries that transformed from a command economy to a market economy. This transformation is normally characterised by the creation of new institutions and private-owned enterprises; changes in the role of the state and different governmental institutions and developing markets and independent financial institutions. Most researchers consider the privatisation of state enterprises as the most significant part of the transition process due to the fact that private ownership is the foundation of market economies and without this, the market cannot exist.

The most significant examples of transition economies are the reforms of the former Warsaw Pact countries as well as China and Latin America. From the simple understanding of the command economy, one can easily determine the tasks of the transition process: just replace inefficiencies in elements of the socialist economies by the excellent solutions provided by the capitalist economies. Nevertheless, transition includes many social processes such as changing political institutions, legal systems, social structure, social policy and allocation mechanisms.

There were many different programmes of transition and the list of actions that governments had to carry out in countries trying the transition to a market economy was astonishing. The list of actions included (Clague 1992): development of the legal infrastructure for the new economy, inventing a new system of taxation, devising rules for the new financial sector, establishing ownership rights to existing real property, setting the rules for import and export operations, reforming prices, creating a safety net for unemployment, stabilising the economy and privatisation.

The transition from socialism to capitalism was a relatively new problem in economics, every country had specific characteristics and different implications for what it was possible to do, and as a result, the process of transition in every country was different. Nevertheless, a few models reveal this process.

Marangos (2004), for example, considers privatisation of state enterprises in transition economies as a result of alternative models of transition, based on different methods of economic analysis and speeds of implementing the transition policies, varying views of what is a good society and ideologies. Consequently, the alternative models of transition are distinguished on the basis of economic analysis, the definition of a good society, speed and ideology.

As a result, five alternative models of transition are considered: the shock-therapy model of transition; the neoclassical gradualist model of transition; the post-Keynesian model of transition; the pluralistic market socialist model of transition and the Chinese model of transition (ibid.). However, one can suggest that these five alternative models of transition are founded by two different economic paradigms namely the neoclassical and the institutional perspectives.

The neoclassical perspective

In 1989, Williamson offered the term 'Washington Consensus' to describe a set of economic policy prescriptions that should constitute the standard reform programme of transition being addressed by Washington-based institutions (IMF, the World Bank and the US Treasury Department) to Latin American countries. Structural adjustment in Latin America had the goal of replacing an established economic system with a market-based economic system (Williamson 1989).

The consensus included ten broad sets of recommendations.

- Fiscal discipline.
- Redirection of public spending from subsidies toward broad-based provision of key services like primary education, primary health care and infrastructure investment.
- Tax reform – broadening the tax base and adopting moderate marginal tax rates.

- Interest rates that are market determined and positive in real terms.
- Competitive exchange rates.
- Trade liberalization – liberalization of imports, with particular emphasis on elimination of quantitative restrictions (licensing, etc.).
- Liberalisation of inward foreign direct investment.
- Privatisation.
- Deregulation – abolition of regulations that impede market entry or restrict competition, except for those justified on safety, environmental and consumer protection grounds, and prudent oversight of financial institutions.
- Legal security for property rights.

This model was broadly accepted as a conventional approach to policies for economic development of post-socialist countries in Europe and Asia. This concept was associated with neoclassical approaches to economics and was implemented in the form of shock therapy under the principle of 'one-size-fits-all' (Stiglitz 1999). The authors of the model note that reforms should be introduced simultaneously and quickly.

Between 1990 and 1993, the shock-therapy model was initiated in the transition economies of Eastern Europe. The shock-therapy programmes included two additional policies: price liberalisation and the establishment of an independent central bank. The supporters of shock therapy considered that the elements of a programme would guarantee economic growth at full employment with low inflation and stability (Marangos 2003).

One of the major ideas of shock therapy in Eastern Europe was that transition economies were experiencing harsh macroeconomic imbalances and could not afford to reform gradually. Moreover, the political situation required a fast reform. As noted by Åslund (1995) no one can tell fire fighters to pour water slowly if your house is on fire. As a result, governments and foreign consultants established extremely short timescales for the transition process.

The shock-therapist strategy was based on the ideas of Coase (1988) who stated that initial ownership was less important as the market rapidly redistributes assets to efficient owners. Coase argues that bargaining will produce an effective result regardless of the initial allocation of property rights when transaction costs are minimal and trade in an externality is possible. However, when applying the Coase construct, the shock therapists did not take into account that the redistribution of asset depends on the availability of contracting and recontracting opportunities as well as an established legal and law enforcement system (Stiglitz 1999).

One of the major problems of the transitive economies lies in the fact that both mechanisms of the state and market regulation are limited. The necessity for forming new institutions and the process of transition create substantial difficulties with the smooth operation of the market economy.

A market cannot operate based exclusively on limited market interest. As noted by Stiglitz (1999), the price system cannot be universal and perfect; therefore, it must be supplemented by an implicit or explicit social contract.

Moreover, he remarks that one of the most difficult parts of the transition from socialism to a market economy is the transformation of the old 'implicit social contract' to a new one. This implicit social contract is essential to a market society and cannot be easily established by a reforming government. Norms and social institutions play critical roles in the success of a market economy. 'Without some minimal amount of social trust and civil norms, social interaction would be reduced to a minimum of tentative and distrustful commodity trades' (ibid.).

Stiglitz summarises two approaches in transition by metaphors. Shock therapy repairing the ship at sea: there is no 'dry dock' or Archimedean fulcrum for changing social institutions from outside the society. Change always starts with given historical institutions. Incrementalism-rebuilding the ship in dry dock. The dry dock provides the Archimedean point outside the water so the ship can be rebuilt without being disturbed by the conditions at sea (ibid.).

The institutionalist perspective

The philosophy of institutionalism based on a strategy of seeing people as a product of culture was created by Veblen. The core ideas concern institutions, habits, rules and their evolution. According to Hodgson (1998), institutions are systems of conventional social rules that organise social interactions and they include formal rules, informal conventions, habits, norms and values. This approach progresses from broad ideas relating to human society, institutions and the evolutionary nature of economic development to particular ideas and theories that are related to specific economic institutions. On the contrary, the neoclassical approach moves from a universal abstract framework relating to rational choice and behaviour and moves straight to theories of price and economic welfare (Hodgson 1998). Institutionalism pays more attention to interrelationships between elements of reforms as well as institutional factors of reforms.

The institutional approach to transformation suggests that transitional economies of Eastern Europe were not homogenous, moreover, every country had an individual logic of transition and there were key dissimilarities. First, there was diversity in the preliminary conditions resulting from the evolution of economies before transition. Second, there were different political, social and economic paths after 1989. Third, there was a variety of external influences. Finally, there were impulsive adaptations and transformations of institutions according to nationally specific societal contexts (Chavance and Magnin 1997). They note common trends in these economies can consequently be summarised under different causal directions: the post-socialist features, institutional movements towards the West, the wish to join the European Union, the influence of international organisations and their conditionality.

All programmes of reform in post-Soviet countries included similar elements because they occurred simultaneously and employed comparable theoretical concepts. As noted by Summers (1992), there was consensus amongst economists about the elements of reform and what had to be done: macro-economic stabilisation, price and market reform, enterprise reform and restructuring (including privatisation) and institutional reform. He adds that despite the fact that there was consensus over the nature of the reforms to be implemented; the chronological sequence of reforms was disputed. One can say that the order of elements of reforms and their timing were the critical factors of success of reforms in all European countries.

Privatisation and transition

Privatisation of state enterprises in transition economies was the key component of transformation. The 1990s revealed a new experience of privatisation that started from a centrally administered economy and undeveloped private property. In general, the prevailing method of privatisation depends on the nature of the country and its government's strategies.

There were a few alternative ways in which privatisation could take place. Restitution-returning a property to former owners who could prove their past ownership before the state expropriated their property, the sale of state property by auctioning state enterprises and the transfer of ownership of enterprises to various financial intermediaries such as pension funds, management funds, banks and government agencies.

Other mechanisms of privatisation include the distribution of different kinds of vouchers, leasing state property to individuals or companies, management buy-out, labour-managed firms and transferring the ownership of the enterprise from the state to the workforce.

Numerous investigations attempt to explain the outcome of the transition in Central and Eastern Europe and different national factors that determined them. A list of factors that could probably have a principal influence on the success of transition as well as the privatisation process has been offered by many researchers. An example could be the list by Rutland (1995) who evaluated the relative success of some European countries in implementing mass privatisation.

Economic factors:

- A stable, convertible currency.
- A stable or growing GDP.
- A boom in exports, generating cash for needed imports.
- Modest unemployment, to avoid social tension.
- The establishment of effective bankruptcy procedures, to accelerate restructuring.

Political factors:

- The emergence of a cohesive, technically competent team of top administrators.
- Support from strong political leadership.
- Conjunctural factors (a window of opportunity).

- Public support for the programme.
- Consensus among the political and economic elite in favour of the programme.

Administrative factors:

- General bureaucratic capacity (efficient, non-corrupt civil servants).
- The laying down of a strict timetable.
- Existence of a clear and reliable legal structure to adjudicate disputes and monitor implementation.
- The creation of a separate specialised bureaucracy tasked with designing and implementing the programme.
- Support from international agencies.
- A decentralised process to minimise opposition while maximising administrative capacity.

Privatisation in Russia

On reflection, the crisis and collapse of socialism in the last decades of the twentieth century was natural and inevitable. The arguments in support of this conclusion are outlined in a number of publications. Gaidar (2005) states that the socialist model of development in the USSR was forged in the model of 'industrialization' and he characterises aspects of the socialist model of economic growth as domination of state ownership, liquidation of private property holdings and a dominant role of the state in mobilisation and distribution of national savings. The model includes the formation of an administrative hierarchy to coordinate economic activities by direct supervision and rigid political control excluded any unauthorised forms of mass activity.

Åslund (1995) also identified how this approach to state enterprise and ownership led to inefficiencies in the economy, which he argues results from the primacy of politics over economics. Managers tried to maximise their loyalty to their political masters who promoted them and economic objectives were focused on quantitative production targets rather than efficiency, profits or future value. Prices played a subordinate role in the process determining the allocation and distribution of resources. Allocation decisions were based on political judgments, and only after these considerations were price issues reviewed. Existing prices served a useful economic function and some had been frozen for decades. As an illustration, at that time, bread cost remarkably little and often private producers used it as fodder for cattle and as a result the country had a large shortage of bread and millions of tonnes of wheat had to be imported.

Between 1989 and 1991, the Soviet price system was in disarray. Some prices floated freely and rose enormously because of the colossal monetary overhang, while most other prices remained regulated. Companies had little incentive to improve efficiency, quality or technology because they were neither oriented toward making profit, nor were they subject to competition. The growth rate declined significantly, however official statistics did not fully mirror this worsening situation.

The basis of growth in the Soviet economy during the 1970s–1980s was in oil revenue and despite the symptoms of an economic crisis emerging, the Soviet government ignored the signals. The decline in growth of the oil industry began at the beginning of the 1980s (see Table 1.3). Growth in oil output halted: 1980 – 603 million tonnes, 1985 – 595 million tonnes (Gaidar 2005). Between 1970–80 export volume had grown by 62 per cent, and consequently favourable dynamics export prices had increased by 370 per cent. Between 1980 and 1985, the volume of exports had grown by only 7.4 per cent reaching a record $91.4 billion in 1983. Thereafter it declined to $86.7 billion in 1985 (ibid.). Instead of directing additional free resources on a painless transition from socialism to the market economy, oil revenues were employed to fund global scientific and military projects, which did not generate market value.

In 1985, Gorbachev's most significant objective was to stimulate the national economy. However, the government made many mistakes such as when there was a decrease of both oil prices and budget income and the government was stimulating investment expenditures; managers of companies were delegated unlimited authority with no adequate system of monitoring their economic behaviour.

After some serious economic failures, Mikhail Gorbachev initiated his political reforms such as the development of education and the spread of information about the wider world to neutralise his opponents within the party elite. These factors are defined within the powerful democratic wave, which quickly occurred after the departure of authoritarian control. According to Mau (2005), the main result of Gorbachev's economic reforms was the dramatic growth of the economic crisis. The features of such a crisis were the beginning of economic decline with rapid growth of the population's nominal income, the rapid decrease of the tax base with a budget deficit approaching 30 per cent of GDP and dramatic growth in external debt.

In 1991, the country was on the brink of widespread hunger, which threatened to also spread to the main industrial centres. In fact, the USSR ceased to exist in December of that year and this left Russia without stable state

Table 1.1 Indicators of the performance of the oil industry of USSR

	1980	*1985*	*1987*	*1991*
Oil output million tonnes	603	595	624	515
price per barrel ($)*	66.1	39.3	24.9	22.9
Export million tonnes	119.1	129.5	136	61

Note: * The price of oil in the prices 2000.
Source: International Financial statistics 2005, IMF; Goskomstat of Russia, Moscow; cited in Gaidar (2005).

barriers, an army and enforcement systems. With a giant shortage of goods and the threat of hunger, there were powerful separatist trends in Russia. Regional administrations wanted full control over their production in order to free themselves from national market or legislative demands. All this resulted in Yeltsin carrying out urgent liberal reforms at the end of 1991.

Stages of Russian privatisation

The starting point of privatisation in the Soviet economy is not one that is easy to identify because this concept did not exist in Soviet economic doctrine. At first, there were only a small number of privatisations and these were often portrayed as administrative innovations rather than privatisations. It is also important to note that from 1987–8 the management committees of state companies began to appropriate at least part of company profits, benefiting from the weakness of the legislation and state control and psychologically they started to feel like owners rather than hired managers.

Kim and Yelkina (2003) write that before Russian privatisation began on a large scale in 1992, there was a pre-privatisation stage called the commercialisation stage or what we might observe as a spontaneous privatisation (1987–92). The large-scale Russian privatisation that followed this process of commercialisation can be classified into two stages: mass privatisation (1992–4) and cash privatisation (1994–7). Later, in 1997 to the present day, the government realised case-by-case privatisation without a strong impact upon the national economy.

Commercialisation (1987–92)

The key target of the Soviet elite at this time, now referred to as the commercialisation stage, was building up capital to prepare the country for subsequent privatisation. One of the key policies was the creation of cooperatives, small businesses and joint ventures. As a result, this stage gave rise to many semi-private enterprises and helped lay the foundation for real privatisation. It should be borne in mind that any attempt at categorising the forms of spontaneous privatisation would be rather conventional. Nevertheless, the following fundamental forms may be chosen as characteristic of 1990–1: bureaucratic privatisation at local and national level; tenders and auctions conducted by local authorities; collective enterprises; privatisation by management also referred to as 'managerial privatisation'.

In 1991, many ministries and departments of national and regional level tried, one way or another, to secure the maximum number of enterprises under their jurisdiction and management. That period alone saw the creation of 126 concerns, 54 associations and about 1,500 amalgamations, many of which were given a right to manage property (Radygin 1995).

Starting from 1991, tenders and auctions conducted by local and city authorities at their own risk were used quite actively and this created numerous new owners. 'Collective enterprise' (the company is owned and controlled by the people who work in it, relatively few employees) was very often used by companies in the areas of retail trade, the public catering and the consumer servicing sectors. In these sectors, enterprises were first leased and then offered as an outright buy-out to work collectives. In the Russian Federation, within the limits of what is termed 'small' privatisation, more than 12,000 (3 per cent of the enterprises of the retail trade) shops were privatised, about 14,000 (7 per cent of restaurants) restaurants and other public catering establishments, and over 12,000 (14 per cent of workshops) tailoring and other workshops (IET 1994).

One more trend in spontaneous privatisation is conventionally known as managerial privatisation. This was a package of measures designed to transfer ownership from state-owned enterprises to private hands without accompanying special permission from the relevant state authorities. In this case, the initiative rested with top executives of the state enterprises themselves.

When spontaneous privatisation was carried out, the following methods could be employed: accumulation of assets to buy out the enterprise through cooperatives' use of state equipment and materials for the manufacture of goods or supply of services within a private enterprise; contribution of a state share to a joint enterprise; creation of various types of private holding companies; registration of a state enterprise with subsequent withdrawal of the state founder; purchase of state property at reduced prices for private use (Radygin 1995).

Mass privatisation 1992–4

On 29 December 1991, the president of Russia signed a decree, causing the privatisation programme of state and municipal enterprises to begin on 1 January 1992 (Collected legal papers 1994). A final version of the programme of privatisation was actually a compromise, on the one hand between paid and free privatisation and, on the other hand, between a model of privatisation for all and the division of property among the workers of enterprises.

Mau (2000) writes that the government did not have control over state assets, which actually had already been allocated to management of enterprises. One of the factors, which had propelled rapid voucher privatisation, was the widespread buy-out of rented assets, a system that had become a free-of-charge transfer of assets. By means of privatisation, the government aspired to solve problems by strengthening their own political position, and formatting a coalition to affect economic reform. These assets acted as a powerful argument in the formation of unions between political forces and influential groups of economic interests. Privatisation was a counteraction to the threat of the restoration of communism where the condition of the state was weak.

According to the programme, the privatisation objectives were the emergence of a socially oriented market economy, together with the enhancement the efficiency of enterprises, social infrastructure development using the revenue from privatisation, contribution to financial stability and a competitive economy, de-monopolisation and the attraction of foreign investors.

In 1992–3, according to the programme, the following privatisation methods were envisaged (Collected legal papers 1994):

- Sale of ownership interests (shares) in the capital of corporatised state-owned enterprises, including private offerings to the management and employees and going public through voucher and money auctions.
- Sale of enterprises at auctions.
- Sale of enterprises through commercial tenders.
- Sale of enterprises through non-commercial investment tenders.
- Sale of property (assets) of enterprises being liquidated and already liquidated.
- Buy-out of rented assets.

All state-owned enterprises were divided into three groups (ibid.):

- Small businesses (with an average workforce of up to 200 employees and book value of less than one million roubles on 1 January 1992) would be sold at auctions and tenders.
- Large enterprises (with an average workforce of more than 1,000 employees or a book value of more than 50 million roubles on 1 January 1992) would be privatised by being transformed into open joint stock companies.
- The remaining enterprises could be privatised by any approach laid down in the programme.

The programme quickly established almost free-of-charge privatisation for most large and medium-sized enterprises. Special lists defined enterprises as available for privatisation and not available for privatisation by decree of the government. The value of an enterprise's property was accepted as a starting estimation of the enterprise's balance sheet. The programme did not permit any methods of privatisation except for those, which were clearly stipulated.

Privatisation vouchers could be used as securities with a limited term of validity. Vouchers with a face value of 10,000 roubles were issued to the bearer with a right of sale. To create vouchers, GKI valued 35 per cent of all state property at 1,400 billion roubles using 1991 balance sheet prices and divided that figure by Russia's population of 148 million (Radygin 1995) resulting in a share worth 10,000 roubles, the voucher's face value.

The goal was to make all Russian citizens owners of private property as quickly as possible with the least amount of social conflict. These vouchers could be used to bid for and buy shares in companies at privatisation auctions and were a compulsory means of payment in the privatisation of state shares. Voucher validity was scheduled to expire on 1 July 1994. In the 20 months of the voucher programme, the voucher price reached a low of $4 and a high of more than $20 (Boycko *et al.* 1995). Citizens had three options with the vouchers: exchanging them for a share in voucher investment funds, selling them for cash or exchanging them for a share in privatised companies.

The infrastructure for a capital market was created according to the presidential decree of 7 October 1992 and other such documents. Russian legislation provided for the creation of investment funds and specialised privatisation funds that would accumulate privatisation vouchers on behalf of the population. In contrast to all other investment funds, a voucher fund had exclusive rights to exchange its own shares for citizens' privatisation vouchers. After collecting vouchers, voucher investment funds participated in privatisation auctions to exchange vouchers for shares in privatised companies.

The exclusive function of the voucher privatisation funds was to carry out mass privatisation because investment resources were dispersed (as was the case with the population's vouchers) and the population lacked knowledge of the investment and securities market.

In June 1994, there were 630 such funds. During 1993 and the first half of 1994 these funds acquired more than 45 million vouchers, and more than 25 million people became shareholders in them. By May 1994, all the funds together had invested as many as 27 million privatisation vouchers (IET 1995). A few years later all privatisation funds were closed and as a result most minor shareholders lost their vouchers.

The actual process of privatisation in 1992–4 was very dynamic. In the course of small-scale privatisation, by 1 July 1994 more than 50 per cent of all small enterprises were privatised. The most common method of small-scale privatisation was a lease with a buy-out right and contest (IET 1995).

In the course of large-scale privatisation, by 1 July 1994, 74 per cent of all state enterprises were privatised, while on 1 January 1993 the corresponding figure was 22 per cent (IET 1995). By the middle of 1994, Russia had about 50 million shareholders in the new joint stock companies or voucher investment funds (Privatisation in figures 1994). The private sector made up 62 per cent of Russian gross national product in 1994 (IET 1995).

Even though the number of companies privatised was very large, funding to the government was not so significant and government receipts from

Table 1.2 Key indicators of privatisation developments in the RF

Cumulative totals since January 1, 1992, as of:	1.1 1993	1.1 1994	7.1 1994
State-owned enterprises (units)	204998	156635	138619
Privatisation applications implemented	46815	88577	103796
State-owned enterprises transformed into OJS Companies	2376	14073	20298
Leased enterprises	22216	20886	20606
Including leased with option to buy (units)	13868	14978	15658

Source: IET (1996), Russia in Figures 1995.

privatisation in 1992–4 were just 1,129 billion roubles (Russia in Figures 1998). This represented around 0.2 per cent of GDP in 1992–4.

During 1992 there began a process of concentration of share capital originally distributed during voucher privatisation. This is evident in the example of the rising share of top management and external shareholders (see Table 1.3).

Privatisation process in 1994–7 (cash privatisation)

Mass privatisation in Russia had all but finished by 1 July 1994, when 97 per cent of vouchers had been exchanged for shares in large- and medium-sized companies. However, a large proportion of securities issued by large- and medium-sized companies belonged to the state. The Russian government controlled 126,000 state enterprises and 19 per cent of shares of open joint-stock companies, which had been created during 1993–4 (Russia in Figures 1997). The most economically significant enterprises were primarily in the fuel and energy, metallurgy, telecommunications and food industry sectors.

On 22 July 1994, the president signed Decree 1535, and a new stage of privatisation began and a change strategy was required for this second stage of Russian privatisation (The Russian Legislation 1995). The new stage of privatisation was known as 'cash privatisation'. This name is connected with a policy on updating the budget. One uses the term 'cash privatisation' to submit to the stage following preliminary configuration of private property, first allocation in voucher auctions, and succeeding redistribution and concentration in the hands of enterprises' directorates and favoured private investors. However, the term is not acceptable for numerous reasons. The price of a privatisation transaction was rarely the major issue in a sale.

Glinkina (2005) writes that more vital was the political component of the privatisation process and the degree of influence of company managers upon political authorities. Usual forms of share redistribution involved lobbying by privileged participants to get substantial shares remaining in the hands of authorities and unfriendly absorption of firms into holdings or financial–industrial groups. Also, legalised dilution of state-owned shares through

Table 1.3 Distribution of share holdings in OJS companies created during privatisation

	April 1994	December 1994	March 1995	June 1995
Internal shareholders	62	60	60	56
Workers	53	49	47	43
Executives	9	11	13	13
External shareholders	21	27	28	33
Institutional owners	11	16	17	22
People	10	11	11	11
State	17	13	12	11
Total	100	100	100	100

Survey of 1000 open joint-stock companies created in 26 regions of Russia. December 1994. Adapted from IET (1994, 1995).

conversion of debt into equity, sale of receivables and manipulation of dividends on privileged shares and unannounced capital increases. All of this was in addition to the purchasing of shares of investment institutions and employees on the secondary market by the company executives.

The major objects of 'cash privatisation' classified into three types: state shareholdings in the privatised enterprises, sites of the privatised enterprises and real estate. All enterprises with a balance sheet value of fixed assets over 20 million roubles as of 1 January 1994 were to be transformed into open joint stock companies (JSCs). Their shares could be sold by any of the methods mentioned earlier.

All other enterprises were considered to be small and were to be privatised through auctions, commercial or investment tenders. The final sale price should be determined during the auctions or tenders. The starting valuation threshold was moved up and was now based on the book value as of 1 January 1994. The enterprises were to be sold employing a sequence of three methods (The Russian Legislation 1995):

- Sale of shares to the employees through a closed subscription.
- Sale of equity (not less than 15–25 per cent of the charter capital) through investment tenders, commercial tenders or auctions.
- Sale of the remaining shares at specialised auctions including ones that were interregional and nationwide.

As a first result of Russian mass privatisation, at many of the privatised enterprises, the structure of equity ownership became such that none of the groups of shareholders had a stable majority. In practice, the positions and influence of the managers who had been in charge of the enterprise prior to privatisation were strengthened.

During 1994 and 1995, two conflicting tendencies surfaced that were connected with the beginning of the process of redistribution of the initial ownership rights: first, a tendency towards the closed structure of the new JSC and second towards the erosion of the initial structure of equity ownership in support of the managers and the large outside shareholders (banks and investment funds). The cash privatisation can be assessed only in the framework of both of the above-mentioned tendencies because it was exactly the struggle for total control over the privatised companies that became the main feature during the remaining sales of the state shareholdings.

Radygin (1996) notes at the same time, taking into account the above-mentioned specific features of the cash privatisation, that one can say the interests of the state and other shareholders during the choice of the secondary sale method were in conflict. The state was interested in the auction-type methods because it was the recipient of the revenues from the sale of its stake. The management, as one of the largest stockholders, was interested in consolidating its control giving preference to the investment and commercial tenders, which gives them the opportunity to formulate special conditions tailored to their buyers. The large outside shareholders preferred specialised auctions, which provided the opportunity for the sudden action in the course of the struggle for the offered stake. In 1995, there were 4,052 cash auctions and 831 specialised auctions in Russia.

During the period 1995–7, the Russian government used various non-standard methods of privatisation such as loans-for-shares schemes, transfers of federal actions to regions as a method of covering federal debt and the converting of debts into securities. In March 1995, the consortium of the largest Russian banks made an offer to the government to transfer ownership of 43 state enterprises (which would be held in trust for five years) to the banks in exchange for a loan to the government equal to the planned budgetary revenues from privatisation. The presidential decree of 11 May 1995 set up a mechanism to hand over the companies' shares in federal ownership to legal persons for the trust management (GKI 1996). During the five-year period, the government could sell the shares to investors and buy back its shares from the banks. In reality, ownership of many main enterprises was transferred to the banks.

Most of these banks grew rapidly during the stages of commercialisation and voucher privatisation. They had a powerful lobby in various levels of government, including President Yeltsin, and emerged as large financial–industrial groups, which included Onexim Bank, Menatep and Alfa (Puffer *et al.* 2000). Most of the enterprises sold during this period, as mentioned, were high-value energy companies, such as Yugansk and Sidanco oil companies. In 1995, 12 auctions contributed 5.1 trillion roubles to the federal budget, accounting for 70 per cent of that year's budget revenues from privatisation (Radygin 1996). In 1995–7, 17,892 enterprises were privatised and 73 per cent of Russian gross national product for 1997 was made in the private sector (IET 1998).

Even though the number of companies privatised was gigantic, funding to the government was not so significant and government receipts from privatisation in 1995–7 were just 27.5 billion roubles. This represented 0.4; 0.071 and 0.73 per cent of GDP in 1995–7 respectively (Russian in Figures 1998).

There was no real competition at these auctions and many participants of these auctions employed money that was effectively from the state budget. The case of Nornickel accurately describes this situation. There were purely political considerations regarding the support of the biggest banking groups in the President Yeltsin elections. Exceptionally attractive chunks of state property were privatised virtually free of charge and these schemes were built in such a way, which minimised public discussions.

Evaluation of privatisation

To evaluate the results of privatisation it is necessary to examine them in the context of the Russian economic and political reforms. The process of privatisation began under conditions of sharp economic and political crises and further privatisation constituted the major element of reforms, which were begun in 1992 by the government of Gaidar. Intriligator (1996) analysed three separate elements of this shock therapy – stabilisation, liberalisation and privatisation and notes that outcomes were different from those expected by reformists. Stabilisation imposed limits on budget deficits and other elements of macroeconomic policy, which were similar to the practices of the IMF to correct structural inflation in Latin American countries.

Birman (1996) highlights the dramatic errors of the monetary and financial policy of Gaidar's government: the reduction of budget outlays that led to the decrease in money supply, the crisis of non-payments, a worsening in the position of population, growth of incomes of the black economy and inefficiency of state administration management of the enterprises that were still under state ownership.

Macroeconomic stabilisation did not stabilise the economy; it resulted in huge stagflation. Inflation between 1991 and 1994 rose to over 1,000 per cent and it destroyed private savings and prevented the growth of middle-class earnings and wealth. Later, between 1997 and 2007, it oscillated around 15 per cent per year. Liberalisation of prices demonstrated that, contrary to theory, prices were not established by the markets but by monopolies and a corrupt bureaucracy. The macroeconomic results of reform are given in Table 1.4.

In general, analysis of statistics, between 1991 and 2008, reveals that the outcome of privatisation and Russian reforms had two stages: deep decline (1992–8) and growth (1999–2008) when the national economy experienced exceptional growth and an average GDP growth rate of about 7 per cent per year. The basis of the growth in the economy during the period from 2000 to 2008 was commodities revenue (Russia in Figures 2010).

Privatisation process in 2000–10

Between 2000 and 2010, privatisation activity was not high. In 2002, the government sold 75 per cent of Slavneft for $1.9 billion and 6 per cent of Lukoil for $0.8 billion. Two years later, in 2004, it sold 7.6 per cent of shares of Lukoil to Conoco for $2 billion. In 2007, the government realised a few people's IPOs. Shares of the two Russian largest banks, VTB and Sberbank, and the largest oil company, Rosneft, were sold for more than $27 billion. However, the income from privatisation was completely gone to the companies themselves, which actually privatised revenues from the privatisation, i.e. the privatisation income was transferred to VTB and Sberbank; and Rosneft's

Table 1.4 Budget deficit and rates of inflation (1989–1994)

	1989	1990	1991	1992	1993	1994
Deficit of the consolidated budget in per cent of the GDP	-8,6	-10,3	-30,9	-29,4	-9,8	-11,8
Inflation per cent per annum	1,9	5,0	161	2506	840	204,4

Sources: IET (1998), Russia in Figures 1999, 2000.

privatisation income was transferred to Gazprom. In other words, the government sold state assets, but the income from the sale was transferred to the buyer, so the buyer got these assets free.

However, privatisation was not the dominant idea of Putin's economic policy, because privatisation decreases bureaucratic control over the national economy and opportunities for using state assets by the bureaucracy for personal enrichment.

In the fat years (2003–8), the privatisation revenue was not critical for the budget because it was in a state of large surplus. Moreover, the dominance of state ownership in the economy and lack of transparency of state corporations create the most favourable environment for corruption and theft by officials.

The next stage of real privatisation can begin when the current political elite realises that the personal profit from asset selling will be larger than their present personal cash flow from the current operations of state companies. Privatisation can be accelerated when the authorities will start wanting to escape from their positions of power due to increasing different geopolitical risks.

Conclusion

In this chapter, we have considered how privatisation was essential to Russian reform and the driver of a process of transition from state-owned asset to private capital and ownership. This process of transition can be understood from a neoclassical and institutional standpoint.

Neoclassical approach

The first point of view suggests that, in the Russian shock-therapy programme, there was too much shock and too little therapy (Stiglitz 1999). In other words, reforms were conducted with an insufficient sense of purpose to establish economic changes. Supporters of the neoclassical approach argued that privatisation should be carried out and completed as quickly as possible.

Advocates of the case for shock therapy argue that quick privatisation would generate the political force necessary to support economic reforms (Boycko *et al.* 1995). The political motions operating in favour of market economy would be an obstacle for a return to communism. However, if there were a long wait for formation of a legal base this could lead to a slowdown in the process of reform. Privatisation could be formally carried out quickly whereas it would take years to create a normative base of institutions to support free market functioning and a legal system to support it.

Quick privatisation was necessary to increase the efficiency of production and prevent massive theft of state assets by managers after the destruction of the Soviet system. Since privatisation by sale of individual enterprises or their shares took time to prepare and since it was not popular with the public, the only possibility turned out to be mass privatisation through vouchers.

The architects of Russian privatisation were concerned about the absence of shareholder rights. For this reason, they concentrated on the policy and predicted that market institutions would arise after the establishment of private ownership (Shleifer and Vishny 1998).

Fisher and Sahay (2000) note that the more rapid reformers located near Western Europe. They had experienced fewer years under the Communist regime and were economically advanced when transition began. Furthermore, the prospect of entry to the European Union apparently generated a strong stimulus for these countries, something again that Russia did not have.

The neoclassical approach to transition suggested broad sets of recommendations such as fiscal discipline, tax reform, trade liberalization, privatisation, deregulation and others. This concept was implemented in the form of shock therapy under the principle of 'one-size-fits-all'. The supporters of shock therapy consider that the elements of a programme would guarantee economic growth at full employment with low inflation and stability and reforms should be introduced quickly, simultaneously and immediately. One of the major ideas of shock therapy in Russia was that the economy was experiencing harsh macroeconomic imbalances and could not afford to reform gradually. Therefore, the government and foreign consultants established extremely short timescales for the process of transition.

Institutional approach

The institutional approach considers that the project of privatisation was adequate for the economic situation but its realisation was unsuccessful. Laws were accepted but were not properly executed because corrupt bureaucrats and the opposition resisted the privatisation project resulting in reforms without sufficient purpose. The medicine has been correctly prescribed, but the patient did not follow the doctor's instructions (Stiglitz 1999).

Kozarzevsky and Rakova (1999) write that the absence of an integrated approach in the carrying out of privatisation led to a decrease in popular support for reform. The basic causes of the failure of privatisation were inadequate aims of privatisation and methods to install privatisation. The social purposes of privatisation had not been achieved although they were considered a priority at the beginning of the process. Slogans of social justice within society were based on expectations that were set too high and, as a result, led to disappointment in privatisation and reforms as a whole. A significant part of society felt deceived because privatisation was often made opaquely, with cases of favouritism within insiders and officials.

The strong opponents of shock therapy consider that the programme of privatisation carried out in 1992–8 was absurd from start to finish; it contradicted not only academic canons but also common sense. Stiglitz and Ellerman (2000) write that the largest mistake of the past decade was the tendency to privatise as soon as possible without understanding the corresponding institutional infrastructure requirements. Historical experience confirms a hypothesis about the stimulus to efficiency; however, the lack of a private market can be a strong stimulus for theft and the disappearance of spheres, which create wealth. Furthermore, there are no theoretical and empirical bases for the statement, that the right of private property automatically creates necessary institutional infrastructure.

The high significance of public institutions and social capital, and that an implicit social contract cannot be simply legalised, decreed or introduced by the decision of reformatory government, which is necessary for a market society, cannot be disputed. One of the most difficult problems of the transition from socialism to a market economy is the transformation of the old 'implicit social contract' into the new contract. Reformers had been destroying old norms and restrictions for cleaning the state. However, they did not understand that the creation of new norms takes a significant amount of time to execute (Stiglitz and Ellerman 2000).

In the opinion of Goldman (1997), the rapid market conversion on unprepared soil was an error because the privatisation of government monopolies was insufficient to strengthen the competitive character of the economy. After liquidation of branch ministries, the authorities quickly discovered that the privatisation of state monopolies often results in simply more private monopolies where privatised enterprises continued to require subsidies from the state budget. The enterprises, becoming private, have almost excluded dismissal of incompetent managers from the practice of running organisations.

Polterovich (2005) writes about the mistakes made during Russian reforms that reform created conditions for illegal activity, lobbying, corruption and growth of criminality; the responsibility and efficiency of bureaucracy decreased at an initial stage of reforms; transplantation of the most advanced Western institutions in the backward institutional environment of Russia was a failure. Reform frequently did not provide a transitive process from old institutions to the new; typical was the situation where simultaneously a law created for the new institutions and a law abolished for the old institutions had no transitional procedures set in place, which resulted in an institutional vacuum, and which brought about losses. He notes that the part of the population that lost out because of the established transformations had not received sufficient indemnification.

2   Winners and losers in the privatisation game

Chapter 2 shows that the Russian reforms established a small number of oligarchs and concentrated enormous riches in the hands of a few. However, it did not contribute to effective management of business and did not make the enterprises attractive to investors. The chapter reveals that the largest private owners and their financial–industrial groups control enterprises in a number of strategic sectors. The process of accumulation is often dependent upon stock market growth, commodity price inflation and leverage.

The chapter discloses that oligarch business is unsustainable because it is not backed by investment in the modernisation of production, labour productivity growth or development of small and medium-sized businesses. The government implements nationalisation only when the owners are not included in its 'favourites' group or when they have inappropriate behaviour. The Russian authority does everything for preserving and strengthening the oligarchs' ownership structure.

Ownership concentration in the Russian economy

Significantly, Russian privatisation concentrated ownership and control of 23 of the largest business groups that control a substantial part of Russian industry with total output about 45 per cent of the Russian GDP (Guriev and Rachinsky 2003).[1] These 23 largest private owners and their financial–industrial groups control large enterprises in a number of strategic sectors such as oil, gas, mining, metallurgy, automobiles and chemicals. The share of these business groups in the national economy was larger than all other private owners, foreigners and regional governments combined. One can conclude that the Russian economy is based on economy-wide conglomerates that own oligopolies/monopolies in several sectors.

Throughout the period 1991 to 1995, modifications to the way in which shares were issued from non-cash- to cash-financed purchases resulted in a concentration of ownership and control. As was noted in the previous chapter, there was no real competition at privatisation auctions, and many participants of these auctions employed money, which was effectively taken from the state budget. Violence during the auctions helped the accumulation of shares in the hands of insiders and the proportion of shares held by employees and ordinary citizens dramatically declined. Earle *et al.* (1996) estimated that by 1994, some 69 per cent of Russian joint stock companies' share capital was held by insiders, and with the loans for shares scheme, this reinforced the strengthening of bank-led financial industrial groups where the ownership structure was even less visible.

In that time, the oligarchs took a significant step from financial to industrial wealth, building large business groups, which have become an economic and politically central factor. Although a few oligarchs had previously been attached to the Soviet nomenklatura, most were young businessmen and created their wealth in the Yeltsin and Putin epochs (Medova and Tischenko 2006). Guriev and Rachinsky (2005) note that, when privatisation occurred, oligarchs had financial capital available to purchase ownership in privatisation auctions, due to the fact that when the Russian reforms started, most of them owned principal trading companies, banks and investment funds.

Position and access to capital were the central ingredients fuelling the accumulation of wealth and a supportive legal framework helped. For example, limited foreign investor access and the restricted rights of minority investors facilitated a market for corporate control. In addition, the Russian law on bankruptcy was actively used by oligarch groups as a means to take over companies. Anti-takeover regulation was weak and easily circumvented. For example, where a takeover raider purchased more than 30 per cent of the voting stock the purchaser has to offer remaining shareholders the maximum of the current market price or previous six-monthly average of the target firm's market value but the market values are difficult to establish in thinly traded markets.

Oligarchs could purchase smaller blocks of shares in their own name or use proxy buyers (employment of raider companies) to conceal their identity and avoid disclosure requirements. A small proportion of these share transfer arrangements were blocked by regional government interventions, and others were frustrated by the fact that minority shareholders also had to be convinced for the deal to go ahead.

Professional raiders were hired by large Russian business groups and former Russian expatriates who wanted to repatriate their capital, usually providing them with funds. During the takeover, they prefer to keep their distance. Moreover, the professional raiders can operate efficiently, already having potential buyers in mind (Guriev *et al.* 2003).

Russian oligarchs very quickly consolidated their positions in industries like oil, gas, non-ferrous metals and ores as the information extracted in Table 2.1 reveals. By 2001, oligarchs dominated these industry sectors in terms of share of sales revenue.

Oligarchs focused on the accumulation of ownership and control in a few significant industrial sectors of the Russian economy where investment generated strong earnings capacity, especially cash extracted from operations, which in turn helped to boost stock market value added and lever additional debt finance to fund corporate acquisitions.

Table 2.1 Oligarchs' control and ownership concentration

Sectors	Share in sales %
Non Ferrous Metals	92
Aluminiun	80
Ferrous Metals	78
Automobiles	78
Ore	73
Oil	72
Pipes	55
Coal	48
Fertilizer	46
Pulp and Paper	30

Adapted from Guriev and Rachinsky 2005.

Because oligarchs tend to operate holding companies and conglomerates, we might expect that they would tend to underperform stand-alone firms that focused on managing core competences and resources. From an agency perspective, however, oligarchs can overcome the separation of ownership and the controlling firm's performance should be stronger (Boone and Rodionov 2002, cited in Guriev and Rachinsky 2005). Guriev and Rachinsky observe that oligarchs are able to restructure organisations because they both own and control corporate capital and thus are able to improve performance. Oligarchs manage their firms almost as well as foreign owners and better than other Russian regionally owned firms.

Jensen and Meckling (1976) classify an agency relationship as a contract under which the principal engages the agent to perform some service on their behalf that involves delegating some decision-making authority to the agent. The principal has to monitor the agent and takes up monitoring costs because the agent may not constantly function in the principal's best interests. The conflict of interests can generate residual losses because benefit is not maximised. They define agency costs as the sum of the monitoring expenditures by the principal, the bonding expenditures by the agent and the residual loss (cost of divergence between the agent's decisions and those decisions that would maximize the welfare of the principal).

Liebman (2003), using the ideas of Jensen and Meckling, describes the typology of agency costs of Russian corporations. These expenditures include monitoring expenditures (payment of remuneration to members of the board of directors and the revision committee, shareholders' meeting and register of shareholders), bonding expenditures (auditor and insurance expenses). In addition to these costs there are the residual costs including the cost of management privileges, cost of resistance to increasing company capital, cost of resistance to the engagement of new executives and resistance to M&A with strong partners. As well as the costs associated with internal power struggles, there is also the cost of investment in unprofitable projects and the development of a company in contradiction to the owners' interests, transferral price and fraud.

Theoretically, the concentration of capital by oligarchs should decrease agency costs because often they connect the roles of owners and executives. However, the analysis of corporate performance shows that companies, as a rule, increase expenditure. The oligarchs' companies need to maintain the monitoring and the bonding expenditures due to their corporate status. In addition, the residual cost has not been eliminated and many expenses have been increased: costs of privilege of a manager-owner and costs of struggles between minority shareholders and large shareholders (Lazareva *et al.* 2007). Moreover, the residual costs have been combined with expenses for defence against external raiders, payments for resistance against state acquisition and payments to state racketeers.

According to the classical definition of Whibley (1971), an oligarchy (Greek *Oligarkhía*) is the 'rule of the few', a form of government in which power effectively rests with a small, influential group distinguished by heritage, wealth, intellectual, family, military or religious domination. Russian modern history presents only one relatively short period (1995–8) when oligarchs could exert influence upon key political decisions. Traditionally, a definition of oligarchs as 'large private owners' excludes bureaucrats; however, it is not absolutely correct because some top state bureaucrats (i.e. Moscow mayor Luzhkov) have relatives who have gigantic assets.

Who created the Russian oligarchs?

The creation of a narrow group of oligarchs who were able to modify government policy to meet their own interests, concentrating their economic power, was possible due to many factors.

First, the sluggish and ineffective economic reforms in Russia undertaken in the initial years of the transition, together with the lack of democracy, decreased the transparency of government actions that created possibilities for rent seeking (Åslund 2007). As result, rent seeking and corruption, as an alternative to non-discriminatory and open competition, have become the key sources of the business success of Russian oligarchs.

Second, an unstable economy and political system has more opportunity for arbitrage between markets where physical, financial and temporal asymmetries are exploited by corporate managers. In the Russian transition economy, there is an enormous opportunity for arbitrage, which involves using confidential information of future economic and political decisions. Large business groups frequently create opportunities for arbitrage, forming and maintaining price asymmetries between markets where they are in a position to profit from their investments.

Third, in Russia growth through acquisitions, often hostile acquisitions, are the dominant strategy of growth. As a result, for oligarchs, M&A are more interesting than long-term organic growth. Additionally, in the process of M&A, politically embedded companies could employ close relationships with authority figures.

Fourth, nepotism that can be determined as favouritism granted to relatives, without regard to their merit (Trefil *et al.* 2002), is a widespread accusation in Russian business and politics when the relative of executives or powerful figures climb to comparable power apparently without suitable qualifications or experience. Aron (2008), using Max Weber's terminology, calls the Russian regime 'sultanistic', which summarises the tendency for Putin's friends and colleagues to rule most of the state corporations.

Fifth, corporation executives' networks with authorities play an essential role in Russian business. Informal relationships of high-ranking executives with authority give insider information about new projects and contracts, different preferences and competitive advantages contrary to under-embedded executives. Often, authority uses the contradictory application of laws and regulations on a non-transparent foundation; nevertheless, informal relationships with authority permit firms to mitigate this problem influencing embeddings and competiveness of the company. However, formal inclusion of executives into authorities can create enormous business opportunities and dramatically reduce political risks. Therefore, there is frequently an intention of oligarchs, executives or people affiliated with them to become involved with authority. Numerous examples show that many oligarchs and executives of large corporations have become the federal ministers, regional governors and members of the Russian parliament.

Finally, there are small oligarch groups that constitute primary level networks. Participants of primary-level networks employ a combination of formal and informal rules and regulations and these institutions are linked by collaboration, regular interactions and cohesion. Oligarchs lobby their interest individually or join unofficial small groups. Oligarchs' networks play a significant role in their business operations because informal interactions perform essential functions such as the transfer of confidential information and reduction of transaction costs.

Since 2000, after Putin's triumph in the presidential election, the role of the state and bureaucracy has been increased. As a result, the position of oligarchs in national politics and the economy has declined slightly. Some members of the oligarch club were eliminated by Putin. For example, Gusinsky and Berezovsky both escaped justice by running out of Russia and the most well-known, Khodorkovsky, was sent to prison after falling out of favour with the Kremlin. However, their places have been taken by some new oligarchs who generally were a member of Putin's team, grateful for the dramatic growth of commodity prices. In addition, the structures of the oligarch have become less transparent; nevertheless, the state authority and the market participants know who the real owners are.

In Putin's time, despite the anti-oligarch rhetoric, the oligarchs have been expanding their areas of influence and establishing strong control over the Russian economy. In the main, Yeltsin's and Putin's oligarchs are similar: they use similar methods of management and most oligarch companies are registered outside of the Russian Federation's tax territory. Putin's oligarch system is characterised by widespread alliances between officials and business, the participation of relatives and friends in management of state assets and the unexplainable allocation of budget funds, creation of unclear state management and its stagnation and deterioration (Nemtsov and Milov 2008).

Between 2000 and 2008, old and new oligarchs, having used the state's financial resources, enriched themselves by the means of stock markets and commodity prices growth. However, in the summer of 2008, when the first wave of crisis swept through Russia, stability of the oligarchic business was destroyed. The reduction of financial income, collapse of the stock markets, problems with debt servicing, the subsequent debt default and margin call for many participants caused a panic reaction. Oligarchs ran to the government with pleas for loans and aid; simultaneously they withdrew money from their companies through enormous dividends and loans to their offshore companies.

Krichevsky (2009) notes that all of these companies transfer assets from corporate to personal property by using preliminary taxes on dividends and personal income, which have been dramatically reduced in Putin's time. However, only a small part of their personal income is declared in the Russian jurisdiction. Significant incomes are accumulated in the accounts of offshore companies, which are used for paying the personal expenses of oligarchs such as yachts, jets and palaces.

Transferring the significant part of Russian companies' assets into personal possessions, as well as the boom in the stock market before the financial crisis of 2008, has created a meteoric rise in corporate borrowing. This borrowing became the main source of financing the investment programmes. From January 2002 to July 2009, the external liabilities of the corporate sector increased 12.3 times from $23.9 billion to $294.4 billion. Reduction of the capitalisation of the Russian stock market, which began in June 2008, has made many large companies technically bankrupt.

Chernykh (2008) notes that many Russian firms are controlled by nameless private owners; business control is applied through extensive use of pyramids. Owners mask their holdings and identities via nominee and foreign offshore arrangements. Her evidence suggests that the legal weaknesses in disclosure requirements are key determinants of country-specific ownership and control structures. The information asymmetry about the identity of the real owners is damaging to market efficiency (ibid.). For example, Surgutneftegas is a large and powerful oil company and it covers 13 per cent of total Russian oil production (61.7 million tonnes of oil). However, Surgutneftegas has never fully disclosed its ownership structure; 71.4 per cent of corporation shares belong to the company itself (treasury stock) (Surgutneftegas 2008).

Conclusion

Oligarchs, by virtue of the sheer scale of their accumulated wealth, stand outside of management and control of state institutions. These institutions, according to Hodgson (2006), embody political settlements and contribute by forming on human performance and thus moulding the abilities and behaviour of agents in essential ways. They have the potential to 'change agents, including changes to their purposes or preferences'. However, the ability of Russian state institutions to regulate the behaviour of oligarchs is reduced the more financially powerful these business elites become.

As a rule, foreign investors increase the volume of privatisation revenues and eventually attract efficient owners. However, due to ideological motives the Russian government ruled out foreign participation. Russian bidders, who benefited from this prohibition of foreign ownership, promoted this negative attitude.

The embedding of a quasi-democratic system in the global capitalist economy forms in the country an oligarchy closely connecting with a corrupt bureaucracy. This alliance for maintaining their position requires stability that can be realised by unmanageable authoritarian power. One can say that oligarchy creates authoritarianism and then authoritarianism itself preserves oligarchy and they become inseparable. The alliance of the authority and the oligarchy has not provided substantial growth and modernisation of the economy. Moreover, it has consistently demanded police regulation of public life, repression of political opposition and direct electoral fraud.

Note

1 This section draws on unpublished Haslam and Glazunov (2009).

3 How successful are Russian companies?

Chapter 3 reveals different factors affecting corporate performance, both internal and external to the enterprise. Internal categories are described as all of the factors that affect the business from within each company, whereas external categories are the factors that determine the business environment in which the companies operate. The internal environment consists of internal stakeholders such as management and personnel while external factors such as conditions within the country, a deficit of modern economic and political institutions, the regulatory policy framework and corporate non-transparency were paramount in determining strategy and influencing outcomes of privatisation in relation to economic productivity and welfare.

External and internal operating context

Corporate performance can be affected by a range of interrelated factors, which should take into consideration the purpose of achieving success and preventing business collapse. The factors affecting corporate performance can be divided into different categories: internal to the enterprise and external to the enterprise. Internal categories are described as all the factors that affect the business from positions inside the companies whereas external categories are described as all the factors that determine the business environment in which companies operate. The internal environment comprises internal stakeholders such as management and personnel while external factors affect firm performance in many macro ways, directly or indirectly (Rockart 1979; Johnson *et al.* 2005).

Kumar and Chadee (2002) provide a more holistic overview of factors that are critical to driving productivity and competitiveness. The list of factors that affect performance and competitiveness of the companies include internal factors (innovation and technology strategy, information and communications, human resources, the financial resources of an enterprise, organisational structure, organisational learning and inter-firm relationships) and external factors (government industrial policy, provision of public goods, export market assistance and financial sector stability).

Berg (2009) identifies factors affecting firm performance – basic industry conditions that include production technologies, input prices, demand patterns and ownership patterns. Additionally, he describes other factors such as market structure, government policies, municipal operation, corporate behaviour, public policies, objectives and priorities, institutional conditions, historical and international experience, international risk perceptions, regulatory governance and incentives, corporate governance, legitimacy and credibility.

In Tibar's (2002) evaluation of the Estonian industry top 50 companies, managers were asked to identify the critical success factors for their organisational level, supporting the realisation of company goals. The statements of respondents analysed and aggregated into the following ten categories: marketing; information management; quality management and quality assurance; product development; technological innovations; personnel; finance; general management; efficiency; pollution-free technology and environmental management.

In addition to these essentially operational issues, there is also the importance of strategy and the direction and scope of organisation objectives over the long term, and how this might achieve advantage through the configuration of resources and competences with the aim of fulfilling stakeholder expectations. Balance between different levels of strategy and the optimal selection of generic strategies are significant factors of corporate performance (Johnson *et al.* 2005). Porter (1985) describes a categorisation scheme consisting of four generic strategies (cost leadership, differentiation, focused low cost and focused differentiation), which are used to help organisations establish a competitive advantage over industry rival companies and that are commonly used by businesses.

One can take into account the variable operating context for each case study firm as shown in Table 3.1. It is possible to set the case study firms within an industry and regional level of analysis, and assess the extent of their institutional embeddedness.

At the industrial level, Porter's five forces model sets a firm in its industry, considering the threat of substitute products, established rivals, new entrants, bargaining power of suppliers and the bargaining power of customers (Porter 1980). These forces determine the attractiveness of an industry and impact upon corporate performance.

In Table 3.1 regions defy governmental boundaries and are linked by intensive interaction such that economic geography and corporate performance are interconnected (Loveridge 2000).

Institutional conditions also play their role in underwriting or frustrating corporate performance, for example, political embeddedness where institutional decisions are formed by a struggle for control that involves economic actors and institutions. The concept of political embeddedness is essential to an appreciation of how companies intersect boundaries between countries in the context of foreign direct investment (Hardy *et al.* 2005). It is possible, however, to employ boundaries more extensively: as borders between regions and districts because in a large country such as Russia there are legislative and administrative differences between areas.

Drawing upon wider literature and personal experience, a number of additional factors of corporate performance have been considered (see the table

Table 3.1 Factors of corporate performance

Categories	Factors	Aspects
	Political	Stability of political institutions
	Economic	Macroeconomics competitiveness and nature of competition
External macro level	Social	Social stratification, social relations, culture and deviance
	Technological	Technological development of the country
	Ecological	Ecological standards and monitoring
External micro level	Industrial	Industrial cluster, nature of competition, technology and labour capacity and skills
	Regional	Natural resources, institutional conditions, financials market, productive resources infrastructure, embeddings, networks with partners, community and authorities
Internal	Strategy	Corporate level, business and functional
	Operations management	Product creation, development, distribution, purchasing, inventory control, quality, storage and logistics
	Marketing	Promotion, location, price structures and nature of product
	Human resources	Availability of skilled labour
	FDI	Access to foreign investment and management skills
	Corporate governance	The nature of a firm's corporate governance and how resources are managed and regulated

Source: Author.

below). This list includes: embeddedness, nepotism, legal nihilism, relationship with authority, non-state institutions, rituals, arbitrage and acquisition as dominant strategy, the nature of power relations and rent-seeking behaviour. Analysis of these factors helps to understand performance outcomes of Russian firms after privatisation.

The sluggish and inconsequential economic reforms in Russia, undertaken in the first years of the transition, created narrow groups who were able to

Table 3.2 Additional influences on behaviour and performance of Russian enterprises

Categories	Factors	Aspects
	Continuation of rent seeking behaviour	Personal gain rather than maximising efficiency of profits
Cultural influences	Arbitrage as dominant strategy	Stagnation of alternative strategies
	Dominating the acquisition strategy against evolution development	Stagnation of evolution development
	Rituals of power	Limitation of business activity
	Nepotism	Decline in quality of HR
Cognitive influences	Legal nihilism	Law enforcement
	Overmbeddedness	Lack of corporate flexibility
	Informal relationship with authority	Law enforcement and deterioration of the investment climate
Institutional influences	Emphasis on including into regional authority	A conflict of interest
	The importance of non-state institutions	Domination of informal relationship in Russian business
	Linkages with national and local government	Involvement in rent seeking activities

Source: Author.

modify government policy to meet their own interests, concentrating their economic power. Additionally, lack of democracy decreases the transparency of government actions, which created possibilities for rent seeking (Åslund 2007). Consequently, rent seeking, as a substitute of non-discriminatory competition, has become the main basis of business accomplishments.

Rent-seeking activity is a compound phenomenon and there are some clear consequences of it: rent seeking raises transaction costs and uncertainty in transition countries; it leads to unproductive economic results, inhibiting foreign and domestic investment; it increases corruption and underground economic activity and it destabilises the state's legality (Tache and Lixandroiu 2006).

Much of Russian industry is concentrated in the hands of large business groups that have an opportunity for arbitrage in different segments of the national economy and between economies of the Russian regions. In addition, they form and maintain price asymmetries between markets and use additional sub-strategies such as the creation by the company itself of conditions for arbitrage.

In Russia, growth through acquisitions has been facilitated by private ownership and the development of capital markets facilitating hostile acquisitions. As a result, for executives, short-term aims such as M&A are more interesting than long-term organic growth. Additionally, in the process of

M&A, politically embedded companies could employ administrative resources (close relationships with the regional authority), which is more effective there than routine organic development.

Aron (2008) notes that political and personal allies of the president-headed companies jointly accounted for 40 per cent of the Russian economy. Similar tendencies have been transmitted on regional and corporation levels. One can suppose that using authorities' relatives, friends or former colleagues by the company will more deeply embed into the region's milieu.

Kertzer (1988) defines ritual as symbolic behaviour that is socially standardised and repetitive. Rappaport (1999) identifies five characteristics of ritual: the rituals' acts and expression are determined by orders, which had to be preliminary set up by others, not by the actors themselves. Ritual includes independent, not accidental, devotion to form; rituals have to involve some unvaried recurrence; ritual must involve both participants and audiences; ritual does not provide a practical result because the aura surrounding the ritual plays a key role.

Rituals of Russian regions are different from each other, although many of them have common authoritarian characteristics. Regional authorities employ many rituals, which maintain functions of control, pressure, creating an atmosphere of mistrust to avoid undesired political alliances, enhancing the authority and the expansion of the region leader and disciplinary actions.

Rituals through which the regional authority emphasises what is particularly valuable for it can be included in different activities such as parties and business meetings, festivals and celebrations as well as informal gatherings. The utilisation of regional rituals by firms may have implications for their embeddedness in localities.

One of the key functions of rituals is to quickly distinguish the suitability of counterparty and to determine their bearing and range that is relatively similar to the military identification system IFF (identification: friend or foe). Additionally, there are two vectors of rituals: internal, which serves the firm itself, and external, which serves external organisations and authorities.

Nihilism in its moral meaning is an absolute rejection of all systems of authority, morals, and social convention (Rosen 2000). Rosen notes that nihilism as a significant political and philosophical movement was created in Russia in the nineteenth century.

Legal nihilism is one of the forms of justice and social behaviour of individuals or groups, characterised by a negative or sceptical attitude towards the law and the values of law. Expressed in contempt, conscious disregard of legal requirements in practice serves one of the causes of delinquent behaviour (*Academic Dictionary* 2009). President Medvedev notes that Russia is a country of legal nihilism and the level of disrespect for the law is highest in Europe (Medvedev 2009).

The opportunities available to an organisation are established by the composition of arm's length and embedded ties making up the network with which it transacts. Strong, dominating, embedded ties could create overembeddedness and an inability for a company to access information circulating in the market and ability to test new trading partners (Uzzi 1996). One can presume that in Russia, companies have a positive attitude towards maximal political embeddedness and trying to increase this by setting solid embedded ties with authorities.

The extent of the embeddedness of Russian enterprises in the regional milieu depends on their extensiveness of relationships and networks with authorities that play an essential role with it. Nevertheless, quality of networks frequently has more influence on the embeddedness. As Moran (2005) notes, the quality of social relations influences upon accessed resources and personal familiarity and interpersonal trust characterise the relational embeddedness of social capital.

Life in the modern world economy is ordered by laws and property rights. However, formal rules establish only a small part of the sum of constraints that shape choices. In day-by-day interaction, the governing structure is strongly defined by codes of conduct, norms and conventions (North 1992). The Soviet Union, as well as post-communist Russia, never suffered from a lack of formal rules in the economy. However, despite that Russia has the numerous formal rules that sometimes are so detailed they permanently leave opportunity for uncertainty, which encourages arbitration on the actual significance of these rules. Moreover, formal rules create supplementary uncertainty and formal rules are mainly substituted by informal ones (Radaev 2000).

Many non-state institutions such as financial institutions, local chambers of commerce, training agencies, trade associations, innovation centres, clerical bodies, unions, government agencies providing premises and land, business service organisations and marketing boards were created at the start of Russian reforms in the late 1980s, but many of them do not work properly and do not influence the embeddedness of companies. This result confirms the suggestion of Hardy *et al.* (2005), that the existence of non-state institutions is an essential but not sufficient condition to embed firms and these institutions need to be linked by collaboration, regular interactions, confidence and cohesion.

Radaev (2000) also notes that there are many recognised business unions and societies in Russia; however, many of them are not powerful because executives prefer to lobby their interest individually or join unofficial small groups. These small groups as well as individuals constitute primary-level networks that, as a rule, include long-term business partners that directly connect with company operations. Participants of primary-level networks employ a combination of formal and informal rules and regulations.

According to Radaev (2000), networks play a significant role in Russian business and informal relationships perform vital functions such as the transfer of confidential information, evaluation of businesses partners, shape of reputations, creation of confidence and reduction of transaction costs. In addition, networks add some privileges to the business partners on an exclusive basis, namely the reduction of price, cancellation of pre-payment obligations, flexibility of payment and delivery terms and additional free services.

Strategy as arbitrage in Russia

According to the common definition, strategy should help the company to tackle the following questions: where should the company compete? How could the company achieve and maintain competitive advantage? What capabilities, assets, structures and culture do companies need to bring the strategy to life? Andersson *et al.* (2008) offer a new look on corporate strategy as a 'process of arbitrage between markets where physical, financial and temporal asymmetries are exploited by corporate managers to boost earnings-capacity'. They propose that arbitrage is a process consisting of buying and selling on different markets with the intention of taking advantage of the differentiation in the price quoted. Also, they reveal three different types of strategy as arbitrage: product, labour and capital market arbitrage, which take advantage of the variability in price structure between product markets, social settlements governing employment, temporal price variations arising from asset appreciation in capital markets and tax, interest and exchange rate variations through transfer pricing.

Ghemawat (2003) writes that arbitrage is not cheap capital or labour; the scope for arbitrage is the differences that exist between countries. He offers a four-dimensional framework for measuring distance between countries, which includes differences in culture, in the administrative and institutional context, geography and differences in economic attributes. Ghemawat emphasises differences that continue between countries; on the contrary one can propose that arbitrage also is the differences that keep on between regions of the one country. In the following section, strategy as arbitrage will be revealed through the experiences of the transitive economy of Russia.

It is a trivial fact that the Soviet economy was managed through the State Planning Commission (Gosplan), which had poor quality of planning and insignificant reliable feedback; industrial goods and military industry were permanently the focus of the Soviet authority and the production of consumer goods was disproportionately low. As a result, there was scarcity of many consumer goods leading to a widespread black market. Some of the black market goods were sold by arbitragers (officially called speculators and prosecuted by the state) who exploited price asymmetries. Generally, this arbitrage and speculation were immanent within the soviet system because they were one of many regulators of economic life.

In 1985, Gorbachev announced the start of the reforms in the Soviet economy and the process of arbitrage was partially legalised. Commonly, between 1988 and 1992, arbitrage was one of the major elements of strategy for new companies because of the collapse of state regulation and undeveloped market economy. Additionally, government policy and regulation gave a large opportunity for strategy as arbitrage. For example, the alcohol reform of 1985 that was designed to fight widespread alcoholism. Prices of alcohol were raised, many wineries were destroyed and sales were restricted. Simultaneously, there was a large disparity between regions of the country in alcohol supply and demand that created price asymmetries and lucky break arbitrage.

Another example is the trade of commodities in the 1990s when there were two different prices: one price for internal operations within the Soviet Union and a global price in Estonia, which at that time was within the economic zone of Russia. As a result, in the 1990s, this gave an opportunity for arbitrage and as a result, Estonia was the largest world exporter of non-ferrous metal.

One more example reveals transfer pricing between subsidiaries, which utilised fiscal differences between one region and another, reducing the company's effective tax rate. After the start of the Russian reforms, few Russian regions created offshore zones that gave opportunities for transfer pricing. The small Russian town Mosalsk, for example, where since 1991 Menatep, one of the largest banks, had been registered and the oil giant Yukos were both controlled by Mikhail Khodorkovsky. These companies received large tax privileges, and yet still paid a large share of the town's budget in corporate tax. Resultantly, the town gained from dramatically increased tax revenue whilst the company benefitted from a substantially reduced taxation liability.

About ten years later Khodorkovsky was found guilty of fraud and sentenced to eight years in prison for a relatively similar financial operation, whereas his business partner Roman Abramovich, who also regularly used this schema, bought Chelsea FC. Moreover, Abramovich developed transfer pricing operations and exploited other price asymmetries. According to the traditional approach, price asymmetries are created by differences in market nature and concrete decision making is eliminated from the analysis. However, the Abramovich case demonstrates how executives can create price asymmetries.

The basic activity of Abramovich in the 2000s was the oil company Siboil that historically was a Russian leader for tax optimisation and it sold oil through the traders registered in the Russian offshore zones. However, in Abramovich's first years in the post of the governor of the Chukotka Region, the company surpassed all of the previous achievements because the governor created its own internal offshore and according to this schema his companies could reduce corporate tax more than $2 billion. In addition, the governor was paid dividends without any taxation. Using tax privileges Abramovich's companies were able to reduce corporate tax from 35 to 5.5 per cent (Accounting Chamber 2002).

This last example shows that strategy as financial arbitrage can include additional sub-strategies such as the creation of conditions for arbitrage by the company itself. In the main, it is more possible in countries with weak institutional and regulatory bodies such as Russia and other countries with transitive economies.

Simplifying, arbitrage is the practice of getting benefits from a price differential between two or more markets and it is possible when two conditions are met: the same asset does not trade at the same price on all markets and there is a technical opportunity of realisation of the arbitrage. Therefore, two parameters determine arbitrage: a price differential and a technical opportunity. In the traditional understanding, arbitrage is the act of buying a product in one market and selling it in another for a higher price and should take place concurrently to avoid exposure to market risk, and so arbitrage as a financial practice has dramatically grown together with the progress of telecommunications, which gives the technical opportunity for the realisation of arbitrage.

To analyse arbitrage, it is possible to build a matrix with two parameters: price differentiation and opportunity. Also, it is possible to select four possible options: absent price asymmetries and strong potential for arbitrage (option 1), absent price asymmetries and weak opportunity for arbitrage (option 3), strong price asymmetries and strong opportunity for arbitrage (option 2) and strong price asymmetries and weak opportunity for arbitrage (option 4). Figure 3.1 shows the matrix of price asymmetries and opportunity with the four outcomes.

Option 1 describes a situation where the opportunity for carrying out operations required for arbitrage exists, but where there are few price asymmetries to exploit. Option 2 is the standard case of arbitrage and it was analysed above. Option 3 could not give arbitrage as neither asymmetries nor opportunity exist. Option 4 is the typical case that determines state and regional regulation, bureaucratic barriers and limitation of infrastructure of the country and region. Often these determinants are positive because they protect ecological and economic interests of the country but often they have strong negative intensions. At first glance, only Option 2 is interesting for business strategy as without price asymmetries or opportunity the operations would not be profitable.

This matrix is analogous to four positions of a treasure hunter. The hunter has both a team and money but he does not know where the treasure is (Option 1); he does not have a team, money or any idea where the treasure is (Pption 3); the hunter knows where treasure is, but nobody believes him. As a result, he cannot organise the expedition (Option 4) and the treasure can be acquired because he has everything he needs (Option 2).

An example could be the forestry industry. China is the biggest market for wood products, which has fuelled growth of timber imports, including a considerable quantity from Russia. Not surprisingly, there is forest cutting carried out with abuse of the existing legislation. However, a major part of the cutting in eastern Russia was made with official permits for logging operations. Russian log imports in China offer very attractive arbitrage but are limited by a weak opportunity for the increase of supply due to Russian state legislation.

This is why many forestry companies have created opportunities for wood-cutting. This was done by obtaining permits for felling in specially protected natural areas where cutting is usually forbidden or without a genuine

Figure 3.1 Matrix price asymmetries and opportunity

Absence of Price asymmetries and strong opportunity for arbitrage (Option 1)	Strong price asymmetries and strong opportunity for arbitrage (Option 2)
Absence of price asymmetries and weak opportunity for arbitrage (Option 3)	Strong price asymmetries and weak opportunity for arbitrage (Option 4)

Source: Author.

assessment of the volume of wood available or by obtaining a permit to cut and transport the wood using relatively non-invasive technology but then using cheaper, more primitive methods. Other firms exploited cutting permits established on dubious interpretations of forest management regulations or by exaggerated the degree to which a forest is afflicted with pests or diseases to the extent that immediate selective felling is considered necessary. As a result, about 40 per cent of Chinese softwood log imports from Russia were of dubious origin (Morozov 2000). This example shows how a weak opportunity for arbitrage was strengthened and, combined with strong price differentiation, strategy as arbitrage was carried out.

Option 2 (strong price asymmetries and strong opportunity for arbitrage) gives the opportunity to create arbitrage, by way of organisation of special conditions. An example of this option is the employment of migrant workers in Moscow and other Russian cites when the construction industry, having had the potential for labour arbitrage, lobbied for special state resolutions to allow the employment of migrants. According to the report Human Rights Watch (2009), there were nine million migrant workers in Russia; 80 per cent of these migrant come from nine countries of the CIS with which Russia maintained a visa-free regime. Approximately 40 per cent of migrant workers were employed in the highly unregulated construction industry, two million of them work in the Moscow region.

Usually, migrant construction workers are young men who leave their family in their home countries and enter Russia for six to nine months of seasonal employment, often for many years in a row. These workers enjoy higher wages in Russia than in their native countries and often send money to their families. Building workers usually live in deprived conditions and many employers commit violations of Russian law such as confiscating passports, withholding wages and forcing employees to work long hours. The absence of a written employment contract leaves migrant workers vulnerable in cases of workplace accidents because workers cannot access state-sponsored accident insurance that depends on employer contributions for legal employees and, in many cases, employers do not provide any assistance to injured workers (Human Rights Watch 2009).

This example shows the well-known type of economic arbitrage that exploits low-cost labour as a reaction to growing competition in markets and strong demand. However, the Russian model of offshoring arbitrage is dissimilar to that observed elsewhere. Russian business transfers labour from developing countries to the relatively more developed Russia. More generally, offshoring transfers capital and technology from advanced economies to developing economies with lower labour costs.

In addition, this case reveals two complementary advantages for companies moving to emerging markets: undeveloped health and safety regulations and labour law. Health and safety compliance is very expensive in manufacturing but is often ignored in developing countries. As a result, relocation into countries with more lenient health and safety regulation can reduce operational expenditure. Labour law in developing and transitive countries does not provide adequate terms of employment, anti-discrimination, unfair dismissal and child labour protection in comparison with developed countries. In addition, trade unions are usually dependent of company executives, reducing union effectiveness. Consequently, companies conducting business in developing countries can often reduce effective labour costs.

In the global market generally, environmental expenditure has been increasing and there are significant differences in environmental standards and control systems between transitive and advanced economies. Multinational companies are arbitraging environment costs, relocating domestic operations into countries with low environmental standards or countries with undeveloped monitoring systems in order to take advantage of international differences in costs of pollution. In the next chapters arbitrage as a strategy will be analysed in the context of case studies.

Conclusion

In this chapter, we have considered the factors affecting corporate performance, which can be divided into different categories: internal, such as strategy, operations management, marketing, human resources, FDI and corporate governance, and external to the enterprise, such as political, economic, social, technological, ecological, industrial and regional. Additionally, there are a number of complementary factors that support corporate performance of Russian firms such as embeddedness, nepotism, legal nihilism, relationship with authority, non-state institutions, rituals, arbitrage and acquisition as a dominant strategy, the nature of power relations and rent-seeking behaviour.

The chapter has studied the concept of corporate strategy as a process of arbitrage between markets where different nature asymmetries are exploited by corporate managers. The scope for arbitrage includes the differences that continue among countries and the differences that exist between regions of one country and the level of the differences depends on size of the country, political system and institutional variation in the culture and geography of the country.

Conditions within Russia, deficit of modern economic and political institutions, regulatory policy framework and non-transparency are paramount factors in determining the strategy. These factors formed and maintained price asymmetries and opportunity for arbitrage in different segments of the national economy. Examples from Russia reveal transfer pricing between subsidiaries, which utilise fiscal differences between one region and another, reducing the company's effective tax rate.

In this chapter, it has been shown that arbitrage is possible when there are two conditions: the same asset does not trade at the same price on all markets and there is a technical opportunity of realisation of arbitrage. Consequently, to analyse arbitrage, a matrix with two parameters is built: those of opportunity and price differentiation, selecting four possible options for arbitrage.

4 Getting into Russian firms

Chapter four reveals the reasons why the particular interdisciplinary approach is chosen and how numerical and narrative accounts are constructed. The author takes a middle-ground approach, where a combination of narratives and numbers are used to construct a series of case studies of several firms. An augmented corporate socio-economic accounting framework is adopted. Such a framework consists of a corporate accounting module for deconstructing firms' financial performance and a socio-economic module for evaluating the internal and external drivers for corporate performance.

This book adopts an interdisciplinary approach to the examination of the dynamic inter-play between agents, interests, incentives, macro- and micro-economic conditions, arbitrage strategies and agent conduct in the privatisation and transformation processes and how such interactions shaped corporate financial performance of firms through case studies. This chapter reveals how five individual case studies across business sectors are selected and adopted for triangulating evidence.

How to examine the outcomes of transformation

Researchers can employ different methodologies and empirical techniques to examine the possible outcomes of privatisation and transformation and these are often connected to other areas of economics. This diversity is seen in the investigation of the comparative economic performance of state-owned and privately owned firms and in the evaluation of the impact of privatisation on financial and operating performance, the development of corporate governance practices and the development of capital markets.

Comparing the performance of government-owned to privately owned companies is one of the methods by which the impact of state ownership on company performance is investigated. Tian (2000) examines 825 companies listed on the Shanghai Stock Exchange: 513 mixed-ownership firms and 312 private firms. He finds that private firms perform better than the mixed ownership firms do and corporate value has a linear relationship with government shareholding. Boardman and Vining (1989) examine the economic performance of the 500 largest non-US industrial firms in 1983. Using profitability ratios, they demonstrate that state-owned ownership enterprises are considerably less profitable and productive than privately owned firms.

Frydman *et al.* (1999) compare the performance of privatised and state firms in the transition economies of Central Europe, surveying data from 506 companies in the Czech Republic, Hungary and Poland in 1994. They evaluate sales revenues, employment, labour productivity and material costs per unit of revenue. The authors contrast the privatised group to the non-privatised group with panel data, controlling for potential pre-privatisation differences between the two groups, and they find that privatisation improves performance.

Megginson (2005) write that there are difficult methodological problems with research in this area such as data availability and consistency. These problems include the insufficiency of information that must be disclosed in most countries, accounting standards that vary from country to country and management that manipulate accounting data. There are also different research methodologies that are used to study how privatisation has improved the performance of divested firms. In addition, they reveal examples, which describe the connections between growth in global market capitalisation, growth in the value of shares traded in the world's stock exchanges and privatisation in the last two decades.

Researchers may examine a single industry, a single country or a small number of individual firms. La Porta *et al.* (1999) offer an example of investigation of industry. They test the performance of 218 SOEs that show performance after privatisation compared with industry-matched firms in order to highlight different levels of success between industry and company-specific influences.

Research approaches and methods

From a legal point of view, privatisation as a process of transfer of assets from the state to private owners was in the main completed in 1995–7. However, there is a transitional process of adjustment for the company to work as an independent manufacturer. This process affects different corporate functions: finance, human resources, operations, marketing and logistics. The success and failure of privatised companies raise the following questions: why is one company successful, yet others fail? Why have some managers managed to reorganise the company and adapt to new conditions, taking advantage of the opportunities created by economic reform, whereas other managers have experienced the opposite? What does business success in Russia mean and how should such success be examined?

While measuring the impact of privatisation on corporate performance, it is difficult to distinguish the effects of economic reforms, competition, regulation and social change. Privatisation has changed the economic business environment in Russia. These processes caused managers to bring about a dramatic change in their management strategy. Moreover, the transition of a company from state to private ownership results in changes in objectives, in corporate decision-making structures and in monitoring systems and these factors also influence post-privatisation corporate performance.

There are two research paradigms in social science: qualitative and quantitative and in literature there is some discussion concerning which methods are more scientific. Qualitative data are usually in the form of words, reached through observation, interviews or documents, rather than numbers. Patton (1990) describes qualitative research in the following terms: that which employs the natural setting as the source of data; when the author tries to observe, describe and interpret settings as they are. The qualitative researcher mostly exploits inductive data analysis and their reports are descriptive with a developing design.

On the other hand, quantitative research uses experimental schemes and quantitative measures to test hypothetical generalisations. Researchers look for causal determination, prediction and generalisation of results, arriving by statistical methods or other methods of quantification. However, statistics cannot take full account of the many interfaces that take place in social situations and furthermore quantitative research does not accept the complexity and dynamics of the world (Patton 1990).

Mixed methods are used in this book that employs qualitative and quantitative data collection techniques and analysis procedures. Although most emphasis in the past has been laid on the financial aspects of privatisation and transformation, this book includes other features that refer to the transitional nature of the programme.

Merton (1968) offered the middle range theory as a solution to the problem of the gap between sociological theory and empirical evidence, and he defined it as a collection of techniques to examine reality and allow for the creation of theoretical explanations and supply ideas for future effort. Middle-range theories and general theories include abstractions; however, the abstractions in theories of the middle range are robustly supported by experiential data and the middle range theory begins its theorising with narrow characteristics of social phenomenon (ibid.).

Middle-range theories should be constructed with an orientation to visible phenomena in order to create an applicable model of theoretical problems. Three techniques facilitate the construction of middle-range theories: working with a minor level of abstraction that increases the probability that propositions will be better cogency; setting limits to the sample structure and endeavouring to control the conditions within which information is collected (Morrow and Muchinskly 1980).

In this book, the author wishes to use the numbers taken from financial statements and narratives from interviews, such as stories about success and failures using a middle-range theory as the guiding research philosophy. This approach tries to preserve the complexity of the universe in which the author operates without the reductionism of positive approaches and simply relying on the interpretation of narratives from interviewees.

One of the aims of this book is to create broad interpretations covering the corporate performance of companies and so enable the reader to connect separate ideas about business practices that illuminate the problem of privatisation and transformation in Russia. To achieve this using only the natural science model (positivistic approach), with strong econometric calculations and representative sampling, would be difficult because the corporate profile also includes human opinions, estimations, motivations and attitudes.

There are several reasons why this study has not adopted a positivistic approach. First, it was difficult to establish causal relations when five case studies across different industry sectors are to be chosen. Second, we did not wish to employ abstraction mechanisms to reduce the complexity of the universe under study. In addition, a positivistic approach usually assumes structural stability in the economic system for the purpose of hypothesising and testing causal relationships. However, this approach is inadequate and inappropriate in a highly dynamic and fluid environment like the Russian economy in the transitional period between large-scale state ownership and private enterprise. The book's orientation goes beyond explanation of a limited range of observations; the application of knowledge and methods used is a significant aspect of this book.

Saunders *et al.* (2007) show links between research philosophy and research practice and his 'research onion' model describes different levels of the research process: research philosophy, approach and strategies, time horizons and data collection methods. There are a number of relatively different methods that can be employed to answer research questions that include experiment, survey, case study, grounded theory, ethnography, archival research and action research. Each method has specific strengths, weaknesses and limitations and these methods can be used to complement each other in specific circumstances, thus forming a single cohesive method.

Case study method

A study of post-privatisation performance and factors, which determined performance, will establish causal relationships between them. Such research may be termed as explanatory studies and use both a quantitative and qualitative approach. To achieve this research objective a case study method was adopted. This method has a particular significance in this research because it offers the opportunity to study companies in their context, both within their industry and in the wider economy, therefore helping to clarify the correlations between these factors.

The case study method is a common way to carry on qualitative investigation. This method brings us to an understanding of a composite problem, and it emphasises comprehensive contextual analysis of a limited number of events and their connections. The case studies in this book comprise a few major analytical components: each case study links the vital events in the life of the company; special emphasis is placed on the most recent 16 years, which are supported by performance data and analysis, undertaken intensively within cases and extensively across cases.

There are numerous definitions of a case study. According to Bromley (1986), it is a systematic investigation into an incident or a set of related events, which aims to describe and explain the phenomenon of interest. Yin (2003) defines the case study research method as 'an empirical investigation that examines an existing phenomenon within its real-life context when the boundaries between phenomenon and context are not clearly evident' and in which numerous sources of evidence are used.

According to Stake (2005), researchers who use the case study approach try to discover the commonality of the case as well as its exclusive character; consequently, the study of a single case could be significant because it might be representative for other cases. He mentions that a case study can be seen as a practical step towards a larger generalisation, but advises against the tendency to over-generalise for the reason that the case study researcher has practical freedom in selecting how much the difficulties of a case will be investigated. The unit of analysis can vary from an individual to a corporation or country and is a critical factor in the case study.

Yin (2003) classifies some particular types of case studies: exploratory cases are occasionally considered as an introduction to social research, explanatory case studies may be used for doing causal researches and descriptive cases, which need a descriptive theory to be developed before starting the project. Moreover, he presents four applications for a case study model: explaining compound causal links in real-life interventions; describing the real-life context in which the intervention has taken place; describing the intervention itself; examining those situations in which the intervention being estimated has no clear set of results.

Yin (2003) distinguishes four types of designs: single-case holistic designs, single-case embedded designs, multiple-case holistic designs and multiple-case embedded designs. Single cases represent a unique and freestanding unit of analysis whereas multiple case studies involve more than one unit of analysis following reproduction logic. Case studies can be holistic or embedded. Holistic case studies concern the organisation as whole, while embedded case studies analyse units of the organisation. This book employs the multiple-case holistic design.

Saunders *et al.* (2007) note that a key question in designing a research strategy is the time horizon; he determines two forms of a time horizon: cross-sectional studies investigate a specific phenomenon at a particular time and longitudinal studies examine change and development over time. Both longitudinal and cross-sectional time horizons are adopted in this book because it is important to evaluate performance changes over time as well as within a specific timeframe.

A 16-year period from 1995 to 2011 is considered sufficient for identifying an analysis of corporate performance and this period was adequately varied in terms of macroeconomic conditions in order to allow for a more generalised statement about corporate strategy and quality of management. The period under study was marked by economic recession, expansion and crises.

According to Yin (2003), the case study design should have five components: a study's questions, its propositions, its units of analysis, the logic linking the data to the propositions and the criteria for interpreting the find-ings. This study utilises standard techniques for posing research questions and defining the unit of analysis.

We use the case study approach to attempt to discover the commonality of the case and its exclusive character; consequently, the study of a single case might be essential because, as said above, that case might be considered representative for other cases. A case study can be seen as a practical step toward a larger generalisation.

Data collection

Documentation, direct observation and interviews were determined as the main sources of evidence for the case study research analysed in this book. This research analyses different documents such as company financial reports, company memoranda and plans as well as the Russian business press. One of the main uses of documents is to support facts collected from other sources and research documents and are a major source of evidence for case studies. Direct observation in a case study occurs when the investigator makes a site visit to collect data. The observations could be formal or informal activities, and reliability of the observations is the main concern.

An interview as a means of extracting different forms of information demands factual interaction between the interviewer and the respondent. Interviews are one of the main sources of case study information and this research in particular.

The fully structured interview is useful in studies of areas where a formal investigation is necessary. It has pre-planned questions with fixed wording in a predetermined order, and it produces specific limitations on a researcher, which depend on what questions the interviewer has asked. A semi-structured interview has predetermined questions, but the order can be tailored based upon the interviewer's opinion on what questions are more suitable. Question phrasing can be changed and the interviewer can include additional questions and exclude any inappropriate questions.

Using an unstructured interview, interviewers could ask for the respon-dent's opinion on events or facts in an informal manner and with only a general idea about the direction of the conversation. Consequently, in order to accumulate data, this study utilised semi-structured interviewing, which combines the benefits of both structured and unstructured interviewing.

The major purpose of qualitative interviews is to assess complex issues and increase understanding. When we use interviews, it is necessary to examine basic questions:

- Whom do you interview?
- How many people are to be interviewed?
- What do you ask them?
- How are you going to record the interview?
- How do you analyse the interview?

Our research employs purposeful sampling, which is the selection of responders who are best equipped to answer the research question.

Yin (2003) suggests three principles of data collection for case studies: employing multiple sources of data, creating a case study database and maintaining a chain of evidence. All of them are suitable to research sources of evidence and can tackle the problem of establishing the construct validity and reliability of evidence.

The basis for using many sources of data is the triangulation of evidence. Triangulation is the application and combination of several research methodologies in the study of the same phenomenon. It can be employed in both quantitative and qualitative studies (Saunders *et al.* 2007). The triangulation method is preferred in social sciences due to its advantages in combining multiple observations, theories, methods and empirical materials in which researchers hope to overcome the weakness and the problems that come from single-method and single-theory studies (Denzin 2006).

According to Denzin (2006), there are four basic types of triangulation: data source triangulation (when the author looks for the data to remain the same in different contexts), investigator triangulation (when several investigators study the same phenomenon), theory triangulation (when researchers with different theoretical viewpoints interpret the same results) and methodological triangulation (which involves using more than one method).

For the interpretation of the research results, it is possible to employ more than one theory and to use different data sources that are applying theory triangulation and data source triangulation respectively. In addition, it employs multiple sources of evidence such as interviews and documentation, which makes up the methodological triangulation.

According to the second part of Yin's principle of data collection, the data need to be organised and documented just as it is in the investigational studies. The data and the report of the investigator are the two categories of the databases that may be required. All types of appropriate documents such as tabular materials, narratives and other notes must be installed in the database.

The maintenance of a chain of evidence boosts the reliability of the case study and the principle is to have an external observer follow the route of evidence from the first research questions to the final case study conclusions. The external observer should be able to discover the steps in either direction and the procedure of acquiring evidence should be similar to collecting criminological evidence. The case study description should have citations in the case study database where the real evidence is to be found (Yin 2003).

A research design of a case study is the logic that links the data and the conclusions to the initial questions of a study and the authors should maximize the quality of the case study (Yin 2003). Discussions about the quality of research begin with the ideas of reliability and validity. Reliability, according to Saunders *et al.* (2007), demonstrates how research data collection procedures will produce stable findings. Joppe (2000) explains that validity in research determines whether the research truthfully measures, what it was planned to measure or how truthful the research results are. Researchers usually determine validity by asking a succession of questions, and will often look for answers in the researches of others. Black and Champion (1976) determine validity as the extent to which a tool measures what it is assumed to measure.

According to Yin (2003), internal validity determines a causal link and in the context of this research, if the study can demonstrate a causal relationship between privatisation and corporate performance it is referred to as having internal validity. There are a few specific tactics for achieving internal validity. In this research, it would be possible to employ two tactics: pattern matching and explanation building. Pattern matching is one of the most attractive strategies for analysis. This technique evaluates an empirically established pattern with a predicted one. If the patterns correspond, the internal validity of the case study is improved. Explanation building is a derivative of a pattern-matching tactic in which the analysis of the case study is performed by building an explanation of the case (Yin 2003). In this research, the actual comparison between the predicted and the actual pattern may have qualitative and quantitative criteria and the discrimination of the pattern is interpreted.

Using Yin's protocol it is possible to employ explanation-building tactics as an iterative process that begin with a theoretical statement, comparing new facts of the initial case in relation to the statement and revising the statement, then repeating this process from the beginning as many times as needed. Construct validity determines precise operational measures for the concepts being examined (Yin 2003). In other words, it is possible to state that the investigation reflects well the research construct of the programme and that the measure reflects well the idea of the research.

Structuring financial analysis

To engage specifically with these arguments about privatisation and transformed performance we first construct a framework of analysis that can be used to investigate the financial performance of Russian firms. This framework requires that we convert Russian financial accounting data reported under Russian accounting principles into formats, whereby we can construct a financial investigation.

The principal accounting objectives under the Soviet economic system were the preservation of collective property, the fulfilment of norms relating to the quantity and configuration of current assets and the production of goods, determining the costs of production and presenting the financial results of business activities to the government organisation (Paliy and Sokolov 1988). The Russian privatisation reforms raised the issue of the significance of accounting information for management of companies, shareholders and government organisations. In 1991, the general regulatory framework of companies and control of the accounting records and their verification in Russia were formed.

According to Enthoven (1999), in the late 1990s, Russian Accounting Standards (RAS) were similar to IAS: a double entry bookkeeping system, balance sheet continuity; recording assets on the foundation of the original cost of acquisition; taking a going concern principle into account and valuing foreign currency assets and liabilities by the current market exchange rate. However, Enthoven also notes that Russian accounting laws did not transform accounting significantly from the needs of government to assess taxes and measure performance with quantitative statistical indicators.

The Russian accounting system was very rigid, particularized and strictly regulated by laws and accounting data oriented towards the past. This is illustrated by the emphasising of the balance sheet and the conservation of company assets rather than the analysis of managerial decisions. Russian accountants did not use these data to undertake comprehensive analyses or to help guide effective decision making, neither did they make the results of this work accessible to outsiders as would be required for the process of corporate valuation (ibid.).

Financial reporting and financial performance

The annual financial statements are the balance sheets, profit and loss accounts and cash flow statements. The accounting policy is declared by management of the company and it must comply with the requirements of completeness, verifiability, emphasis of substance over form, non-conflicting data, rationality and also the operational charter of accounts of the firm must be included in the accounting policy (Paliy and Sokolov 1988). In the main, the accounting policy is similar to Western accounting practice. Russian companies are obliged to abide Russian laws and incorporate accounting regulations and standards of the Ministry of Finance.

KPMG (2005) observes that Russian requirements are obligatory and whilst a number of requirements pronounced formally follow IAS, their application and interpretation may be different. Enthoven (1999) notes that Russian companies have often manipulated financial data to strengthen their position when bargaining with state authorities, whether the company is looking to pay less tax or is seeking more subsidies. Obtaining dependable account information about Russian companies is difficult and available information about many of them fails to give a clear picture of the company.

The analysis carried out in this book utilises company reports and accounts that were prepared according to RAS, translated Russian terms into English and converted financial statements from RAS to IAS.

Deconstructing firm financial performance

Financial analysis starts with a bottom line measure of corporate performance, the return on capital employed (ROCE), return on equity and return on total assets (ROTA). Profit margin measures the percentage of each sale in roubles that goes to trading profit, where trading profit is the profit before interest charges; and tax and sales exclude VAT and inter-company transactions.

Return on capital employed (ROCE) is a ratio, which measures overall firm performance by relating some measure of profit to capital employed, estimated as a long-term debt plus shareholder funds. Andersson *et al.* (2006) observe how the ROCE can be broken down into its constituent elements using the so-called Pyramid of Ratios. This concentrates upon one or two overall ratio measures of corporate performance (profit and cash return on capital employed) and then deconstructs these to identify the drivers of financial performance.

ROCE is a key shareholder value ratio because both cash and capital employed numbers in shareholder value metrics. The objective is for firms to generate improved earnings capacity in order to increase returns to shareholders both by boosting market value and by increasing the capability of a firm to absorb market value (from acquisitions) on behalf of shareholders (ibid.).

The framework for deconstructing the ROCE shown in Figure 4.1 starts with the bottom line ROCE but then deconstructs this ratio into its constituent elements using a 'nature of expenses' rather than 'function of expenses' approach. This approach avoids the problems attached to using the 'function of expenses', where allocations to expenses can be arbitrary, and helps to identify the drivers of strong and weak financial performance.

The financial performance of five Russian company cases are considered using this financial framework of analysis covering the period of 1994 to 2011 to establish the extent of the Russian transformation.

Structuring the case studies

The presented case studies do not have a broadly established fixed reporting format because each case study is unique. We employ a journal format that is appropriate for this work. It is important to stress that this research method is a middle ground approach where narratives are from interviews and numbers are from financial analyses. Both the numbers and narratives collected are used to assess company performance after privatisation.

We have outlined the framework of analysis to construct an assessment of financial performance for the case study firms. This is followed by a consideration of the literature that emphasises the importance of external, internal, behavioural and institutional characteristics.

Choice of case study companies

In the first stage of sampling, the author determined general principles of selection of companies for the investigation:

- a company had to be privatised by being transformed into open joint stock companies;
- a company had to exist throughout the period 1990 to 2011;
- a company had to be not significantly transformed during this period of time;
- a company had to be relatively large (with an average workforce of more than 1,000 employees);
- a company had to have an impact upon regional and national economies;

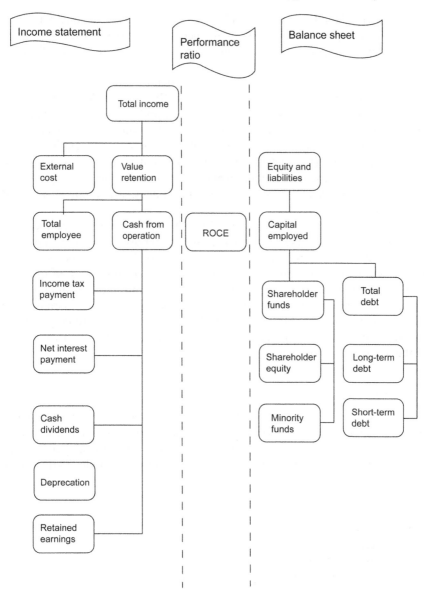

Figure 4.1 Framework for deconstructing the ROCE
Source: Adapted from Andersson *et al.* (2008).

- a company should not have had a large share in the defence industry because the industry operates under state control hence it does not disclose information;
- the selected companies had to present different regions and industries of Russia.

Employing these principles, five Russian companies were selected: Arkhangelsk Pulp and Paper Mill (APPM), Norilsk Nickel (Nornickel), Kondrovo Paper Company (KPC), Avtoelektronika (AE) and Avtovaz. The choice of these firms is governed by the practical issue of gaining access to interview senior managers. These companies are of different sizes, from relatively small (AE) to very large (Nornickel), producing different types of products: cars, consumer goods, electronic components, metals and pulp. Each firm also operates with a different type of operation, strategy, geographical, regional and climatic conditions.

The author collected financial data for each firm covering the period from 1995–2011. It was anticipated that company reports and other financial papers would not be easy to retrieve as paper-based annual reports are not always kept by the companies; therefore, the author obtained this information from other sources. To collect narratives, it was the author's intention to conduct semi-structured interviews with executives of the companies. The interviews, corporate publications and direct observations were employed to establish factors, which impacted on post-privatisation corporate performance of the five selected companies.

Interviews

The research questions have been drawn from the analysis of business practice and this list of questions constituted the framework for interviews where attention is given to the narratives and explanations given by the participants. The basic questionnaire for the semi-structured interview includes 74 questions, classified into ten groups:

- industrial factors;
- regional factors;
- managerial influence;
- corporate and business unit strategies;
- operation management and manufacturing;
- management style and organisational behaviour;
- marketing;
- structure of the company and staff;
- finance;
- personal strategy of the principal shareholders or executives.

The interview sampling focused on the decision-making persons of the companies. In each case, a few persons were interviewed, such as top managers, major shareholders or an expert who had been working with the company for more than five years. All interviews covered different aspects of the companies in different times (1991–2010). They were conducted, recorded and transcribed in Russian, mainly between 2008 and 2010. Then, they were translated into English.

All of the quotes used from the informants' interviews have been minimally edited to preserve the original content. The information obtained during the interviews have been verified by interviewing other respondents and other relevant sources such as documents and press publications.

The interviews were translated from Russian into English with financial and management definitions and phrases being translated with consideration of occasional discrepancies between them. The quality of translation and conversion of definitions have been ensured by an expert analysis.

Analysis of interview data

The structuring of a respondents' judgment was a complicated task. The main aims of the analysis of interview data were:

- interpretation of the results in accordance with the objectives of a specific study;
- identification and assessment of textual material, allowing the drawing of conclusions;
- the logical linking of the data to the propositions of the cases;
- evaluating capacity of the factors of corporate performance by using content analysis of the interviews' answers.

The analysis of interview data consists of three stages:

- Preliminary evaluation of capacity of the factors of corporate performance. Again, this was carried out in consultation with the respondent.
- Evaluation of the quality of answers by comparison with other respondents' answers (data triangulation) or other sources of information (methodological triangulation).
- Evaluation of capacity of the factors to corporate performance (scoring of the factors).

We used the content analysis of the interview for the evaluation of the corporate performance's factors' capacity. Content analysis of the case study interviews is based on a study of sentences and words, focusing the author upon the interview content. However, there was the problem of an appropriate evaluation of factors – the author needed to decide whether a particular factor contributed to a positive or a negative impact on the corporate performance. In this case, it was necessary to evaluate not only each factor of performance of the organisation, but also their capacity. A particularly difficult component of this task is in the longitudinal research of corporate life.

The degree of influence was measured by a scale from one to five. A value of one means that the impact of a factor is very strong, a value of two – strong, three – middling, four – weak and five – insubstantial. As noted above, many factors that affect the privatisation and post-privatisation performance were selected by the respondents. Additionally, these factors were separated into internal and external categories and all were further classified by the respondents and the author into two groups: crucial and minor factors. Minor factors were employed as narratives in the case study, whereas the key internal factors of corporate performance were employed for analysis across cases.

Below are the examples from interview questionnaires and transcripts, showing the process of selection of factors and the estimation of their capacity:

Question: *Was the production process efficiently configured?*

Answer: *Operating segments were aggregated into three main production lines: production of paper, production of board and production of sulphate-bleached pulp.*

Answer evaluation: minor factor, which was used in this case but was not used in the cross-case analysis.

Question: *How efficiently did the company employ manufacturing capacity?*

Answer: *The management of the company released numerous projects such as putting into operation two container factories, introduction of elementary chlorine free pulp bleaching at the mill and reconstruction of the paper machines. The environmental policy was not a principal part of the company's strategy and in reality, APPM did not create safe operating conditions for its personnel nor it protected the health of local residents in its areas of operation or preserved a healthy environment.*

Answer evaluation: Score 4 (positive): a key factor, which was used in the case and in the cross-case analysis.

The results of the evaluation were used for constructing a web diagram. Figure 4.2 below shows the model key factors of corporate performance, where factors are represented in the form of questions.

In Chapter 10, the web diagrams of key internal and external factors are revealed in different configurations.

Conclusion

The research method has focused upon the construction of five firm-level case studies that were in turn the product of both narratives and numbers. The narratives used in the case studies were collected and summarised from semi-structured interviews carried out with managers and executives of the various

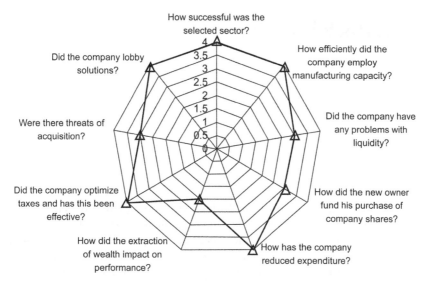

Figure 4.2 Key internal factors of corporate performance (example)
1 = Extremely negative, 2 = Negative, 3 = Relatively positive, 4 = Positive, 5 = Extremely positive.

privatised Russian companies selected. In addition, this book has collected financial information from the case study firms covering the period 1994 to 2011. This financial information was structured into key performance ratios employing a nature of expenses approach with a view to triangulating the interview material. The objective was to employ a rich financial dataset and utilise this information to highlight corporate performance in the five case study firms. This approach reveals the internal details of the dynamic process of privatisation and transformation in Russia.

One can pose a question: is it possible to obtain explanations that allow a confident generality and still respect the particularity of the case under study? To respond to this challenge this book employs both narratives and numbers to develop a critical reflection of the policy of Russian privatisation to explore the ambiguity between policy initiatives and outcomes.

We now turn in the following chapters to construct a series of five company case studies that combine narratives and numbers to explore corporate transformation after privatisation in Russia.

5   Avtoelektronika

The case study examines how the Kaluga electronic plant 'Avtoelektronika' was transformed from a relatively small auto-components supplier in the Russian car market to the large and successful company it now is, controlling more than 50 per cent of its market segment. The case shows a sustainable development of the company and the key component of its success.

Privatisation

Avtoelektronika (AE) was created in August 1990, based on the department of design of electronics in the auto electro-component plant 'KZAME' in the city Kaluga, for the production of modern electronic systems for vehicles. The first mass production of the plant was voltage regulators, control units of economiser, pressure and temperature sensors. In November 1992, the company was turned into a joint-stock company.

The distribution of shares at the first stage of privatisation was made according to 'option 2' of the law on privatisation and all the members of the company were given a right to acquire common shares for vouchers, which constituted up to 51 per cent of total shares of the authorised capital. Another 20 per cent of the ordinary shares were offered for sale at auctions against privatisation vouchers to private companies, some of them were close to executives of the company whereas others were independent investors. Additionally, 5 per cent of total shares were allocated amongst all the company's workers and 20 per cent of shares were offered as investments to business partners of AE. A small percentage of shares were sold to different companies and citizens in cash auctions (AE SR 1998).

After privatisation, the exact ownership of the company was clear: about 70 per cent of the shares belonged to executives and personnel of the company and this ownership was reflected by the structure of the board of directors, which included major representatives of the executives. In 1996 and 1997, an additional 12,000 issued shares increased the share that was controlled by the executives (AE SR 1998).

The major shareholder of the company was General Director Perchan, who for seven years saw his share increase from around 7 per cent to 31 per cent.

Other executives such as the commercial director, personnel director, financial and a few other executives accumulated more than 40 per cent of shares. The distribution of company shares to executives avoided many privatisation conflicts. Furthermore, in 2003, executives founded the management company and their shares were transferred to the new company (AE SR 2004).

Regional factors

AE was based in Kaluga (population 334,751), which is only 160 kilometres from Moscow. The town and the region did not have extensive natural, financial, consumer or production resources, which could have positively impacted corporate performance. The region did not have strong industries that dominated in the regional economy but it had a relatively strong machinery-building industry and benefited from a good supply of highly skilled specialists, created by the Soviet military industry. Beside this, the region had a moderate level of social, economic, ecological and criminal risks. Consumer and production resources of the region were weak and did not generate any demand for AE products.

After 2004, the regional authority started to promote the development of automotive-related industries, boosted the implementation of assembling plants and assisted in the development of regional transport infrastructure and technical services (ASM 2002–5). Between 2005 and 2007, Volkswagen, PSA-Peugeot and Mitsubishi Motors announced their decisions to build new assembly plants in Kaluga (PSA Peugeot Citroën 2007), which were built in 2007–10. There was a regional automotive-industry cluster and AE would be a participant in this cluster.

The executives of AE set a very positive relationship with the town and regional authority and this helped the company to get some privileges such as tax exemption and receive industrial properties and land on regional tenders. Additionally, the company's CEO was a member of the regional parliament and was nominated for the position of mayor of Kaluga where he took second place (AE 2004).

Industrial factors

The automotive industry of Russia included 226 enterprises, 28 research and design organisations and more than 770,000 people. More than 75 per cent of the workforce worked in auto-components manufactories. From 1990 to 1995, Russian car production fell sharply from 1,074,000 to 834,000 cars, affecting final assembly production and component manufacture (ASM 2000).

The Russian car industry, particularly the auto-component segment, had inherent characteristics: the mass production of cars with a limited model range and state financing of research and development. In addition, in comparison with its foreign counterparts, Russian automotive components and parts had inadequate ecological, ergonomic and safety characteristics and weak quality and reliability.

After 1992, the Russian automotive industry became more open, globalisation impacted upon the industry and product development and a new generation of composite material and electronic components were introduced. From 1993, there was strong competition between companies in the same industrial sector because there had been many supplies of auto components for a few assembling plants.

There were no strong barriers to new entrants into the auto-component segment. As a result, many companies from the Russian military industry started to produce auto components, whereas foreign manufacturers started to manufacture 10 years later because huge uncertainty about the future of Russia paralysed any activity of the leading international car manufacturers in the country. Between 1993 and 1998, the companies of the auto component segment did not have any opportunity for working with other buyers or changing their products unlike assembling plants that were more flexible.

The financial crisis in 1998 strongly impacted on the development of the auto component segment, and after 1999 many Russian car assembling plants refused to buy imported foreign auto components because of a sharp price increase and instead focused on domestic producers. As a result, the share of import components declined from approximately 20 per cent to 8 per cent (ASM 2000).

By 2000, about 90 per cent of cars produced in the European Union were equipped with a system of direct fuel injection and electronic engine management systems. European emission standards define the acceptable limits for exhaust emissions of new vehicles sold in the EU but Russian cars did not comply with any European standards regarding pollution. Only in 1999 did the Russian government establish Euro 1 for domestic auto producers. This created a strong demand for electronic fuel injection systems and microprocessor control systems. AE was founded for the production of modern electronic systems for vehicles and this was in line with the general developing trends of the car industry (AE SR 1998, 2001).

Business strategy after privatisation

To establish a competitive advantage over rival companies, between 1994 and 2004 AE employed a focused low-cost strategy and according to this strategy, the company targeted a few Russian assembling plants. The strategy was successful, particularly in the light of strong competition between auto-component producers. The company employed strategic methods for selection, development and coordination of the portfolio of businesses and a relatively high quality of strategic planning impacted encouragingly on corporate performance.

The company had sufficient ability to maintain the long-term competitive advantages and the impact of this strategy on corporate performance was strong. Since the first years after privatisation, corporate strategy was included as a part of constant management activity and it was paid attention to by the company executives. The quality of strategic planning was reasonably good and as a result, the company synchronised the corporate strategy and methods of its implementation.

There was an effective implementation of strategy in the vertical management functions such as marketing, investment management, personnel and quality control. The executives established a professional administration and monitoring of the company's assets and created a corporate centre that developed a uniform strategy. The opening of the Russian market generated the most vital challenges for the company because the Russian automakers lost their position therefore potential demand for AE products declined. In addition, threats for the company included strong competition from both domestic and foreign competitors and a rapid increase of consumer requirements for quality products.

The opportunities faced by the company from 1993 to 2005 were of tremendous potential for the growth of the Russian car market and an increasing market of auto components because car ownership per person in Russia was one of the lowest in Europe. Additionally, there were numerous highly skilled specialists in the region and an ability to attract investment. By 2002, opportunities increased with the signing of a cooperation agreement with Siemens (AE SR 2000).

The fundamental weaknesses of the company during that period were a large percentage of outdated equipment, undeveloped design and tool departments, the long cycle of placing products on the production line and the tremendous dependence on a few customers. By contrast, the strengths were the image of the company as a reliable supplier to major Russian car manufacturers, relatively high quality products, a secure financial position and high competence of executives.

After 2000, the executives decided to expand the business and the company's strategy of diversification included an internal development of new products such as electromechanical steering systems for the new model VAZ-2110, a new market as a manufacturer of electronics units for Uz-Daewoo (Uzbekistan) and ZAZ (Ukraine). In addition, it included an alliance with the design company ELCAR (Moscow), development of new products using technological similarities between industries such as electronics control units for refrigerators and the joining together with a design organisation (AE SR 2004). These combinations were determined by available opportunities with the objectives and the resources of the company. Between 1999 and 2004, the new company businesses were integrated and managed properly and there were synergies by sharing resources across business units.

A few years later in 2003, the company started to market many new products and services that had no technological synergies with its current products with the intention of improving the profitability and flexibility of the company and its influence in regional politics. These included the production of agricultural products and a tool plant 'INSEL' that designed and produced various types of tools and accessories for industry (AE SR 2004). In addition, 'Trade Centre Orbita-Service', specialising in the maintenance and repair of household electronic appliances, was bought as well as a 53 per cent share of 'Commercial Bank Kaluga'. The new firms had only a loose relationship with the company's current business and were not integrated and managed appropriately, preventing synergies across business units.

Management of operations

After privatisation, the company manufactured rather sophisticated products, such as controllers for internal combustion engines and controllers for car heating. In the late 1990s, the company established a system of management for intellectual property and registered 28 patents. In 1999, the automatic production line FUJI was bought and new technological opportunities for Avtoelektronika were opened (AE SR 1998, 2004).

Since its foundation, the company has maintained a stable growth rate and production volumes increased more than sevenfold in 15 years and it continually carried out work to improve its quality of production introducing the ISO 9001 quality control system (AE SR 2004). AE resourcefully employed manufacturing capacity and had a high-quality manufacturing schedule. In addition, the company employed highly qualified human resources: more than 30 per cent of the employees had a university degree (AE SR 2004).

The company could not quickly convert a product idea into a new product or improve already existing products and technologies. Additionally, operational management was made difficult by the fluctuation in quality of materials and components, a strong dependence on monopoly suppliers and their cartel agreements and stringent terms of payment. Levels of inventory were not optimised given that the AE production planning system did not work in harmony with the supply system of materials and components.

In 2006, the company finished modernisation of its workshop and installed new imported technological lines. As a result, the company began to manufacture electromechanical steering systems for a new model VAZ-2110 and doubled sales (AE SR 2006).

Marketing

Between 1994 and 2003, the company was dependent on the major consumer Avtovaz that purchased about 65 per cent of the total sales; later the company slightly decreased this share (AE SR 1998–2004). Sales were affected by prices of cars in the domestic market, exchange rates, tariff and tax that were set by the government and prices of raw materials. Since 1990, the company sold products directly to the major auto producers of Russia. However, after 2002 the exclusive company's trader 'AVTEL-Trade' sold more than 50 per cent of products (AE SR 2004). In addition, 'AVTEL-Trade' was a major supplier (36 per cent of the total volume) of AE and it was affiliated with AE's principal owners. It sold the electronic components from European firms to AE at prices that were at least 15 per cent higher than the market rate. This policy resulted in accumulated profit by the executives and helped the company effectively optimise duty and corporate taxes.

The situation in the automotive industry was characterised by stiff competition between suppliers of automotive components, therefore AE policy was to improve products and optimise the product value for money. As a result, until 2004 the company maintained at least a 50 per cent market share in core products, such as temperature sensors and light regulators (AE SR 2004).

It is important to note that the top Russian car manufacturers wanted to have not more than 50 per cent of deliveries from one national supplier so AE had several competitors for different types of products. By 2002, the company had begun to sell its products for private clients and small auto workshops using retail networks and this provided 14 per cent of total revenue (AE SR 2004).

AE did not have a solid research and development department. Therefore, in 1999 the company came together with design company ELCAR to found a Joint Venture 'AVTEL' of which AE had 50 per cent of the shares (AE SR 2000). The main goal of this business was the design, manufacture and supply of components of ECSE (electronic control systems for internal combustion engines), produced by the domestic plants.

The joint venture was the first integral ECSE supplier on the Russian automotive electronics market, granting both AVTEL and AE considerable competitive advantages. Moreover, AVTEL was able to compete in the domestic market of ECSE with the global giant Bosch. In October 2006, 51 per cent of the shares of AVTEL were bought by the German conglomerate Siemens with the aim of development and manufacture of electronics components for foreign car companies.

The consumer value of products was relatively high because the company produced reliable low-price products. However, there was no differentiation between AE's products and products of major Russian competitors. In addition, foreign manufactures were ahead of their Russian counterparts in durability and reliability. In the main, three major factors: quality, price and R&D impacted on corporate performance.

Financial management

In 1993–2003, 60–65 per cent of the total production cost of AE was the cost of electronic components, 10 per cent of the cost was labour and R&D and less than 3–4 per cent of the cost was amortisation, whereas foreign counterparts had greater labour costs, R&D and amortisation (AE SR 1998, 2000 and 2004).

The company effectively managed to control expenditure such as labour and administration costs. A major method of financial management was the rationing of the elements of working capital by the establishment of standard stocks in various stages of production, receivables and stocks of finished products. Additionally, the company paid attention to the correction of technological norms and discipline settlements with consumers.

As was noted above, in 2003–6, the company created numerous new subsidiaries in different areas such as agriculture, tourism, the food industry, banking and car retail. Substantial funds were invested both in new production and the acquisition of new businesses. This combination contributed to the growth in sales of the company and required additional finance. In the main new businesses did not generate sufficient cash flow; however, they maintained the image of a socially orientated company.

The company had a low risk of liquidation or acquisition due to a strong political position of the major shareholder. As well as this, the withdrawn wealth by the management was comparatively insignificant and it did not impact on corporate performance. Since 2005, the company made relatively large investments to launch the new products, therefore AE had a problem with working capital and desperately needed short- and long-term loans. Additionally the company funded itself by selling different assets (Interview AE 2010).

Financial analysis

AE operated with the intertwined problems of: a strong dependence on monopoly customers and their cartel agreements, fluctuations in the quality of materials and components of suppliers and problems with logistics. Nevertheless, sales revenue grew constantly due to strong demand for the company's products, devaluation of the rouble in 1998 and the Russian automotive boom during the period 2000–7 (see Figure 5.1 and 5.2).

As can be seen from Figure 5.3, in 1995–2007, the operating profit also increased, although during the period of 1998 and between 2001 and 2003, this profit was negatively affected by a reduction of a demand from Avtovaz and other Russian car assembly plants. Also in 2003–4, a large modernisation of the company's plants increased the resources cost and reduced reported operating profit.

Resource costs (see Figure 5.4), which includes external material and services purchased, and employee compensation accounted for approximately 85 per cent of total income in 1996–2011 (excluding the crisis 2008).

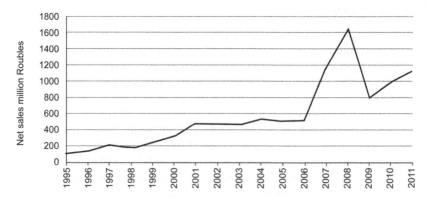

Figure 5.1 AE net sales (nominal)
Source: AE annual and special reports.

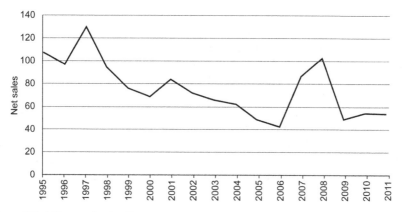

Figure 5.2 AE net sales (real)
Note: AE net sales in terms of purchasing power of the rouble as of 31 December 1995.
Source: AE annual and special reports. Author's calculation.

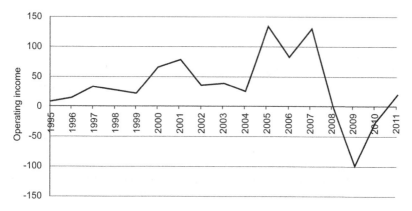

Figure 5.3 AE operating income
Source: AE annual and special reports.

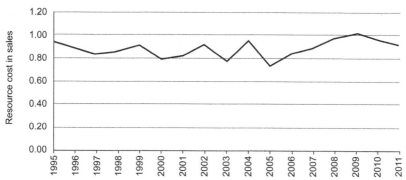

Figure 5.4 AE resources cost in sales
Note: resources cost in sales is defined as the sum of external material and services purchased and employee compensation divided by sales revenue.
Source: Author's calculation.

Value retained in income can be determined as the sum of EBITDA and labour cost divided into sales revenue. Between 1995 and 2004, the ratio fluctuated around 30 per cent and only during the crisis of 1998 did it reach a nadir of 20 per cent (see Figure 5.5). Later, it gradually improves to an average level; in 2006, this index peaked to 60 per cent, which was created by significant growth of EBITDA.

Figure 5.6 shows that external costs from 1995 to 2004 fluctuate around 70 per cent and thereafter (2005) it reduces to 48 per cent.

The company's share of labour costs in value retained is one of the key financial ratios employed by the company (Figure 5.7). It was relatively unstable between 1995 and 2007, fluctuating between 40 per cent (1998) and 73 per cent (2004).

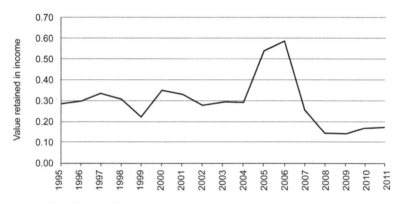

Figure 5.5 AE value retained in income
Note: Value retained in income can be determined as the sum of EBITDA and labour cost divided into sales revenue. Source: Author's calculation.

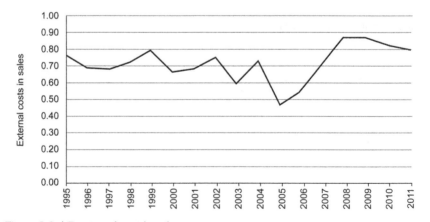

Figure 5.6 AE external cost in sales
Note: External cost is defined as raw materials and consumable divided by sales. Source: Author's calculation.

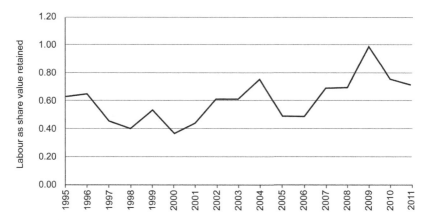

Figure 5.7 AE labour as share value retained
Note: Labour costs share of value retained is defined as personnel costs divided by operating result before depreciation and amortisation plus personnel costs. Source: Author's calculation.

Figure 5.8 shows that return on capital employed had a moderately cyclical pattern and the average ROCE for the company placed at about 30 per cent, which was comparable to the average levels of Russian car assembling plants. In 1999 and 2004, ROCE reached its minimal levels and after it relatively rapidly recovered to 50 per cent (2000 and 2005) for the reason that the company sales generated healthy gross profit margins.

Between 1995 and 1997, the company had a moderately low share of profit pre interest and tax in sales (ROS) which reached approximately 15 per cent (Figure 5.10) and relatively low capital employed as a share of income (Figure 5.9)

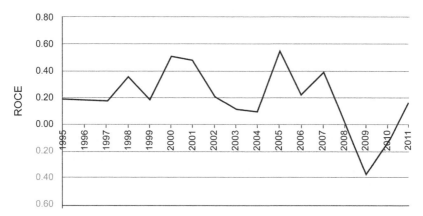

Figure 5.8 AE return on capital employed
Note: ROCE is defined as operating result before depreciation and amortisation in relation to the sum of equity and long-term debt.
Source: Author's calculation.

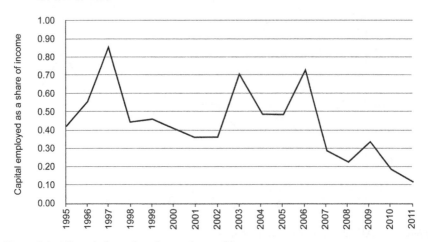

Figure 5.9 AE capital employed as a share of income
Note: Capital employed as a share of income is defined as total long-term debt plus
shareholders fund divided by sales.
Source: Author's calculation.

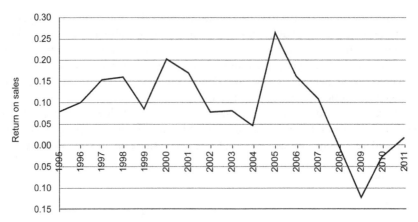

Figure 5.10 AE return on sales
Note: Return on sales is defined as operating result before depreciation and amortisa-
tion divided by sales.
Source: Author's calculation.

which was about 0.5–0.6. This combination boosted ROCE on a positive level
and additionally, in 2000 and 2005, growth of ROS lifted ROCE to a 50 per
cent level. In 1994–2006, the company constantly used about 0.5–0.6 roubles
of capital for every rouble of sales revenue.

Conclusion

Every year, AE maintained its position on the rapidly growing Russian auto
market and its market share was 50–60 per cent in different auto components.

Moreover, the company managed to dramatically increase a quantity of its products. Sales increased more than sevenfold in 15 years due to strong demand for the company's products and the Russian car boom. Return on capital employed had a moderately cyclical pattern at about 30 per cent, comparable to the average level of Russian car assembling plants.

The fundamental weaknesses of the company were a large percentage of outdated equipment, undeveloped design and tool departments, the long cycle of placing products on the production line and the tremendous dependence on Avtovaz and other Russian assembling plants.

By contrast, the strengths were the image of the company as a reliable supplier to major Russian car manufacturers, relatively high quality products, a secure financial position and high competence of executives. In addition, the company had a high intellectual level of human resources.

Threats to the company were strong competition in all major types of products and powerful foreign competitors. The opportunities faced by the company from 1993 to 2005 were tremendous potential for the growth of the Russian car market, an ability to attract investment and the cooperation with Siemens. The critical success factors of the company were control for expenditure and optimal relation between price and quality.

After 2000, the executives decided to expand the business and the company's strategies of diversification during the next five years included: internal development of new products and a new market, creation of an alliance with a complementary design company and development of new products using technological similarities between the industries.

In 2003–6, the company created numerous new subsidiaries in different areas such as agriculture, tourism, the food industry, banking and car retail, which had no technological synergies with its current products. Moreover, substantial amounts of funds were invested in new production and the acquisition of new businesses.

Managers established timely and regular feedback from their customers, resourcefully employed manufacturing and capacity effectively controlled the expenditure. Additionally, they set up standards of stocks in various stages of production and paid attention to correction of technological norms. The executives established a very positive relationship with the town and regional authorities and this helped the company to get some privileges such as tax exemption and the acquisition of an industrial property and land on a regional tender.

6   Avtovaz

This case study illustrates how the largest Russian car company Avtovaz managed its business during the various phases of the Russian transformation. Avtovaz was a long-standing Russian firm that built and assembled cars from parts that were made in Russia. Avtovaz controlled more than 60 per cent of the Russian car market and was protected significantly from overseas competition. The Avtovaz case is a story of a 'good deal gone bad' because privatisation did not create a stronger company fit for a competitive market. An opportunity was turned into a threat when senior managers lost sight of strategic and operational priorities as they concentrated their efforts on the struggle to extract wealth from within the company.

Privatisation

Avtovaz is a Russian automobile manufacturer that was built on the banks of the Volga River, 1,100 kilometres south of Moscow. The first car model, the VAZ 2101 was introduced in 1970. It is based on the 1966 Fiat 124; it was adapted to mitigate unsafe Russian driving conditions and is still the car associated the most with its Lada brand. On 19 April 1970, the factory was officially inaugurated, and mass production started. This plant was one of the biggest in the world, having three assembly lines, over 90 miles of production lines, a large power station, a foundry, a centre for stamping and a workshop for production of plastics and various chemicals. What distinguished this company from its competitors in the automotive industry was that most of the components for the cars were made by the company itself (Pleshanov 2001; History of Avtovaz 2007).

In 1975, just five years after opening, the target level of production was reached. As a result, nearly 750,000 Ladas left the gigantic assembly lines making this plant the third most productive in the world. The cars were distributed throughout the world, mainly in communist countries. During the 1970s and 1980s, the company updated the initial VAZ-2101 model incorporating different interiors and new types of engines. By 1986, more than 10 million cars were built using the Fiat 124 platform and by 2001 this figure had doubled to 20 million cars using not only Fiat but also other platforms (Pleshanov 2001; Shavrin 1996).

In the late 1980s, Avtovaz continued to remain a leader of the Soviet economy; however, the company had serious problems, for example, deterioration of tools and machinery, poor quality of manufactured products, unproductive management and an absence of market competition in the Soviet economy. The first problem was connected with low expenditures on renovation of equipment over a long period. For example, the wholesale price in 1985 on the model 2103 was 2,481 roubles and the cost price was 2,079 roubles. This included the materials used for manufacturing (24.5 per cent), purchased accessories (49.5 per cent), wages (3.8 per cent), charges on operation (8.6 per cent) and only 2.2 per cent was spent on the amortisation of the equipment (Shavrin 1996, 1998).

In October 1992, the presidential decree 'Avtovaz privatisation' was passed after successful lobbying by Vladimir Kadannikov, the head of Avtovaz since 1988, who became general director and chairman of the board of directors of the new company. He had several decades of experience at Avtovaz, having started out as a shop floor apprentice in his youth. This lobbying provided the company with particular terms and conditions for its privatisation. From January 1993, the company officially became an open joint-stock company, 'Avtovaz' (Pleshanov 2001, Shavrin 1996).

The final share distribution at the first stage of privatisation allowed for 25 per cent of company shares (5,354,161 of preference shares) to be distributed free to workers of Avtovaz. In addition, 10 per cent of ordinary shares were offered at a 30 per cent discount by a closed subscription to members of the workforce (Avtovaz AR 1997, 1998).

Another 10 per cent of ordinary shares were sold to employees at face value and a further 5 per cent of ordinary shares were offered to senior managers under an option scheme. Company executives controlled the share allocation and had the opportunity to take up shares.

At the first stage of privatisation the state continued to own half of the company equity, however, it was restricted to only 20 per cent of voting shares, which resulted in limiting state power and a high level of control by the management of the company. The system of hiring executives comprised of two stages: first, the State Property Committee (GKI) concluded an agreement with the general director and second, the general director arranged contracts with the managers already employed and gave them the right to buy shares. This system increased the real power of the general director above any other senior managers.

Following this first stage of privatisation, the company was controlled by Avtovaz management. Kadannikov owned about 10–15 per cent of Avtovaz shares through different companies, which enabled him to control the company's financial flows. However, there was a high risk of losing control because the state had to sell 50 per cent of the company equity in the following three years and the future purchaser could be another oligarchic group. Therefore, in order to secure future control of Avtovaz management, they had to find finance for the next stage of privatisation (Interview Avtovaz 2010).

In the absence of state and shareholders, the highest ranking executives had taken the 'I manage. Therefore, I own' approach in order to achieve their objectives, and senior management designed a number of ad hoc performance schemes for personal enrichment.

Industrial and regional factors (1993–7)

After the disintegration of the USSR, precarious economic situations in the country resulted in a decline of manufacturing. From 1990 to 1995, Russian car production fell sharply from 1,074,000 cars to 834,000 (Russia in Figures 1997). Avtovaz reduced its production over the same period from 734,588 to 609,213 (Pleshanov 2001). Since 1990, the market for the Russian automotive industry had significantly decreased. Export of Russian cars shrank from 55 per cent of total production to just 17 per cent over the period of 1990–5 (Russia in Figures 1997).

Deliveries of cars from Russia to former Soviet republics were reduced tenfold so the Russian car industry refocused on the domestic market (Avtovaz AR 1995). The automotive industry was affected by new state boundaries and lost markets in the Far East of Russia and the Kaliningrad enclave. These lucrative markets were taken over by Japan and Germany respectively (Avtovaz AR 1995, 1998).

After 1992, the Russian automotive industry had become more open, and globalisation had begun to impact on this industry and Avtovaz in particular. At that time, leading car manufacturers were merging and consolidating their operations on a large scale. This had given rise to remarkable economies of scale and the accumulation of resources required for research and development of the next generation of cars. Major international automotive companies had improved quality, safety, reliability and ecological parameters more rapidly than those in Russia. New models were constructed as a rule every two to three years and tailored much closer to customer needs; as a result, Avtovaz and other Russian carmakers could not compete in these events.

In the first years after Russian reform, there was no competition between the companies in the same industrial sector because there was a strong specialisation in different cars plants, as planned by the state. It could be argued that there were no hard barriers to new entrants into the Russian automotive industry. However, huge uncertainty about the future of Russia paralysed any potential activity from leading global automobile manufacturers.

Avtovaz was built in the Samara region where aerospace, automotive and oil industry activities dominated. According to Expert RA (1996), the region had high investment potential due to favourable factors such as natural resources, good finance, innovation, infrastructure, high productivity and a high level of regional consumer and skilled labour force. The degree of political, social and economic risk was not strong, but there were relatively high ecological and criminal risks.

Avtovaz played a key role in the regional economy by providing about 40 per cent of total production of the machinery-building industry in Samara

(Avtovaz AR 1998, 2000, Shavrin 1996, 1998). The company also promoted the development of automotive-related industries, boosted the implementation of advances in science and technology and assisted in the development of regional transport infrastructure and technical services. There was a regional automotive-industry cluster, and Avtovaz was the centre of this cluster. During the 1990s, about 200 suppliers of Avtovaz located in this region, which supplied about 40 per cent of all purchased components and materials used by the company. About 400,000 jobs throughout the region depended on the company's success in maintaining stable performance and growth of its business (Avtovaz AR 1998).

In 1993–5, suppliers of the company did not have opportunities to work with other car manufactories. Senior management of Avtovaz was fully aware of the importance of the company's contribution to the Samara regional economy and exploited their dominant position. The company had an exceptionally strong impact on the overall Russian economy and a strong influence in the federal capital and the region. The human resources of this region were sufficient to satisfy the company's requirements, and they had contributed positively to the financial performance of the company. This automotive company generated more than 35 per cent of the total budget of the Samara region (Shavrin 1996, 1998, Pleshanov 2001).

At the same time (1993–5) the company created a number of joint-stock companies, investing its own capital but also giving these subsidiaries legal independence. Among these were the Serpukhov, Scopin and Dimitrovgrad auto plants that were constructed during the Soviet years and traditionally had been working with Avtovaz (Avtovaz AR 1998, Shavrin 1998).

In addition, building, transport and catering retail departments had been outsourced to separate business units. Many subsidiary companies with an unclear purpose were created by Avtovaz executives and were governed by former and current managers of the company. Those companies operated without strong official management control and rigid supervision of their budget. Moreover, these companies created new independent organisations and transferred Avtovaz assets to them without permission of the possessor (Interview Avtovaz 2010).

Business strategy after privatisation

When the USSR bought the FIAT 124 model, no consideration was given to long-term cooperation with leading foreign motorcar manufacturers. When auto manufacturers produce models under licence, fundamental problems arise not at the initial stage of a project but at the intermediate stage. Avtovaz could exist for some time using one platform after the purchase of this readymade model, especially in the absence of competition. Difficulties only emerged when the time came to change the model that, unfortunately, coincided with the breakdown of the political system in the USSR. The automobile companies of the Soviet Union lacked sufficient funding for significant modernisation of production and always had to rely on the socialist government for financial assistance.

In non-socialist developing countries, car companies exchanged the right to make the cars under licence in exchange for equity participation by the foreign licensers. In addition, the foreign corporation provided consultation, watching over the 'younger brother' and periodically transferring technology. For example, the Turkish subsidiary of Renault produced the Renault 12 under the name 'Broadway' and then the Renault 19, by which time Renault France had begun to assemble the Megane. Likewise, Huyndai, produced in South Korea, was based on the outdated Mitsubishi models.

In the final years of the Soviet era, Avtovaz created the new 'Samara' platform, development of which was funded by the government. In the 1990s, it became clear that the socialist economy could not create the next generation of cars and, therefore, to promote Avtovaz development, the government could have invited a foreign investor and could have sold that investor equity participation and passed on Avtovaz's problems. However, the government and company management decided to proceed with the next model – 'model 10' – instead.

General Director Kadannikov, talking about the problem of model 10 with the company employees, noted:

> [I]t is necessary to tighten our belts because all the profit of Avtovaz should only be used on the model VAZ-2110. This is a difficult decision, but we cannot reject the model 10 because we have invested too much: the new engine plant has been constructed, the main assembly plant has been increased and we have already provided our suppliers with the new equipment.
>
> (History of Avtovaz 2007)

The main argument for continuing this project was the risk of losing the investment, but the company did not have the funds to complete this project and, from a marketing perspective, this model did not perform well because of its price. The company could not terminate the 'model 10' project. This strategy depressed corporate performance and only imposed import duties have improved the price competitiveness of the new model in the domestic market.

Despite this failure, Avtovaz, which was relatively successful in the B-class car industry sector, tried to diversify its position into the A-class car range by participating in the project 'People car' together with the Russian government in Elabuga town. Avtovaz planned to assemble 900,000 cars similar to the Fiat Panda that exceeded the production capacity of the Tolyatti plant (History of Avtovaz 2007; Pleshanov 2001).

The search for a foreign investor was not successful and making the new model without sufficient internal and external resources was an extremely difficult task for the company. This attempt by the company to create such a large project with insufficient resources appeared as management chaos, but in reality, the Avtovaz executives' aim was to acquire government funding.

The company did not employ strategic methods for the selection, development and coordination of the portfolio of businesses. Often the personal interest of the executives, the principal shareholders and the government bureaucracy connected to the corporate strategic solutions and projects.

To establish a competitive advantage over rival companies, Avtovaz used focused low-cost strategy and, according to this strategy, the company targeted a customer sector of individuals with an annual salary of between $3,000 and $12,000, who were the Russian middle class, and this was a successful strategy particularly in the light of weak competition. However, the company did not have sufficient ability to maintain the long-term competitive advantages and corporate strategy did not feature as a part of regular management activity.

The quality of strategic planning was poor, and as a result, the company could not synchronise corporate strategy and methods of management to measure the process of implementation of corporate strategy. There was no guaranteed or effective implementation of strategy in corporate business units in the vertical management functions such as marketing, investment management, personnel and quality control.

The executives of Avtovaz did not establish efficient administration and monitoring of the company's assets. They did not create a corporate centre that could develop a uniform strategy and make strategic management available. The critical success factors of the company were the monopoly position in the Russian market, the low level of consumption of cars and the ability of the company to struggle against the increase of imported cars. The opening of the Russian market generated the most significant challenges for the company. The opportunities faced by the company from 1993 to 1997 were of tremendous potential for growth of the Russian car market because car ownership per person in the country was one of the lowest in Europe. The fundamental weaknesses of the company during that period were the low quality of production, old-fashioned models and deficit financial and intellectual resources for making new platforms. By contrast, the strengths were recognition of the brand, a significant share of the domestic market and low cost of production, service and operation.

Management of operations (1993–7)

As stated above, Avtovaz production had declined dramatically in the 1990s and in 1994 reached its nadir: 528,845 cars were assembled, almost 30 per cent less than the average volume over the past ten years (Avtovaz AR 1995).

Since 1993, the assembly lines of the plant had been regularly halted by strikes; moreover, in 1994 the strikers stopped production for an entire month. The workers demanded an increase in salary, regular and timely wages, and they accused the executives of corruption and poor management.

Apart from these labour difficulties, Avtovaz had to address problems of efficiency in operations and production: namely, they had to improve the

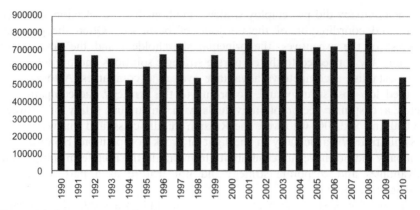

Figure 6.1 Avtovaz car production
Source: Avtovaz annual reports, History of Avtovaz.

components supply system as many parts and components were delivered by more than four or six suppliers, so the selection of supply was irrational and taken on the spur of the moment.

Organisation and discipline were not controlled and seemed anarchic. For example, management was incapable of controlling informal arrangements on the site where consumer goods and foods were brought and sold near the workplaces, disrupting work zones in a chaotic and an uncontrolled manner, even stopping labour shifts. This situation was in a direct contradiction with numerous company rules and regulations as well as those of federal health and safety. Nevertheless, for a long time the administration turned a blind eye to these violations.

At that time, Avtovaz frequently could not pay suppliers on time thus paralysing delivery of parts and units. Regularly, company personnel had to halt production on main assembly lines due to the depletion of inventory. To overcome this chronic shortage, panic orders were placed for express delivery by air, dramatically increasing the cost of parts. This lack of inventory was completely predictable yet emergency freight orders had to be placed several times a month. This situation was further exacerbated by failure on the part of suppliers to implement a new quality control system – the ISO 9000 – generating an enormous problem with the quality of the cars.

The management system of Avtovaz was not responsive to the specific requirements of their consumers because Avtovaz did not establish timely or regular feedback from their customers through dealers and their service companies. The company could not provide the foundation for a flexible plan of operations that could then be incorporated into production programmes. Consequently, levels of inventory were not optimised, given that the Avtovaz production planning system did not work synchronically with the supply system of materials and components. In particular, it did not establish a balance of components and material between suppliers' stock in their warehouses and the company's own stock in the production zone.

The company could not quickly convert a product idea into a new product or improve already existing products and technologies. An example of this was seen in the case of the VAZ-2110. The initial stages of this model's development began in 1986 (History of Avtovaz 2007). From 1993 'model ten' has began to be shown widely at motor shows but mass production did not start until 1996, the result of this severely affected its market position because the car's principal characteristics were outmoded in relation to their European competitors. It was only in 1997, when the five years of crises were overcome, that Avtovaz reached the production level of 739,600 cars, which preceded the pre-crises level (Avtovaz AR 2000).

Marketing (1994–7)

In 1994, Russia had a comparatively underdeveloped car market and according to official statistics, car market penetration was at 83 cars per 1,000 people, considerably lower than that in other European markets. For example, in Germany for every 1,000 inhabitants there were approximately 500 cars (ASM 1995). This factor created a large demand for cars in Russia, because national manufacturers did not have an adequate capacity and the quality of cars could not satisfy the consumers.

From 1993 to 1997, despite a decline in the Russian economy and the automotive industry, the car market in Russia was steadily growing because of a considerable increase in car imports. In 1996, there was an enormous growth in foreign second-hand motor vehicles, which rose to 457,000 (about 50 per cent of the market). Consequently, the market share for foreign cars grew from 2 per cent to 18 per cent; it was a serious threat to the domestic automotive industry and for Avtovaz in particular (ASM 1998).

From 1994 to 1997, the retail price of 95 per cent of cars was less than $8,000, and the market, in the main, consisted of the C sector, which included LADA vehicles representing 70 per cent of the market. The E sector (Volga and foreign vehicles) represented 12 per cent and the SUV sector (Niva, UAZ and foreign vehicles) represented 10 per cent. In terms of production and sales of passenger cars Avtovaz was the unquestionable leader and its share of the market was about 75 per cent for new cars and about 50 per cent of all sold cars in that period (Avtovaz AR 1995, 1999). However, the company significantly lost position on the European market. For example, between 1994 and 1996 in Bulgaria, the share of 'Lada' and 'Samara' decreased by 40 per cent, in Hungary by 70 per cent and in Central Europe Avtovaz market share became negligible (ASM 1998).

From 1993 to 1997, the company's model mix consisted of vehicles from three generations as follows: the 'classic' Lada vehicles (VAZ 2104, 2105, 2106, 2107) and the off-road VAZ-2121 and 21213 models, which were designed and put into production in the early 1970s. The front wheel drive platform was represented by the models VAZ 2108, 2109, 21099, which were designed and put into production in the early 1980s, and the VAZ-2110, which was designed and put into production during the 1990s (Avtovaz AR 1996, 1999).

The domestic distribution network included about 300 trading companies comprised of regional distributers, direct dealers and dealers many of which were started by managers of Avtovaz, who teamed up with friends and relations as partners. However, corporate sales did not generate high gross profit because trading companies often bartered components and materials for cars directly with a 25 or 30 per cent discount from the wholesale price.

The company sold cars to distributors at an average price of $3,500 per unit (ASM 1998); the official retail price was approximately $5,000, and in reality, the average price of Lada was about $6,000. Whereas trading average expenditures and profit amounted to approximately $900 per vehicle. As a result, the company lost more than $1,300 on each car. Moreover, the executives did not attempt to change this pricing strategy because the company managers profited from these sales (Interview Avtovaz 2010).

In the 1990s, the company's network of customer services in Russia consisted of about 675 technical service stations and 3,972 service outlets, located in 71 regions of the Russian Federation, employing 14,000 employees (Avtovaz AR 1999). However, Avtovaz did not control the quality of its technical services, and the management system was not responsive to the requirements of its consumers. The company did not create a strong marketing function nor did it develop its skills in market research and the monitoring of macroeconomic trends.

In the period of 1993 to 1997, the Avtovaz dealers had been severely affected by the company's crisis management and its failure to honour deliveries of cars and spare parts. The situation worsened due to the erratic pricing policy, which resulted in more than ten variants of car prices depending on personal relationships between dealers and Avtovaz executives. In addition, many dealers received cars under special bills and payoffs with the terms of sale, which demanded one-third more if the cars were not bought by cash. As a result, many traders started to trade imported cars instead of Lada; what is more, they preferred to buy cheaper spare parts in Finland.

Criminal wars

The homicide rate in Russia more than tripled between 1988 and 1994 and was among the highest in the world. However, the level of criminal activity within Tolyatti exceeded the national average. From the late 1980s, Tolyatti was well known for racketeers who demanded money from buyers, transporting their cars from the plant (Soldatov 2002). Shortly thereafter, these criminal gangs started demanding $100 commission per car from trading companies to guarantee safe delivery.

Although untypical for large Russian companies, Avtovaz had its own police department, which included 155 professional police officers. Despite this police presence, every year about 1,700 crimes were registered, approximately 85 per cent of which were thefts. The official corporate losses from thefts in 1997 amounted to about 90 billion roubles ($20 million), as a rule, large thefts of 300–400 million roubles were prevented twice a week (Trifonov 1998).

The head of the Avtovaz police department noted that by 1995 criminal organisations controlled car sales, distribution of spare parts and car shipment. Gangsters in the service of trading companies delivered cars to buyers with specification and colour pre-ordered by dealers, charging extra for particular colours for example. Furthermore, bandits frequently delivered spare parts when the plant had experienced shortages or stoppages; this resulted in the bizarre situation where criminals acting upon car dealers' orders were the driving force behind the assembly line production. The management of Avtovaz needed to accept this criminal–economic situation because of the close relationships that existed between certain managers and criminal elements. Moreover, executives used gangsters to break strikes and prevent deviant behaviour of employees (Interview Avtovaz 2010).

Executives employed criminals as debt collectors, but on occasion this created other forms of economic crime. For example, in December 1995, dealers' liabilities to Avtovaz exceeded $800 million, and the financial controller Vladimir Nesterov suggested to the criminal leader Vogel to organise the collection of these outstanding debts (Trifonov 1998). According to the contract, Vogel was authorised to recover outstanding payments from corporate debtors and charge a commission of 10 per cent on amounts recovered. As a result of these operations, the company lost $1,300,000 as prepayment to Vogel for his work, which he was not going do. Only in 2001, after a five-year investigation, this most controversial criminal trial finally came to an end.

From 1993 onwards, the criminal situation escalated. In 1997, there were 200 murders in Tolyatti alone, 65 of which were of company managers, dealers and business rivals including two Avtovaz board members: Oleg Shevtsov and Vladimir Shishkov. In that year, Avtovaz perhaps had become the most gangster-ridden leading industrial company in Russia; therefore, the executives had to admit that the company had serious problems with gangsters and asked the Russian government for assistance.

In 1997, the Ministry of Internal Affairs (MVD) launched 'Operation Cyclone' (Trifonov 1998), a combined-forces attack on criminal groups with 3,000 operatives from MVD being involved in this operation. After the opening of this criminal investigation, over 50 people were arrested. The investigation brought clear evidence that gangsters infiltrated Avtovaz management. It was discovered that an additional 500 cars had been manufactured but were not registered in the company's documents because computer information had been deleted at regular intervals, thus omitting them from production statistics (Trifonov 1998).

The extraordinary level of criminal activity in the city and the company was a result of the specific conditions in the region as well as unprofessional conduct, corruption and fraud in the company itself. For years, the federal government had ignored the conflicts of interest and even the relationship between the criminal element and managers because the government wished to gain their support for policies (Interview Avtovaz 2010).

Financial management (1993–7)

From the start of privatisation, the company had serious problems with liquidity, which is the ability to convert assets into cash. Therefore, the company could not meet its commitments on time, either for third party contracts or wages to employees. For example, during the period of 1995–6, the company paid monthly salaries two months in arrears and this practice sometimes gave rise to strike action by the workforce.

To improve liquidity, in 1993, Avtovaz issued bonds with repayments of loans being made in Avtovaz cars. The total amount of the bond issue was equivalent to 300,000 cars (Avtovaz AR 2000); however, over three years the company could only sell 42,755 bonds because few people trusted Avtovaz.

From 1993 to 1997, the company's fiscal indebtedness grew both at federal and local levels. When the former Avtovaz president Vladimir Kadannikov was appointed vice premier of the Russian government, he used his authority to allow an exception for Avtovaz to have a full tax write off. However, after the swift departure of Kadannikov from the government, the company was reassessed and its tax liabilities had ballooned to 4,600 billion roubles. In light of this, the new first deputy prime minister of the Russian government, Potanin, suggested that the company went into liquidation. However, Avtovaz was a significant test case for the government, which decided finally that it could not risk closing a company that employed 120,000 people. As a result, the government passed legislation to enable a rescue package for Avtovaz that included an extension of tax repayments over a long period.

In October 1997, the government allowed Avtovaz to restructure repayments totalling to approximately 4,650 billion roubles. Additionally, the company was allowed to postpone payment of these debts for ten years. This restructuring was guaranteed by the issue of additional shares, and subsequently the Russian government took a 50 per cent shareholding in the company (Avtovaz AR 2000).

At the same time, Avtovaz executives were fearful that the government might sell its shareholding to third parties. To protect their own shareholdings, executives' assets were transferred to corporate entities affiliated with these executives, the largest of which was 'Sok'. It was supposed that this disposal of assets would protect the company from hostile acquisition. If the government had decided to sell corporate shares, it would have been too problematic because of non-transparency within the automotive giant.

According to interviews and company data, there were many methods for appropriation of assets by the management, the proceeds of which were used for share purchasing and other purposes. Company executives created a number of firms located in Germany and Italy whose basic function included sale of the cars, purchase of accessories, materials and industrial equipment.

Illegal income was formed by overestimated invoice pricing for equipment delivered to the company.

Special investigation by shareholders showed that the volume of annual contracts on each of the specified firm-suppliers amounted to between $100 and $240 million, and the overestimated price for the ordered equipment was more than 20–30 per cent. Therefore, the annual commission on each contract could be worth $20 to $65 million (Trifonov 1998).

Berezovsky, the principal non-official shareholder and a close partner of the company's president, offered a scheme known as re-export. Avtovaz export contracts normally specified lower price for Ladas than domestic dealership contracts and offered extended grace periods for foreign dealerships in their credit terms. Berezovsky's company actually sold its cars in Russia, but the cars never physically crossed the Russian border, although trade documentation showed them as exported and then imported back into Russia.

As a result, Avtovaz had an export price per car of approximately $3,000 thereby losing $160 million per year, with more than $300 million in unpaid invoices; this outstanding debt was attributed to sales problems. Supported by some Avtovaz managers, the private trading companies siphoned off profits by buying company cars at below-market prices and reselling them to retailers at a giant gain (Interview Avtovaz 2010).

As mentioned above, many dealers close to executives could sell their Ladas for $6,000 or more, making 50 per cent gross margins, much more than a dealer would get in Western countries. By 1995, Berezovsky's Logovaz and other dealers owed the automaker $1.2 billion, representing one-third of its annual revenues (ibid.).

In addition, an extremely popular method of sale involved traders buying cars with defects at discounts of 30–40 per cent of the normal sale price and after minor repairs by a mechanic at a cost of just 2–3 per cent; these cars were then sold in mint condition. Because of these financial operations, Kadannikov and Berezovsky set up a company, called the All-Russian Automobile Alliance (AVVA), which steadily amassed a 34 per cent stake in the company. Avtovaz managers and employees owned 35 per cent of the company, and Automobile Finance Corporation, which was affiliated with Avtovaz and headed by Kadannikov, held 19 per cent (Avtovaz AR 2000). Thus in 1996 Kadannikov and Berezovsky held more than 50 per cent of shares and had full control of the auto giant.

Industrial and regional factors (1998–2002)

In August 1998, the Russian economy was hit by the financial crisis that was intensified by the Asian financial crisis of 1997 and the global recession of 1998. However, the primary causes of the financial crisis were budget deficit and the extreme level of inflation, which reached 84 per cent per year. In addition, the national economy was affected by the sharp decline of world commodities prices, which accounted for more than 80 per cent of exports and they were a significant source of the government tax revenue (Åslund 2007).

However, Russia recovered from the financial collapse unusually quickly due to the devaluation of the rouble. The growth of import prices in domestic industries such as motor, food processing and textiles recovered their capacity. Moreover, for the first time in many years, unemployment in 2000 had declined. Surprisingly, the financial crisis did not have such a strong impact on many manufacturers as it would have had if the Russian economy was dependent on a banking system because the economy was operating with a significant level of non-monetary instruments such as barter and bills.

In 1998–2002, the regional factors were similar to the period of 1993 and 1997, which were analysed above. The industrial factors had been transformed by the financial crisis, which gave a large opportunity for the motor industry and auto-component producers. All car manufacturers improved their financial position, implemented modern technology and improved quality.

From 2000, consolidation and integration had become a trend in the motor industry. For example, the main Russian steel producer 'Severstal' acquired a controlling stake in 'UAZ' and 'Siberian Aluminium', took over 'GAZ', and several bus and engine plants (ASM 2000). The new executives of these factories improved management, reduced debts, made better marketing strategies and eliminated barter schemes. However, most domestic automotive makers did not have funds to invest in a new car development and in the upgrading of production facilities.

Since 2000, all the major world car manufacturers have paid increased attention to the Russian market. By the end of 2002, there were already six foreign car assembly operations in Russia. Ford started to assemble the Ford Focus in the Leningrad region; General Motors, jointly with Avtovaz, produced cars in Tolyatti; 'Autotor' in Kaliningrad assembled Kia, BMW and Hummer; Moscow's 'Avtoframos' assembled the Renault-Megane; the Taganrog car plant assembled motor vehicles for Hyundai and Izhevsk car plants assembled the Kia Spectra (Kansky 2004). As a result, in 2002, there were 11,000 cars assembled by foreign car manufacturers (ASM 2003).

Business strategy (1998–2002)

The financial crisis gave Avtovaz a new impulse to employ strategic methods for development of the company. The executives saved control in the company, and the risk of non-friendly acquisition had dramatically declined. The private aims of the executives changed from control of the financial flows and withdrawal of wealth to incrementing of the value of the business. Consequently, the company became more transparent and the corporate strategic solutions and projects became more understandable for outsiders.

As a result, it was possible to generate a new vision for the company. The owners of the company began to search for a foreign partner for Avtovaz, and this was officially declared as one of the strategic tasks – to actively seek opportunities to form strategic alliances with large investors (Avtovaz AR 2001).

From 1998 to 2002, the company established a two-level management system of corporate centre and business units, completed the first stage of modernisation of business units and made them independent. The leading consulting company of the world car industry, A. T. Kearney, was engaged as a creator for a new strategy of the company that included an evaluation of its current condition and business environment, minimisation of expenses, creation of a portfolio of investment projects and the complex analysis of business strategies (Avtovaz AR 2001).

Nevertheless, the quality of strategic planning and implementation of corporate strategy was limited; many strategic purposes of the company were unclear and time frameworks of the strategic purposes were incomprehensible. In addition, the purposes did not contain target values and ineffectively corresponded with the accepted strategy.

The strategic targets of the company were rather short-term and were focused more on operational activities such as improvement of a financial condition, reduction of costs and restructuring the company's dealership network. To establish a competitive advantage over rival companies, Avtovaz employed a focused low-cost strategy (Avtovaz AR 2000).

After 1998, an optimal strategy for Avtovaz could have been a strategy to hold the market position. In this case, the growth of efficiency was possible both due to improvement in working with clients and the optimisation of internal business processes and investment projects could have been directed on expansion of capacities. Therefore, there could have been a growth of market share and operating profit, growth of profitability of capital, separate products and business as a whole.

However, the company selected the strategy that was more suitable for 'stages of growth', which presumed the possession of the essential potential of growth, the significant volume of investments with the purpose of promotion of new types of production, development of a distributive network, expansion of capacities and the creation of a wide client base. Nevertheless, the company did not have resources for implementing the 'stages of growth' strategy.

The opportunities faced by the company were the growth of the Russian car market. Moreover, Avtovaz had opportunities in the expansion of the market due to the growth of the small business sector, manufacturing of accompanying goods, work with certificated Russian suppliers, reception of financial and political support from the Russian government, raising funds from private investors and an increase in the personal income of Russian citizens.

The fundamental weaknesses of the company were the low quality of cars and spare parts, a lack of clear functional strategy, low consumer loyalty, old-fashioned models, deficit of financial and intellectual resources for building a new platform and scarcity of manufacturing capacity. By contrast, the company's strengths continued to be brand recognition, a significant share of the domestic market and low prices of products and services. Importantly, the most significant threats for the company were the appearance of new competitors and the changing requirements and attitudes of consumers.

Management of operations (1998–2002)

In line with general economic growth in Russia, Avtovaz production had been increasing significantly since 1998; in 2001, a record level of production was achieved when some 768,000 vehicles were assembled, almost 6 per cent more than the theoretical capacity of Avtovaz (Avtovaz AR 2002). Additionally 60,000 old-fashioned cars were assembled by the external subsidiaries in Russia and Ukraine.

Between 1998 and 2002, the Avtovaz model mix consisted of vehicles of three generations that were quite similar in the previous five-year period and the share of the new front-wheel family of VAZ-2110 reached 25 per cent of the production (Avtovaz AR 2002).

After the crisis of 1998, Avtovaz improved the monitoring purchase costs for materials and components, transferred production of some components to third-party suppliers, increased the turnover of the inventory and updated the Enterprise Resource Planning systems. In addition, the company eliminated barter transactions and managed to replace the majority of foreign suppliers to Russian suppliers. Therefore, the share of cost of imported components at Avtovaz reduced from 25 per cent to approximately 5 per cent.

During 2000–1, the majority of the company's production divisions and a number of suppliers were certified for compliance with ISO 9002. However, Avtovaz could not significantly improve the quality, and in 1999, there were 49,917 cases where vehicles were originally assembled with missing parts (Avtovaz AR 2001). The dealers had to spend a few hours on pre-selling preparation for each car and an extra payment for recovering missing spare parts and Avtovaz never compensated their dealers for this expenditure.

Marketing (1998–2002)

Selling in that period was relatively stable, it was equal to approximately 1,300,000 cars annually, and after 2000, the domestic car market was worth about $9 billion in terms of sales (ASM 1999). New vehicles that were made in Russia accounted for about two-thirds of total vehicle sales. Sales of second-hand foreign vehicles grew by 87.3 per cent. It remained the most serious threat to Avtovaz (ASM 1999). The underdeveloped Russian car market created a large demand for cars and price asymmetries between domestic and external markets. Consequently, numerous entrepreneurs employed opportunities for arbitrage; there was colossal growth in foreign second-hand motor vehicles that was a serious threat to the company.

In order to prevent the significant growth of used-car imports Avtovaz lobbied the government programme about encouraging domestic production of cars. As a result, tariffs on used cars were increased by 35 per cent to protect domestic producers from inexpensive used-car imports. However, the limitation of sales of second-hand cars could not support domestic markets because the demands for used car imports were shifted towards the low-priced foreign new cars.

The Avtovaz case reveals two outcomes: on the one hand, it demonstrates strong price asymmetries and a robust opportunity for arbitrage in the undeveloped Russian market. On the other hand, it shows a strategy of defence against arbitrage. This case clearly discloses the Avtovaz competition strategy – increasing the trade barrier for second-hand foreign cars. The history of Avtovaz shows that the company maintained competitive advantages for ten years by using anti-arbitrage strategy.

After the crisis and devaluation of the rouble, 'Lada' and 'Samara' quickly filled in the niches that had been released by foreign cars; Avtovaz sales in 2001 reached its peak – 774,000 cars, almost 30 per cent more than before the crisis year. The company innovated many slightly modernised models that were extremely profitable because the costs of new models and old were almost the same, but their prices were considerably different. In addition, the company had reduced the discount to wholesalers from 15 per cent to 10 per cent respectively. However, Avtovaz's share in the Russian market decreased steadily from 58 per cent in 1998 to 49 per cent in 2002 (Avtovaz AR 2001, 2002).

The company created the trade network in all Russian cities and modified significantly principles of car sales. First, the dealers got an opportunity to sell cars assembled specially for them by their order, which reached about 90 per cent of production volume. Second, a special pricing system based on principles of geographical position of the dealer was offered. Finally, Avtovaz got an opportunity to inspect the price policy over all dealers of the country in order to exclude dumping from the dealers. In those days, the company deliberately raised actual export sales (over 83,000) of vehicles, primarily in CIS countries because the devaluation of the Russian rouble in 1998 benefited the company significantly by overseas sales (Avtovaz AR 2002).

The company did not employ the broad implementation of consumer credit and leasing, marketing research techniques such as a consumer satisfaction index and loyalty index and did not use the e-commerce instruments. The implementation of corporate image and independent segments of the distribution network were inadequate, and the quality of after-sale services needed substantial improvement.

Financial management (1998–2002)

Between 1998 and 2002, the company's majority tax and debt obligations had been restructured, the distribution system had been significantly reconstructed and ruinous debts had been reduced. The successful negotiation with the government, resulting in the abolition of a restrictive credit on the company's share capital, consequently it made possible to raise finance. Additionally, for acceleration of the company's cash flow, the company demanded prepayments for most cars shipped to domestic consumers and these approaches resulted in a reduction of debtors' collection period from 50 days in 1997 to 26 days in 2001 (Avtovaz AR 2001).

Growing sales volume and the increasing output of higher margin new models were the main factors that contributed to the maintenance of net income. Optimisation of production processes and better than early allocation of resources gradually decreased the share of production overheads. However, this significant decrease in production overheads was balanced by increasing variable costs such as components and metals that were often growing in excess of the rate of inflation, and as a result, overall gross profit did not transform significantly.

Avtovaz created a joint venture with General Motors (GM), which launched production of the Chevrolet-Niva SUV in September 2002. The new company had to produce 75,000 vehicles annually, and planned to expand volume to capture 20 per cent of the Russian passenger car market by 2007. GM and Avtovaz each owned a 41.5 per cent stake in the joint venture, initially valued at $99 million each and the European Bank for Reconstruction and Development owned the remaining 17 per cent of shares (Avtovaz AR 2003).

The company had a relatively complicated ownership structure compared to other major Russian giants. Majority control of Avtovaz was held by its subsidiaries: AVVA held 38.2 per cent in Avtovaz and Automobile Financial Corporation (AFC) had 23.6 per cent, whereas Avtovaz owned about 85 per cent of AVVA and 49 per cent of AFC (Avtovaz AR 2001); 26 per cent of AFC belonged to Avtovaz top managers, including Kadannikov. The remaining stocks were split among the minors, of which top Russian financial organisations had about 22 per cent including nominal holding and around 15 per cent of Avtovaz stocks were circulating on the stock market (Avtovaz AR 2005). Because of this share distribution, Avtovaz management, led by CEO Kadannikov during that time, exercised majority voting rights.

Avtovaz (2003–6)

The Russian new car market steadily posted strong rates of growth throughout the 2003–7 period. In 2007, the total sales of new passenger cars constituted 2,000,000 units and the domestic plants made up only 30 per cent of them. In that time, Avtovaz maintained its volume of production, which fluctuated between 600,000 and 700,000 although the company dramatically decreased its market share from 50 per cent to 24 per cent (ASM 2007).

The financial capacity of the Russian market was growing faster than the volume indexes of sales. The Russian new car market generated total revenues of $24.6 billion in 2007, representing a compound annual growth rate (CAGR) of 31.3 per cent for the period spanning 2003–7 and market consumption volumes increased with a CAGR of 19.7 per cent. The company increased sales from $3.3 billion to $5.1 billion, but the share of LADA by financial volume decreased from 32 per cent to 20 per cent because it could not make the expensive models and managed to maintain position only in the cheapest market niche (ASM 2007).

Despite high duties, which were reducing demand for second-hand foreign-made cars, Avtovaz could not save its position because growth of the national economy shifted consumer preferences toward new foreign-made cars of the low and average cost segments. Additionally, after years of protecting the domestic car industry through prohibitive tariffs, the government reduced the duty on imported auto components virtually to zero. This motivated the world's car producers to significantly increase production facilities in Russia. In the struggle for Russian customers, foreign companies used all possible trade methods: building car assembly plants in Russia, offering consumer credit on a wider scale, improving and developing dealer networks, selling new models in the Russian market simultaneously with sales in markets of Western countries and using a wide range of aggressive marketing techniques (ASM 2003–7).

Avtovaz fought back to retain its market share; the company built an entirely new factory, equipped with new technology to build the new model 'Kalina', which included features like antilock brakes, power steering and air conditioning, all rarities in previous Russian models. However, Avtovaz was limited by an inability to bring new designs to the market in time. The 'Kalina' was originally designed in the early 1990s and built on the basis of an old platform, with an old engine and gearbox; its launch was repeatedly delayed, and the price was inadequate for the characteristics of the model.

In addition, it had strengthened control over the quality of components, which were produced by Avtovaz, and by third-party companies. Because of this activity, in 2004, the number of complaints about new cars fell by almost 50 per cent. Service and sales networks were improved significantly; the company employed only certificated resellers with modern showrooms. Nevertheless, the gap between Avtovaz and its foreign competitors continued to grow.

Nationalisation

In 2003, the economic principles of Putin's government dramatically changed, and a bureaucratic–oligarchic regime was established that had the dominance of state monopoly, and as a result, many private companies were nationalised.

As was noted above, more than 61 per cent of shares belonged to two subsidiaries of Avtovaz, AVVA and AFC, which were controlled by Chairman Kadannikov. In October 2005, the board of directors of Avtovaz was forced to agree to a transfer of control over the auto plant to the state enterprise 'Rosoboroneksport', the state arms trading agency (Belikov and Ryzhkin 2005).

Kadannikov and most executives were dismissed. The sum of the deal for the sale of two Avtovaz subsidiaries that controlled more than 60 per cent of its stock was over $700 million. Moreover, the motive of Kadannikov and his team for the decision to sell the company could be seen as the money paid personally to executives and at least a part of $700 million paid as compensation to Kadannikov, who led the company for 17 years (Belikov and Semenov 2005).

The new management team did not have experience in the car industry and it was not deeply integrated into the regional context. In general, the new team maintained the vision and strategy of the previous Avtovaz executives (Avtovaz AR 2007). However, the new executives realised some new ideas: purchasing licenses from foreign car manufacturers for parts production, building inexpensive car plants and obtaining government support of $5 billion, which would be used for development of new models, retooling the plants (Belikov *et al.* 2005). Additionally, the new executives of the company tried to optimise expenditure and management without serious result. In September 2008, the main shareholders were Renault (25 per cent), Russian Technologies (25.1 per cent) and Troika Dialog (25.64 per cent) (Avtovaz AR 2010).

The 2008–9 financial crises (see Chapter 11) dramatically exacerbated corporate performance. As a result, the government needed to inject billions of dollars to the company and sell 25 per cent of company shares to Renault. In November 2009, it was announced that Avtovaz was going to produce different models (Renault, Nissan and Lada) on the Renault platform B0 and that the Russian government saw the development of Avtovaz as deeper integration with Renault-Nissan (ibid.).

Financial analysis

Analysis shows that every year, Avtovaz concedes its position on the rapidly growing Russian auto market. However, sales had grown constantly due to strong demand for Avtovaz cars, vigorous protection of the domestic market in 1994–2003, devaluation of the rouble in 1998 and the Russian financial boom during 2000–5 (Figures 6.2 and 6.3).

Analysis of the company's operating profit from 1995 to 2000, in terms of purchasing power of the rouble as of 31 December 2000, shows that operating profit was not stable and it amounted to about 5–10 billion roubles per year.

The decline of operating profit in 1997–8 (see Figure 6.4) was created by the large extraction of wealth by the management from the company and serious problems of operation management. In addition, this decline was accelerated by the macroeconomic situation in Russia during this time. However, by 2000,

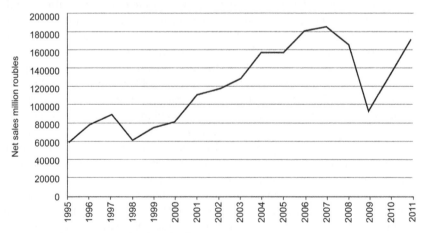

Figure 6.2 Avtovaz net sales (nominal)
Source: Avtovaz annual reports.

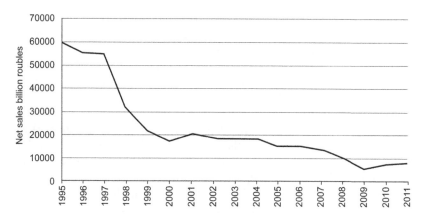

Figure 6.3 Avtovaz net sales (real)
Note: Avtovaz real net sales in terms of purchasing power of the rouble as of 31 December 1995. Source: Avtovaz annual reports, author's calculation.

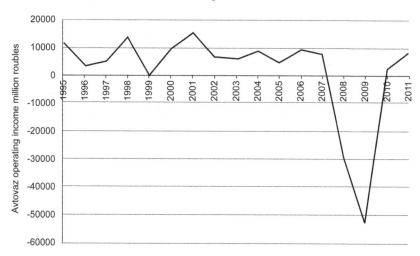

Figure 6.4 Avtovaz operating income
Source: Avtovaz annual reports.

Avtovaz had managed to achieve operating profit higher than the pre-crisis levels due to the devaluation of the Russian rouble. In addition, the peak of 2001 was created by a situation when prices of finished goods were rising faster than prices of materials and components. For example, in 2001, prices of cars increased by 9.1 per cent whilst the average cost of materials and components grew by 1.2 per cent.

The foundation of the decline of operating profit in 1997–8 was generated by a robust attack of the foreign manufacturers and dramatically reduced duty on imported auto components.

Total cost had grown constantly due to weak control of expenditures and constantly growing price on raw materials, auto components and energy. Only in the financial crisis of 1998 did Avtovaz dramatically decrease the total cost. Resource costs (see Figure 6.5), which include external materials, services purchased and employee compensation, accounted for approximately 80 per cent of total income in 1995, and fluctuated around this level. Resource costs increased rapidly to 117 per cent by 2009. After the crisis, resource costs relatively quickly recovered to 100 per cent.

Value retained in income can be determined as the sum of EBITDA, labour cost and R&D divided into sales revenue. Between 1995 and 1998, this index (Figure 6.6) has a falling trajectory; during the crisis of 1998, it reaches 9 per cent. Later, it gradually improves to the average level and after 2001 this index peaks to about 18 per cent, which is created by a significant growth of labour cost and expenditures for start-up of the new model. In 2008, the index dramatically declined.

There was a strong negative correlation between labour cost and the company's gross profit. Even though the company significantly decreased its share of labour expenses as a proportion of net sales, it still absorbed a major part of gross profit and as a result, decreased operating profit (Figure 6.8).

Analysis of return on capital employed (ROCE) (Figure 6.9) shows that it has a moderately cyclical pattern and in the period of 1995–8, the average ROCE for Avtovaz placed at about 10 per cent. In that time, ROCE was on a falling trajectory from the height of 20 per cent in 1995 towards a negative 1 per cent in the crisis of 1998, because the corporate sales did not generate healthy gross profit margins and the company had serious problems with liquidity, marketing and operation management. However, in 2000, the ratio quickly recovered to 19 per cent due to a considerable growth of company earnings and relatively slow growth of capital employed. In the years of 2002–5, Avtovaz could not improve its ROCE and it fluctuated between 3 and 8 per cent.

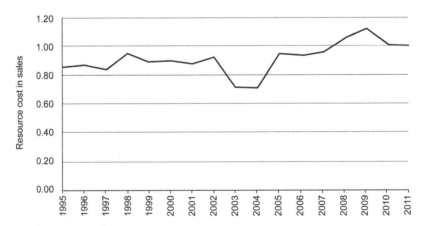

Figure 6.5 Avtovaz resource cost in sales
Note: resources cost in sales is defined as the sum of external material and services purchased and employee compensation divided by sales revenue.
Source: Author's calculation.

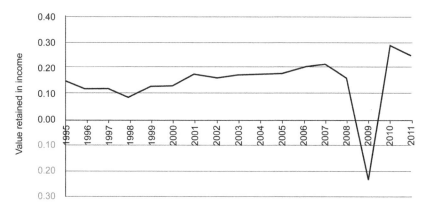

Figure 6.6 Avtovaz value retained in income
Note: Value retained in income can be determined as the sum of EBITDA and labour
cost divided by sales revenue.
Source: Author's calculation.

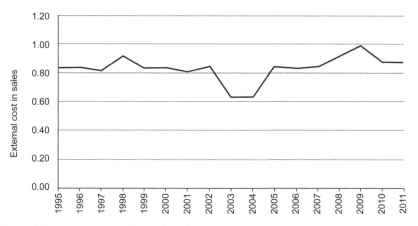

Figure 6.7 Avtovaz external costs in sales
Note: External cost is defined as raw materials and consumable divided by sales.
Source: Author's calculation.

The time between 2001 and 2006 was when a comparatively low share of profit
pre-interest and tax in sales (Figure 6.11) and a relatively low capital
employed as a share of income (Figure 6.9) combined to support a stable ROCE.

Between 1995 and 1997, ROS of Avtovaz has a falling trajectory and
during the crisis of 1998–9, it reaches a nadir of 0 per cent (Figure 6.11).
Later, it quickly recovers to pre-crisis level and, between 2001 and 2007, ROS
fluctuated around 5 per cent because the relatively high growth of net sales
was maintained, in practice, by a growth of profit.

The return on capital is a result of combining the return on sales and capital
intensity (capital employed/sales). In 1995, the company used about 0.8 rouble

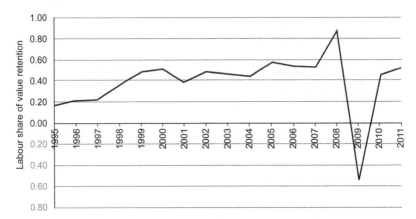

Figure 6.8 Avtovaz labour share of value retention
Note: Labour costs share of value retained is defined as personnel costs divided by
operating result before depreciation and amortisation plus personnel costs.
Source: Author's calculation.

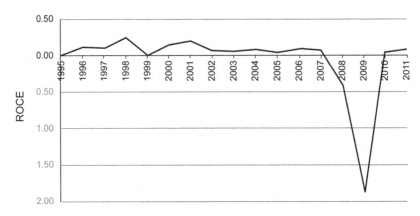

Figure 6.9 Avtovaz ROCE
Note: ROCE is defined as operating result before depreciation and amortisation in
relation to the sum of equity and long-term debt.
Source: Author's calculation.

of capital for every rouble of sales revenue and by 2006 this had decreased
gradually to 0.6 rouble of capital for one rouble of sales (Figure 6.10).

During that period, Avtovaz had a relatively low sales profit (see Figure
6.11) and a comparatively low share of capital employed to sales; this combination boosted ROCE of the company.

Conclusion

Avtovaz was a long-standing Russian firm, which built and assembled cars from
parts sourced within Russia and its satellite countries. Avtovaz output was

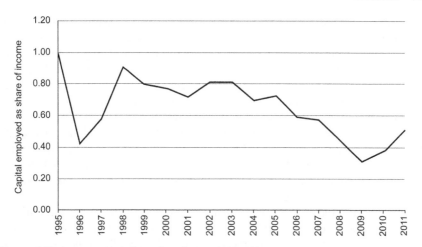

Figure 6.10 Avtovaz capital employed as a share of income
Note: Capital employed as a share of income is defined as total long-term debt plus
shareholders fund divided by sales.

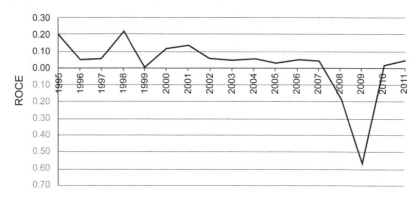

Figure 6.11 Avtovaz return on sales
Note: Return on sales is defined as operating result before depreciation and amortisa-
tion divided by sales.
Source: Author's calculation.

similar to that of Peugeot or BMW, and it had been operating in a sheltered
environment and unexposed to foreign competition. It should also be noted
that the growth in the volume of car production was restricted by household
income levels in Russia, which acted as a brake on capacity expansion.

After privatisation, Avtovaz was still protected from the full heat of foreign
competition on its home market and the level of average household income
started to increase as economic reforms adjusted income and patterns of wealth
accumulation in Russia. In the years immediately after privatisation, Avtovaz
controlled more than 60 per cent of the domestic market. A combination of
strong market share, protection and favourable currency movements against

the dollar ensured a strong sales revenue trajectory for Avtovaz. Sales revenues grew by a factor of three–four in the ten-year period of 1995 to 2005.

However, strong revenue growth did not translate into strong profit cash and return on capital employed. During this period, the company was weakened by its own managers who have not established clear strategic objectives, operational efficiency and new product development. These were crucial to strengthening the company during the period when the firm was being protected from competition. The narratives extracted from interviews with those directly and indirectly involved with the company reveal how Avtovaz was used to extract wealth for a few senior managers. This lost income weakened the company when substantial sums would be required to modernise production, improve processes and deliver new car platforms.

Operating income and cash generated out of income were erratic and untransformed during the period of 1995 to 2010. Cash generated from income is a significant indicator of corporate financial health and especially in the car business, cash is an important lever required to finance (via debt) new product development.

Without a reliable source of internally generated cash, it is increasingly difficult to finance the cost of debt, which was needed to build and develop new cars for the Russian consumer. Avtovaz did not have the financial resources to create new cars, and interviews with managers at Avtovaz revealed their frustration in not being able to renew the model range.

It is not surprising that operational controls restricted the Avtovaz ability to maintain a strong cash return on capital employed. In 1995, the company ROCE stood at 20 per cent. After collapsing throughout the 1990s, there was a period of brief recovery of the ROCE before it went down again and settled in the range of 5–10 per cent, even though the market was sheltered from foreign competition.

The short-term recovery in finances towards the end of the 1990s came too late because the Russian market was now open to foreign competition, both direct imports and assembly operations within the Russian market. Russian consumers, now with higher incomes, were able to purchase new and used cars imported directly into Russia or buy European or US products assembled in Russia. The share of imported and foreign assembled products soon took a significant fraction of the home market demand and this damaged Avtovaz considerably. After a period of 15 years of protection, Avtovaz had failed strategically to prepare itself for this critical moment because the opportunity had been squandered by managers whose priorities were not aligned with those of the company. The Avtovaz case is a story of a 'good deal gone bad' because privatisation did not create a stronger company fit for a competitive market. It is significant that an opportunity was turned into a threat because senior managers lost sight of strategic and operational priorities.

In 2005, the company was again taken into the state's hands primarily because it still employed over 100,000 skilled workers. However, without a clear sense of business strategy it is not clear what the future holds for Avtovaz in a market where foreign competitors are offering relatively low-priced quality products.

7 Kondrovo Paper Company

This case study illustrates how a Russian paper company managed their business during the post-privatisation development. In the first years of the Russian reforms, the company, having had a large share of the Russian consumer paper market and technological advantages, successfully operated in six different sectors of the paper industry. However, remarkable opportunities were not realised and the company's market share in its major products was in constant decline. The case shows the complicated situation when the executives could not control company expenditure and the quality of operations because of poor management and discipline. Poor management was created by the executives' lack of qualification and a deficit of highly skilled managers and engineers.

Privatisation

Kondrovo Paper Company (KPC) is situated in the Kaluga region about 180 kilometres from Moscow. Before the start of mass privatisation, it had been mainly engaged in the manufacturing and marketing, throughout the former Soviet Union republics, of a wide range of products for personal and industrial uses. Most of these products were made from pulp and synthetic fibers.

The company was organised into operating segments based on product groupings. These operating segments had been aggregated into six business segments: personal care products, tissue products, health care, packaging, paper and utility services (KPC SR 1998).

The personal care segment included disposable diapers and feminine sanitary care products whereas the tissue segment consisted of toilet paper and napkins. Both segments manufactured products only for household use and their products were sold directly and through wholesalers, department stores, supermarkets, drugstores and other retail outlets.

The health care segment manufactured and marketed disposable health care products, such as absorbing nappies, obstetrical bedding, sterile wrap and sterile surgical packs (KPC SR 1998). Health care products were sold to distributors, hospitals and health care organisations.

The paper segment included printing papers, correspondence papers, specialty papers and related products; the packaging segment manufactured and marketed boxes made from corrugated fibreboard, which were used for protective and transport purposes. Products of both these segments were sold directly to users, manufacturers and sales agents.

Other products and the service segment included different businesses, such as power and water supply, agriculture production, construction, building material production and transport services. In addition, the company's assets included property where more than 10,000 people had lived; the stadium, two culture centres and many other businesses that were used by citizens of Kondrovo.

In 1993, the company was turned into a joint-stock company. The share distribution at the first stage of privatisation was made according to 'option 2' of the law on privatisation. All the members of the company were given a right to acquire common shares for vouchers, which constituted up to 51 per cent; that was 59,885 of total shares of the authorised capital. Another 24 per cent of ordinary shares were offered for sale at auctions against privatisation vouchers for other investors (KPC SR 1998). Approximately 4 per cent of shares were sold to citizens; another 20 per cent of the total shares were bought by a private company, which was created by the executives and trade unions. The basic functions of this small-scale enterprise included the sale of paper, purchase of raw materials and the accumulation of income by over-estimating prices for raw materials delivered to KPC.

At the first stage of privatisation, the state continued to own 25 per cent of the company's equity and according to the privatisation law, the State Committee for State Property Management of the Russian Federation (GKI), had to offer for sale 20 per cent of the state's shares within a three-year period. The last 5 per cent of total shares had to be allocated equally among all the company's workers (KPC SR 1998). The system of hiring management comprised of two stages: first, the share meeting chose a general director who appointed executive managers. The members of the board then arranged the contracts with the executive managers. This system did not increase the real power of the general director above any other senior managers.

After the first stage of privatisation, exact ownership of the company was clear: about 70 per cent of the shares belonged to actual and former workers of the company and this ownership was reflected by the structure of the board of directors, which included three representatives of the trade union, three executives and one representative of the regional authority.

In 1995, about 35 per cent of shares were bought by the trading company Incombi, based in Moscow, from the company's workers; 11 per cent of the shares were bought by British company Davis Smith (KPC AR 1997). Additionally, 20 per cent of the state's shares of the company were sold to Incombi in a cash auction for $1,400,000 by the state property fund. As a result, the share distribution in 1996 was as follows: Incombi had 55 per cent of shares and this allowed Incombi to have the majority on the board of directors and to appoint the general director of the company.

Industrial factors

As was noted above, the company operated in the five different sectors of the paper industry.

Tissue products

Between 1993 and 2004, the world market of tissue had shown continuing growth from 4 to 5 per cent and the average consumption of tissue products in Western countries had reached about 20 kilograms per person (kg/pp) whereas Russia recorded 12 per cent growth and individual consumption of 1.6 kg/pp (Risi 2007 and author's calculation). In addition, the global market was characterised by the high concentration of business, with 45 per cent of world production being shared between just four leading manufactories.

Low consumption in the Russian market can be explained not only by the comparatively recent arrival of mass production of tissue on the domestic market, but also poor-hygiene culture and low levels of income and consequent wide-spread use of substitutes such as newspaper and wrapping paper. In addition, the tissue sector comprised a large number of small regional manufacturers who produced extremely poor-quality products at a low price; 75 per cent of the Russian tissue-based market was single-layered and low quality toilet paper of the lower price category and was made from unselected recycled paper.

The other 25 per cent of the market consisted of wipes (representing 12 per cent), paper towels (representing 10 per cent), facial tissues and pocket hand-kerchiefs (representing about 3 per cent). KPC had a relatively large share of the Russian market and in 1997–8 reached its zenith: 30 per cent of the market, later its share had declined dramatically and in 2004 reached its nadir, approximately 8 per cent (KPC SR 1998).

Prior to 1998, Russian companies only produced consumer tissue for household use and these products were not sold under recognised brands. Since 1998, tissue for away from home (AFH), and products under recognised brands started to be manufactured because the largest world paper manufacturers such as SCA and Kimberly-Clark began trading new tissue products in Russia.

Personal care

Before 1995, only three companies in Russia produced outdated disposable diapers and feminine sanitary care products, the share of the KPC was about 35 per cent. After 1993, the top three world manufacturers, Procter & Gamble, Kimberly-Clark and SCA Hygiene Products, came to Russia and established their strong leading position selling well-known brands. These companies offered the market numerous new sanitary protection products, previously completely unknown to customers, and they spent vast amounts on advertising campaigns. This was central to building a solid image for its brands.

As a result, they remained the unconditional leading manufacturers of personal care products in 2003 and they retained 65 per cent of the market share (KPC SR 2003). Between 1993 and 2003, the Russian market of personal care products saw continuing dynamic growth of approximately 20 per cent per year in volume terms and totalled $600 million in 1998. The market share of the company steadily declined and in 1999 it was only 4 per cent (ibid.).

In August 1998, the rouble was devalued and the price of personal care products rose fourfold whilst actual wages remained unchanged. Accordingly, sales were seriously affected because of the high proportion of imports; however, the market of these products regained pre-crisis sales levels in a short period.

The Russian market of these products was far from saturated. Growth was underpinned by changing attitudes towards disposable paper products, linked to the adoption of Western lifestyle values where fashion and usefulness take a definite place. However, substitutes continued to be in favour with lower-income consumers. Quality was a major factor in the selection process of consumers, closely followed by price and in general, most low-priced products had poor quality.

The domestic brands were moderately popular among lower-income consumers and were broadly available across the country; these consumers remained loyal to inexpensive domestic products, because they were price sensitive. However, none of the Russian brands were being developed sufficiently to increase sales because of lack of appropriate equipment to produce competitive products and strong promotion.

Paper

Before the 1990s, 90 per cent of the traditional paper products, which included newsprint, offset and speciality papers, had been produced by the 10 large pulp and paper companies that had full technological continuous production chains from logging saws to cellulose manufacture and then to paper production and sellers (Butrin 2004b). In addition, about 100 relatively small paper companies produced numerous kinds of paper with the majority of them having out-of-date equipment and technology, high direct raw material costs and overhead expenses that meant they could exist only with financial support from the state.

The transition towards a market economy caused problems for the paper enterprises, and over the period of 1990–8, the volumes of paper and paperboard halved. Privatisation of the majority of pulp and paper companies occurred in 1993–5, when the world paper industry faced a crisis because the price of bleach pulp plunged from $800 per tonne to $400. In 1996, the crisis in the industry was at its highest and operations in many Russian mills were shut down for several months as the Russian parliament needed to make immediate resolutions for state support of the industry. The financial crises of 1998 and the increasing world pulp price helped the Russian industry avoid total collapse.

Packaging

The Russian paper packaging industry was quite a new phenomenon. During the Soviet period, the relatively undeveloped market did not form a demand for modern packaging. This was one of the fastest growing sectors of the paper industry, which, from 1993 to 2002, experienced annual growth rates of approximately 11 per cent (KPC SR 2000). The country had increased consumption from 40 to 80 kilograms per capita, although it remained substantially less than in West Europe. The board-converting segment where KPC had a market share of 1 or 2 per cent was quite fragmented, with more than 150 companies producing various types of packaging, predominantly corrugated board and boxes with an output of less than 10 million square metres (KPC SR 2000). Nevertheless, the six largest companies, including one of the largest world producers, Stora Enso, had nearly 50 per cent of total output with productivity of more than 100 million square metres. Larger players had a significant advantage in corrugated production, as they were able to meet the requirements of large customers and finance capacity expansions.

About 70 per cent of paperboard packaging production on the market consisted of corrugated board, 80 per cent of which was exploited for shipping purposes. Moreover, the food industry was the largest Russian market for packaging – approximately 50 per cent of packaging used. Productions were located primarily in Russian industrial centres, including nearly a quarter in Moscow and surrounding areas.

Health care

Strong price competition affected personal care products, tissue products and packaging market segments, whereas in the health care segment competition was due to its strong monopoly position in the domestic markets.

In addition, there was an absence of strong competition between companies in the same industrial segment. There were also strong barriers to new entrants because of the high capital requirements of installing advanced technology, the scarcity and cost of highly skilled personnel and inadequate infrastructure. These factors also negatively impacted on corporate performance when companies tried to increase capacity or introduce new products.

Significant increases in the price of raw materials, energy, transportation and other necessary supplies and services adversely affected the corporate financial results. Waste paper and cellulose were significantly employed in KPC's tissue products. They were subject to considerable price fluctuations due to the cyclical nature of these markets. Increases in pulp prices negatively affected the company's earnings because the selling prices for its finished products were frequently not adjusted or else such adjustments did not significantly follow the increases in pulp prices.

Regional factors

KPC was based in the Kaluga region, which is only 150 kilometres from Moscow, which was a main market for KPC and a high number of regional businesses. In the main, the region did not have natural, financial, consumer or production resources, which could have positively impacted on corporate performance. However, the region enjoyed a good infrastructure including railway connections, good roads as well as gas and electricity supplies.

In the 1990s, Kaluga benefited from a good supply of highly skilled specialists, created by the Soviet military industry and this labour force was half as expensive as in Moscow. As well as this, the region had a moderate level of social, economic, ecological and criminal risks (Expert RA 2003). Consumer and production resources of the region were weak and did not generate a strong local demand for KPC products. The scarcity of regional finance increased the cost of corporate borrowing and consequently impacted on corporate performance.

The company's executives were unable to form close relationships with the regional authorities. Therefore, in 1995 the regional government filed a bankruptcy petition against KPC in an effort to recoup a short-term debt of about $100,000. It was an unusual case because the company had quite a strong financial position. However, the government's major target was to change the company's owner.

Between 1996 and 1999, the relationship between the company and regional authorities was positive due to a change of governor and active participation of KPC in regional charity programmes. After 2000, the company became the target of hostile acquisition from companies that had close links with the regional authority. This negative environment increased the company's owner risks and prompted executives to create a new project outside the Kaluga region thus increasing the transaction costs of the business.

Business strategy after privatisation

As stated above, in the first three years after privatisation the company had been controlled and managed by its workforce, which employed a strategy that was known as 'business as usual'. The main principle of this strategy was using the Soviet business model, which emphasised retaining labour and low-skilled managers, maintaining numerous non-profitable businesses and preserving all social benefits without evaluating their efficiency. In the main, the management system was a bad hybrid of the Soviet 'collective farming' with an absence of control and evaluation of business.

The company did not employ strategic methods for selection, development and coordination of the business' portfolio. The company had tried to maintain numerous projects with insufficient resources and often the personal interests of the managers were connected to these projects. During the three years after privatisation, corporate strategy was not presented as a part of regular management activity and company executives paid it little attention.

In addition, in order to establish a competitive advantage over rival companies, KPC used the 'focused low cost strategy', according to which the company was targeting individuals with an annual salary less than $2,000 and, surprisingly, this was a successful strategy to maintain long-term competitive advantages.

Between 1993 and 1997, the critical success factors of the company were a significant share of personal care, tissue and health care products in the domestic market, the low level of consumption of these products, exceptional geographical location of the company, high qualifications of employees and reliable infrastructure (railways, power station, power and water supply). On the other hand, the most significant challenges for the company were the rise in the cost of raw materials and energy and an inability to maintain favourable supplier agreement. Additionally, technologies of personal care and paper products were in a declining stage of their life cycles, labour capacity of these products were comparatively lower than the other main competitors and the company did not have a strong market position in personal care, packaging and paper segments.

The opportunities faced by the company presented remarkable potential for the growth of the Russian market (KPC AR 1997). The fundamental weaknesses of the company were the absence of brands, old fashioned design and packaging, and a deficit of financial and intellectual resources for modernisation of the business. By contrast, the strengths were the low cost of manufacturing, service and operation. Moreover, the company had strong technological advantages and core competencies in the tissue and health care sector.

Since 1996, the new management team had begun to form a new vision and strategy for the company including a change in generic strategy from 'cost leadership' to 'focused differentiation strategy', a decrease in the number of the business segments and selling or liquidation of non-specific business (KPC AR 1997). The board of management had established an efficient administration and monitoring of company assets and consequently created a corporate centre in order to develop a uniform strategy.

Having used focused differentiation strategy the company had employed products and marketing as areas of differentiation. Furthermore, the middle-class segment of the market was targeted by the company for personal care and tissue products. In packaging and paper segments, 'a focused low cost strategy' was used; the company specified a number of customers that were based in a radius of 200 kilometres around Kondrovo. However, the implementation of this strategy was poor and there were no synergies across business segments. Conclusively, the strategy did not include plans for branding and product positioning, cost reductions including supply chain management and capacity and capital investments for the business.

Management of operations

From 1993 to 1995, operations of the company had been maintained successfully, but KPC was increasing its cost of production because of poor operations management, inappropriate discipline and losses from theft. During that period, the manufacturing capacity of KPC was not employed efficiently because manufacturing was often disrupted by irregular fibre materials supply. The loss of manufacturing rhythm impacted on corporate performance because the production cost had been dramatically increased in arrhythmic operations.

After 1995, the company had improved regularity of manufacturing, efficiency in operations and quality output by utilising the control system more powerfully. KPC had realised numerous quality improvement programmes but still, it was not up to the mark.

The company was slow to convert ideas into new products or improvements in technology; for example, implementation of new disposable diapers was extended from an estimated six months to eight months. Usually, a slow implementation of innovations was determined by the deficit of financial resources and properly trained workers (KPC AR 2000).

From 1996, the strategy of the new management team led to a decrease in the number of employees from 2,500 to 1,600 and reduced numbers of managers. In addition, the company incurred substantial development costs in introducing new and improved products and technologies. For example, three paper machines were modernised, disposable diapers, feminine incontinence and a lot of tissue-converting equipment had been bought (KPC AR 2000).

As a result, the tissue products segment had begun to manufacture and market more expensive paper towels, napkins and a range of products for use away from home. Additionally, the health care segment started to manufacture and market new types of disposable medical products such as face masks, sterilisation wrap and surgical gowns. In addition, the paper segment started to manufacture new types of paper based on the use of recovered fibre. Consumer products were sold with new brand names and under new packaging.

The company's manufacturing operations utilised electricity, natural gas and petroleum-based fuel, but the power infrastructure had been sufficiently amortised. In order to guarantee that KPC used all forms of energy cost-effectively, the company needed to maintain ongoing energy efficiency improvement programmes at the power station and utility supply systems (KPC AR 2000).The company's energy costs were affected by availability of supplies of natural gas, energy prices and local regulatory decisions.

Productivity fluctuated because the manufacture had not been efficiently planned; many projects that were intended were not realised, and some departments could not produce according to the required standard of quality. In addition, personal care and paper manufacturers could not reach estimated capacity because the company's sales did not occur as planned and positive supplier agreements could not be maintained constantly and so there was a halt in the supply of raw materials and power and this affected corporate performance.

Marketing

As noted above, from 1993 to 2003, Russian paper consumer products had dynamic growth due to the low level of consumption of these products and the changing attitudes of buyers. From 1993, the company's market shares in its major products were in constant decline until 1996, but then stabilised until 1999.

Surprisingly, until 1997, the company did not differentiate between KPC's product and the products of its main competitors in most segments and, as a result, price and distribution of the products determined the volume of sales. In general, the main competitors were larger and had greater financial resources than KPC and consequently they introduced new products more quickly and responded more effectively to the changing environment.

After 1996, the management team changed generic strategy from 'cost leadership' to 'focused differentiation strategy' and started to realise a new marketing policy that included creating branded products, production of tissue goods for 'away-from-home' and manufacturing in the higher price segment. However, the company's consumer products had been sold in a highly competitive market with branded products, which experienced consolidation of retail trade and increased concentration of large-format retailers and discounters. As a result of this, since 1999 there was an increase in dependence on key retailers.

These large-format retailers negatively affected the corporate performance of the company because some of them had bigger bargaining power than KPC, which led to higher trade discounts. Additionally, since 1996, the foreign competitors had spent more on advertising and promotional activities; for example, the Russian division of P& g had an annual advertising budget of more than the total revenue of KPC (KPC SR 2000).

As a result of increased price pressure and intense competition, corporate performance was affected strongly. Sales did not match forecasts because the company was unable to anticipate consumer preferences and estimate sales of new products; consequently, the company's products were not accepted in new markets.

In 2001, the company began to cease its operations in paper sectors because the products were not competitive on the market. In 2003–4, the company discontinued production in the personal care and health care sectors for similar reasons.

Financial management

The company was affected by economic and political instability in Russia, and it faced increased risks in its domestic operations, including hyperinflation, inconsistencies in taxation policy and trade barriers. All these factors negatively affected the company's corporate performance.

From 1993 to 1996, the company experienced some liquidity problems that resulted in late payment to suppliers and contractors, as well as delays in payment of wages to employees. In that time, the rouble suffered from instability that was exacerbated by domestic hyperinflation, which resulted in devaluation against major currencies. To mitigate this, the company used barter, which in some months amounted to more than 80 per cent of sales.

Mostly, barter did not contribute positively to corporate performance because of overestimated prices of supplies and inaccuracies in execution. The great sensitivity to both changes in pricing and demand for the company's key products were significant factors in the company's ability to generate operating cash flow.

In addition, the company could not effectively decrease production and administration costs because it utilised Soviet manufacturing and technological standards, which were often overstated, and yet the financial results of KPC were still relatively profitable. Moreover, the company had no method to decrease inventory, improve credit control or reduce wages.

From 1995 to 2000, the company worked in close alliance with the major shareholder Incombi, its principal distributor, which wholesaled approximately 40 per cent of KPC products. As part of a special discount, Incombi earned in the region of $500,000 annually and to offset this Incombi invested $900,000 per annum in KPC. This approach provided the opportunity to minimise corporate tax using the specific tax privilege enjoyed by Incombi that also benefitted from cheaper credit in Moscow.

As mentioned above, the Kaluga region was a depressed region of Russia with insufficient financial recourses. These factors were reflected in the higher cost of borrowing for regional companies, some 15 per cent higher than for those in Moscow (KPC AR 1997).

Between 1996 and 2000, the company developed too fast and did not have the ability to borrow money on the financial market. As a result, the company constantly had problems with working capital. During that time, the company decreased its share of labour costs by dismissing 30 per cent of personnel, implementing new technological standards and decreasing its inventory and receivables. However, capacity utilisation never got over 80 per cent and this dramatically increased the share of overheads and power expenditure (KPC AR 1997–2000).

After the Russian crisis of 1998 and the devaluation of the rouble, the company had to pay four times as much for imported equipment. As a result, terms of delivery were changed, many machines were supplied much later than usual, and many projects were terminated. Additionally, devaluation of the rouble increased the cost of imported raw materials that was a significant part of production expenditure for many products.

After 2000, the company became the target of hostile acquisition. The investment company Basic Element, having made the new Russian pulp and paper holding, decided to acquire the 30 top Russian paper companies, which manufactured more than 75 per cent of the paper industry's products.

Consequently, KPC was attacked by Basic Element, which employed Russian traditional approaches such as manipulating courts and media. Because of the threat of acquisition, after the end of 2001, the company halted all investment programmes and its financial standing fell dramatically because all resources of the company had been used for defence. Finally, after 18 months of this defence, about 80 per cent of the company's shares were sold much cheaper than the market price.

Under the roof of Basic Element

Between 2003 and 2007, the Russian paper market had annual growth of more than 15 per cent, dramatically boosted by the growth of the pulp market price; as a result, KPC managed to increase sales in the packaging segment (KPC SR 2006). The new executives could not control the company's quality of operations and expenditures because of poor operation management and technology discipline. The management team tried to optimise expenditures by reducing the number of employees, but without a sufficient financial result.

At that time, the company could not maintain the rhythm of production. There were large deviations of actual output from the planned one due to a lack of raw materials, pulp and waste paper, which was generated by a shortage of working capital. In addition, the increase in the technological downtime was accelerated by a lack of highly qualified workers, because the company radically reduced the workforce. For instance, in 2003, the company decreased the staff numbers by 18 per cent and the quality of the products declined. For example, more than 17 per cent of produced sanitary papers were not meeting quality standards (KPC AR 2003–6).

In 2003–4, many executives and principal engineers left the company and, as a result, a deficit of highly skilled managers and engineers partially paralysed the business of KPC. Additionally, the owner of the company appointed four different CEOs for a two-year period and needed to provide extra funding to keep the business afloat (ibid.).

The different approaches taken to improve the situation, such as decreasing the personnel's salaries, simplifying products and technology and reducing the amount of the product, did not have a positive effect on corporate performance. As a result, KPC lost some major segments of the market and managed to maintain positions only in the cheapest market segments, which could not generate sufficient profitability.

The faulty operation management dramatically limited funding for maintaining stable and safe equipment and buildings. Consequently, there was a dramatic increase in different risks of an accident occurring, such as environmental risks, which are caused by overflows of the landfill designated for storing the technological sludge and a possibility of industrial areas flooding by the nearby river's flood waters. Also, there were energy risks caused by the significant deterioration of power and water equipment and risks caused by the disintegration of building panels and support-suspension systems.

In 2009, due to the financial crisis, the management slightly improved the performance of the company. It prepared an anti-crisis programme for KPC, which included a more efficient employment of energy resources and raw materials and reduction of the salaries (KPC AR 2009–11). However, the improvement from the anti-crisis programme was short-lived and in 2010 the company performance considerably deteriorated. In 2011, the company went bankrupt.

After privatisation, KPC had an excess of personnel and, as a result, labour cost as a share of value retained was more than 60 per cent. Later, in 1995–6, the company managed to decrease the number of staff and the ratio declined to 30 per cent of the value retained (Figure 7.7). In 1999–2007, even though the company significantly decreased the share of labour expenses in net sales, personnel wages absorbed a major part of gross profit, and as a result, there was a growth of labour cost as a share of value retained.

Financial analysis

The only period in which the company maintained its volume of sales at a relatively high level was between 1994 and 1997. After the devaluation of the rouble in 1998, sales (Figure 7.1 and 7.2) had declined to 300 million roubles per annum and over the next five years fluctuated around this level, and it was only after 2003 that the company managed to increase sales.

Analysis of the company's operating profit (Figure 7.3) from 1995 to 2000 shows that operating profit declined progressively from its zenith in 1995 to zero in 2002. Nevertheless, it is important to note that the price index for the pulp and paper segment of the national economy in 1994–7 was significantly lower than the average industrial index due to a deep crisis in the world paper industry.

Later, after the company's change of ownership and the management collapse, operating losses deteriorated to 74 million roubles and it remained in a loss-making situation for the next three years.

As can be seen from Figure 7.3, operating profit was negatively affected by the 1998 crisis. In that year, the operating profit dropped to a third of that of the previous year because the company could not increase product prices due to the collapse of the domestic consumer market.

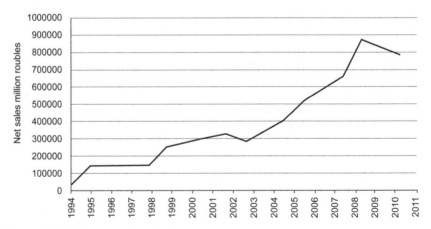

Figure 7.1 KPC net sales (nominal)
Source: KPC annual and special reports.

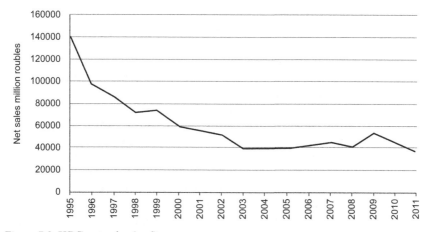

Figure 7.2 KPC net sales (real)
Note: KPC net sales in terms of purchasing power of the rouble as of 31 December 1995.
Source: KPC annual and special reports.

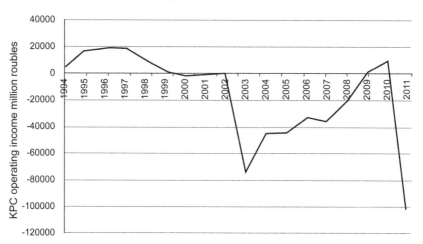

Figure 7.3 KPC operating income
Source: KPC annual and special reports.
Source: Author's calculation.

The operating profit was further eroded by the higher cost of raw materials caused by the increase in pulp prices on the world market, and the company had increased sales expenditure. Thus, KPC was unable to restore the profitability of pre-crisis levels. The financial collapse of the company in 2003 was caused by a considerable decline in operating profits and serious problems in the management of its operations.

From 1995 to 1998, the total cost constantly declined due to strong control of expenditure, the absence of growth of the price of raw materials and weak growth of energy prices. Additionally, the executives managed to substantially decrease the number of employees. Since the financial crisis of 1998, KPC had dramatically increased the total cost because devaluation of the rouble increased the cost of imported raw materials and energy, which was a sufficient part of production expenditure.

Resource cost (see Figure 7.4), which includes external material and services purchased, and employee compensation accounted for approximately 80 per cent of total income in the positive company years of 1995. This rose steadily to 126 per cent by 2003. After the crash of 2003, resource cost recovered somewhat to 110 per cent and fluctuated about this level.

Value retained in income (Figure 7.5) has a similar pattern as the operating profit and the peak of the ratio (1995–7) was created by high profitability of business and low expenditure for raw materials and power. Since 1998 and after the crisis in particular, this index had a falling trajectory; during 1999, it reached a local minimum of 22 per cent. Later, it fluctuated near the 25 per cent level and then in 2003 this index fell violently when the value retained was equal to zero because EBIDTA declined strongly.

After privatisation, KPC had an excess of personnel and as a result, labour cost as a share of value retained was more than 60 per cent. Later, in 1995–6, the company managed to decrease the number of staff and the ratio declined to 30 per cent of the value retained (Figure 7.7). In 1999–2007, even though the company significantly decreased the share of labour expenses in net sales, personnel wages absorbed a major part of gross profit, and as a result, there was growth of labour cost as a share of value retained.

Analysis of the return on capital employed (ROCE) in Figure 7.8 shows that in the first years after privatisation it had a moderately cyclical pattern and the average ROCE for KPC was about 10 per cent, slightly lower than

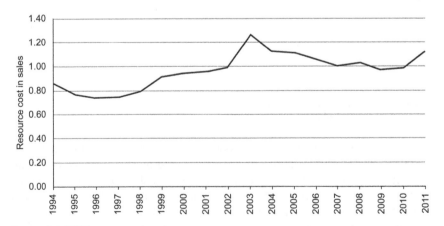

Figure 7.4 KPC resources in sales
Note: resources cost in sales is defined as the sum of external material and services purchased and employee compensation divided by sales revenue.
Source: Author's calculation.

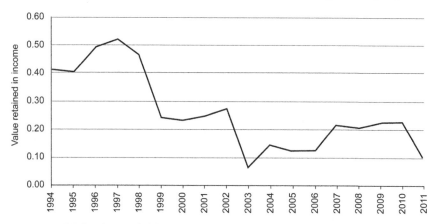

Figure 7.5 KPC value retained in income
Note: Value retained in income can be determined as the sum of EBITDA and labour cost divided by sales revenue.
Source: Author's calculation.

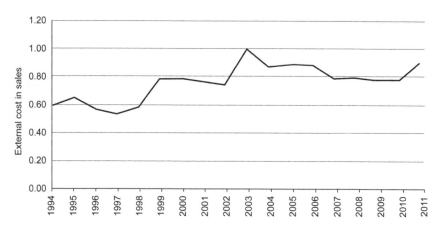

Figure 7.6 KPC external costs in sales
Note: External cost is defined as raw materials and consumable divided by sales.
Source: Author's calculation.

the average level of Russian companies included in the Russian stock market index RTS.

In 1998, ROCE reached a new level of about 0 per cent and oscillated around this level until 2002, when the ratio began to fall rapidly to a strongly negative position of minus 70 per cent (2004) because corporate sales did not generate healthy gross profit margins and the company had serious problems with liquidity, marketing and operation management.

Even in successful years, the company had a comparatively low share of profit before interest and tax in sales (ROS), which fluctuated at approximately 12

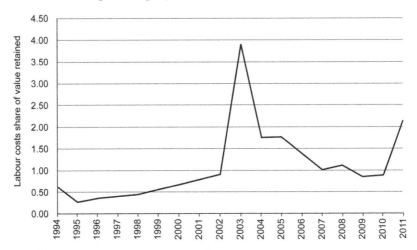

Figure 7.7   KPC labour as share value retained
Note. Labour costs share of value retained is defined as personnel costs divided by operating result before depreciation and amortisation plus personnel costs.
Source: Author's calculation.

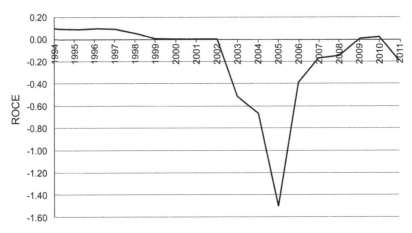

Figure 7.8   KPC return on capital employed
Note: ROCE is defined as operating result before depreciation and amortisation in relation to the sum of equity and long term debt.
Source: Author's calculation.

per cent (Figure 7.10). The return on capital is a result of combining the return on sales and capital intensity (capital employed/sales). In 1994–7, the company used about 1.3 rouble of capital for every rouble of sales revenue. By 1999, this had decreased gradually to 0.4 roubles of capital for each rouble of sales (Figure 7.9).

As noted above, the company maintained ROS between 1994 and 1997. Afterwards, during the crisis year, it quickly reached a zero level because the

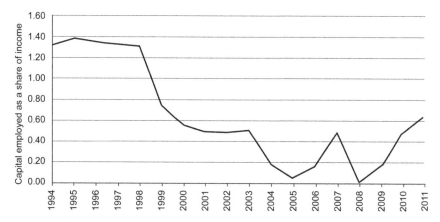

Figure 7.9 KPC capital employed as a share of income
Note: Capital employed as a share of income is defined as total long-term debt plus shareholders fund divided by sales.
Source: Author's calculation.

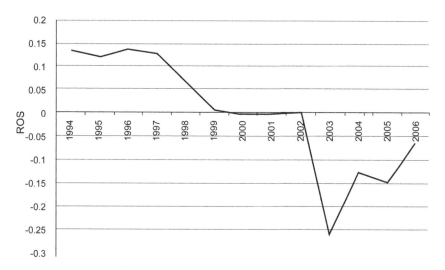

Figure 7.10 KPC return on sales
Note: Return on sales is defined as operating result before depreciation and amortisation divided by sales.
Source: Author's calculation.

growth of net sales was maintained by a negative growth of profit. Later, by the end of 2002, it fell to 6 per cent due to a huge decrease in profit (Figure 7.10).

In the main, the company until 2003 did not have sufficient long-term debt (LTD) because there were difficulties with obtaining credit on the Russian financial market. As a result, between 1997 and 2001, a deficit of external financial resources did not allow a boost to the company's working capital;

sales grew more slowly than resource costs (see Figure 7.4) so that the company could not work at full capacity. Consequently, operating profit (see Figure 7.3) decreased rapidly. Later, in 2003, due to KPC's very active borrowing, LTD/Equity ratio reached four to one.

Conclusion

In the first years of the Russian reforms, KPC had a large share of the Russian consumer paper market and technological advantages. Additionally, from 1993 to 2003, there was continuing dynamic growth of the Russian market due to the low level of consumption of paper products prior to this period and changing attitudes of buyers. However, remarkable opportunities were not realised. The company's market shares in its key products were in constant decline, due to the fact that after 1993 the world's top manufacturers came to Russia and established their strong leading positions selling well-known brands.

The company had little chance to find a solution for the new challenge, because of the absence of brands and old-fashioned design together with a deficit of financial and intellectual resources to allow modernisation of the business. Additionally, the company was not adequately managed; the quality of strategic planning and implementation of this strategy was poor; there were no synergies across business segments and the corporate strategy did not include plans for product positioning.

From 1993 to 1997, operations of the company had been maintained successfully; in 1995–7, the company managed to improve regularity of manufacturing, efficiency in operations and quality of output and reduced certain levels of management. However, the company incurred substantial development costs in introducing new and improved products and technologies. In addition, many projects that were planned were not realised and some departments could not produce to the required quality standard.

After 1996, the management team changed the generic strategy and started to realise a new marketing policy, which included creating branded products, goods for 'away-from-home' and manufacturing in the higher price segment. However, the company's consumer products had been sold in a highly competitive market with branded products and the new policy did not create competitive advantages. As a result, KPC lost the key segments of the market and maintained a position in the cheapest segments that could not generate a sufficiently large profitability. Moreover, the company's sales did not occur as had been estimated because the company was not able to anticipate consumer preferences, estimated sales of new products and the company's products were not accepted in new markets.

Between 1996 and 2000, the company decreased its share of labour costs by sacking 30 per cent of its personnel, implementing new technological standards and decreasing its inventory and receivables. However, capacity utilisation never exceeded 80 per cent and this dramatically increased the share of overheads and power expenditure. In addition, the company developed too fast and did not have the ability to borrow money on the financial market and therefore it constantly had problems with working capital.

After the Russian crisis of 1998 and the devaluation of the rouble, the company had to pay four times more for imported raw materials: a major part of production expenditure for many products, as well as import equipment. Evidence from this period shows that every year KPC was surrendering more and more of its position in the rapidly growing Russian consumer market. Its market share decreased to less than a third of what it was at the start of privatisation and the company ceased trading in many segments of the paper industry.

Poor operations dramatically limited funding for maintaining the business and dramatically increased different business risks. Many executives and top engineers left the company and a deficit of highly skilled managers and engineers partially paralysed the business of KPC.

In the case of KPC, a complicated situation was created, when the executives could not control the company's expenditures and quality of operations because of poor management and discipline. Poor management was created by the lack of qualification and a deficit of highly skilled managers and engineers. Deficit of highly skilled staff was created by reduced wages and the scarcity of finance for human development.

Different approaches for improving the situation, such as decreasing the salaries of personnel, simplification of products and technology and reducing the amount of the product did not have a positive effect on the corporate performance. As a result, KPC lost significant segments of the market and managed to maintain positions only in the cheapest market segments.

8 Norilsk Nickel

This case study examines how Nornickel, which is one of the biggest mining companies in the world, carried out its operations and development between 1994 and 2011. The company has been able to access natural resources and has benefited from inflated global market demand and commodity prices. However, it is worrying that Nornickel is dominated by oligarchs where there is a high level of lobbying, which may damage the long-term condition of this company.

Privatisation

In 1989, the State Concern for Non-Ferrous Metals Production Nornickel (Nornickel) was created by the Council of Ministers of the USSR. The basis of Nornickel was Norilsk Mining and Metallurgical Plant (NMMP) – a leading enterprise in Russia for production of non-ferrous metals. NMMP was the largest company in Siberia and was located in the Krasnoyarsk region. The enterprise included five underground mines; it had two ore concentrate plants and three metallurgical plants and employed about 120,000 people. The second enterprise, Mining and Metallurgical Plant Pechenganikel, was located in the north-western part of the Kola Peninsula near the border with Norway. The composition of the factory consisted of four mines, a concentrate plant, smelting plant and a sulphuric acid plant, accessible by road and rail and employing 10,000 people. The third large enterprise of Nornickel was Severonickel Plant that was founded in 1938 in the Kola Peninsula; it processed a rich copper-nickel ore from Norilsk and Pechenganikel plants, as well as scrap and raw materials for both domestic and foreign suppliers (Nornickel AR 1996).

In July 1993, the presidential decree 'On Special Features of the Sale of Shares and Privatisation of the Russian State Nonferrous and Precious Metal Concern Norilsk Nickel' was passed, and this provided the company with particular terms and conditions for its privatisation. From April 1994, the company officially became an open joint-stock company, Nornickel (ibid.).

The final share distribution at the first stage of privatisation allowed for 25 per cent of company shares (preference shares) to be distributed free to workers of the company. In addition, 15 per cent of ordinary shares were offered at a discount by closed subscription to members of the workforce and another 12 per cent of ordinary shares were sold on the cheque auction to Russian and foreign investors (Sorokin 2000). At the first stage of privatisation, the state continued to own 48 per cent of company equity; this resulted in encouraging state power and intervention in the management of the company.

In March 1995, a consortium of the largest Russian banks made an offer to the Russian government to transfer ownership of 43 state enterprises to the banks in exchange for a loan to the government. The presidential decree of 11 May 1995 set up a mechanism to hand over the companies' shares in federal ownership to private companies for the trust management. In a few years, the government could sell the shares to investors at a special auction and buy back its shares from the banks. In reality, it was the privatisation of state enterprises by selling shares to the large financial–industrial groups, which were close associates of the Russian authorities.

One of these banks was Uneximbank, which was created with the active participation of Norilsk Nickel's capital, and grew rapidly during the first years of Russian reforms as it had a powerful lobby in federal and regional governments (Puffer *et al.* 2000). The president of Uneximbank, Vladimir Potanin, received the right to control the organisation and conduct a number of special mortgaging auctions, which included Nornickel.

In November 1995, 38 per cent of the total shares (51 per cent of the voting shares) were offered at the mortgaging auction; consequently, Uneximbank won the auction, paid $170 million, and became the nominal holder of the controlling stake with the prospect of acquiring the whole company. Russian Credit Bank, which was a main competitor of Uneximbank, offered $355 million, however this was not accepted by the organiser of the auction (Sorokin 2000, Butrin 2004a).

Shares of Nornickel had been underestimated because, in that time, net income exceeded $500 million, the turnover of the company was about $3 billion and capitalisation was about $1 billion. Moreover, according to the agreement with the GKI, this money was not transferred from the bank to the state because GKI had accounts in this bank and it deposited money with low interest (Sorokin 2000). A few months later after the victory in the auction, the banking group lobbied benefits for Nornickel (and also for itself), which included delaying return of a number of loans amounting to $100 million and also delayed interest and penalties on those loans and reduced customs duties.

In order to force the resignation of Nornickel's President Anatoly Filatov, representatives of Uneximbank initiated a mass media campaign against him that accused him of collapsing production, completely disrupting financial flows, making irregular payments of salaries to workers and causing a growing tax debt. Additionally, in January 1996, the Norilsk prosecutor initiated a criminal case against Nornickel's managers, accusing them of improper use of funds, and three months later president Filatov was dismissed by government orders and the company's board of directors was replaced. The new president was Uneximbank's representative Aleksandr Khloponin, who was the head of the company until 2001.

Under the terms of mortgage auctions, after one year the mortgagee has the right to sell shares received as a loan if the government does not return the loan. Understanding this, in February 1997, the Russian Parliament passed a resolution that de facto nationalised Nornickel and Uneximbank were required to return the state shares of the company that the bank held in pledge. However, at that time, former Uneximbank president Vladimir Potanin was appointed the first deputy prime minister of the Russian Federation and he used his authority to allow his bank to win the battle for the nickel giant. Therefore, after the loan period had ended, the mortgagee Uneximbank exhibited the controlling share at the commercial auction in August 1997; the controlling share was acquired by Uneximbank's subsidiary 'Swift' for $270 million (Sorokin 2000).

Under the terms announced, Uneximbank had to transfer to Nornickel (essentially to itself) $300 million for the development of condensed gas fields near Norilsk, and about $80 million to maintain the social infrastructure of the Norilsk industrial district and to recompense debts of the company. One month later, a 100 per cent additional issue of Nornickel shares increased the share that was controlled by Potanin and his companion Mikhail Prokhorov to 60 per cent and the giant Russian industry ceased to be public (Butrin 2004a).

Boldyrev (2000) notes that privatisation of Nornickel gave a reason to believe that when the Russian government was considering the 'loan for shares' deal, it initially has not planned to return the loan, thereby after a certain time the assets transferred to the pledge. Also, he concludes that the global leader in the non-ferrous metallurgy, with colossal reserves for more than 40 years of rich ores and an annual net profit of nearly half a billion dollars, was sold for $180 million and the state had not received any real money, but even if they actually had the $180 million, it is only crumbs.

Industrial factors

Non-ferrous metallurgy was one of the most significant industries for the national economy and Russian companies were the key players in the global market. The industry accounted for 8.9 per cent of GDP in Russia (1999), with a total annual turnover of more than $11 billion and was strongly export-oriented; more than 70 per cent of the nonferrous metals were exported (Butrin 2004a).

The industry was growing dynamically; it was not in a deep crisis as were many other Russian industries and its output volumes increased annually by an average of 7.1 per cent from 1995–2005. In the first years of the Russian reforms, the effectiveness of this segment of the national economy was a result of relatively inexpensive energy and mineral raw materials, enormous Russian mineral reserves, low labour costs, low state standards of environmental pollution and weak control over them.

Nornickel was a significant part of the Russian nonferrous industry and had a dominant share of nickel and platinum production on the global market. Therefore, corporate performance strongly depended upon market competition on the external market. The company produced about 96 per cent of Russian nickel, 55 per cent of copper and more than 95 per cent of platinum and palladium. However, only 15 per cent of sales were made on the Russian market; Europe accounted for about 55 per cent, North America 16 per cent and Asia for 11 per cent (Nornickel AR 2000, 2002).

There were vigorous barriers to new entrants such as difficult technology and a deficit of highly skilled personnel and infrastructure. Considerable increases in prices of raw materials, energy, transportation and other necessary supplies and services adversely affected the corporation's financial results. Metals were subjected to considerable price fluctuations due to the cyclical nature of these markets; as a result, the decrease in metals prices negatively affected the company performance.

Despite the crash of the Soviet system and financial crises in Russia, the company maintained stable production and, between 1989 and 2006, it produced 220,000 tonnes of nickel, 410,000 tonnes of copper and 670,000 ounces of platinum per year. Moreover, production of palladium doubled in the 1990s due to a huge demand from the auto and electronics industries and this reached 4.5 million ounces (Nornickel AR 2000).

Generally, the situation in the base and precious metal markets was favourable between 1993 and 2006. The decisive factors that influenced the world prices for the main products of Nornickel were stable growth in China, strong demand from major developed economies and increased impact of operations conducted by international investment funds on the metal markets.

Between 1994 and 2006, the world production of major metals of Nornickel steadily increased, and the company saved its market share accounting for approximately 20 per cent of global nickel supply, 55 per cent of global palladium and 3 per cent of global copper. However, the company could not maintain its share on the global market of platinum due to the dramatic growth of African suppliers; as a result, the share of platinum being produced by the company on the global market decreased from 22 per cent in 1990–5 to 12 per cent in 2006 (Nornickel AR 2000–6).

The price of metals was the key factor, which determined the corporate performance of mining companies. Figures 8.1 and 8.2 show the changes in metal prices; one can see that the average annual nickel, copper and platinum prices have a slightly growing trend; changing in 2001 to an extremely high growth, when prices of metals (nickel and copper) increased by around 100 per cent per year, and their prices hit record high values. The palladium price had a peak in 1997–2003 due to a huge increase in demand from auto component producers.

Regional factors

The most significant production of the company is situated in the extreme conditions of the Taimyr Peninsula above the Arctic Circle. Therefore, the company was constantly required to guarantee its own stable power supplies and reliable transportation links. The company is based in Norilsk in the Taimyr Autonomous region, and it is the northernmost city on the planet

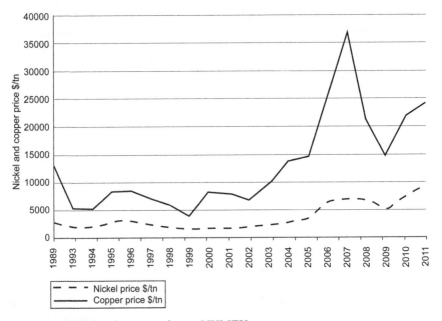

Figure 8.1 Nickel and copper price on NYMEX
Source: Nornickel annual reports (1995–2011).
Author's calculation.

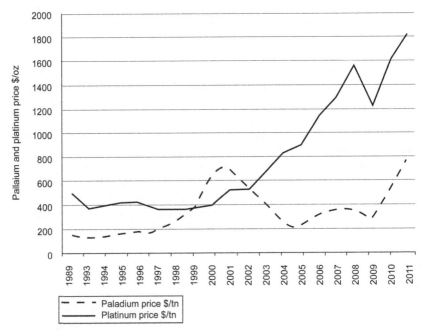

Figure 8.2 Palladium and platinum price on NYMEX
Source: Nornickel annual reports (1995–2011).
Author's calculation.

with a population of over 200,000. Nornickel was the principal employer in the Norilsk area. In addition, Port Dudinka and the railway were built to support the company and the town. From the port, enriched nickel and copper are transported by sea to the Monchegorsk enrichment plant on the Kola Peninsula, while valuable metals are transported by river to the Kransnoyarsk plant (Nornickel AR 2000, 2003). Importantly, these transportations only take place during the summer months when the river is navigable.

The nickel deposits of Norilsk-Talnakh are the largest nickel-copper-palladium deposits in the world, and the current resources overstep 1.8 billion tonnes. The ore is mined via numerous shafts, which are located more than 1,200 meters below ground. Norilsk-Talknakh mines had a significantly high level of accidents, for example there were 2.4 accidents per thousand workers in 2005 (Nornickel AR 2000–6). In addition, part of the nickel ore was smelted in plants near Norilsk. The smelting was directly responsible for harsh pollution that included carbon oxides, sulphur dioxide, phenols and a high concentration of heavy metals.

The Blacksmith Institute included Norilsk in its 2007 list of the ten most polluted places on Earth (Bryan 2007). Mortality from respiratory diseases is much higher than the average in Russia. Within 50 kilometres of the nickel smelter there is not a single living tree. Norilsk has an extremely difficult climate; the area is covered with snow for about 250–70 days a year and average temperature is approximately minus 10 degrees Celsius and winter temperatures can fall to minus 55 degrees Celsius (Norilsk 2008).

All resources of Taimyr, whether financial, labour related or mineral, depended on Nornickel. Additionally, consumer demand of the region, migration of people, education, industrial production and infrastructure were determined by the company. As a result of this monopoly, the region did not have sufficient high-quality labour. The region had the lowest level of crime because of its geography and closed regime of working. Bellona (2010) notes that in the Norilsk area, where the company's plants are located, the human rights movement is fragile. Citizens completely depend on the company, which makes them afraid of speaking out and providing truthful information.

The strong economic and social position of the company provided total political control of the region, and it helped the general director of Nornickel, Aleksandr Khloponin, to win the election for the governor of the Taimyr Region in 2001. The new governor changed the distribution of regional taxes and used a major part of them for the social, ecological and infrastructural programme of the company. The executives of the company created arbitraged fiscal differentiation between the Norilsk region and other regions of Russia and as a result sufficiently reduced the company's effective tax rate.

Business strategy after privatisation

Before Russian reforms, the majority of company products were used domestically for military uses. In addition, all platinum and palladium were acquired by the Soviet government to form state reserves. After the collapse of the Soviet economy, the market changed rapidly, and the company became one of the leading European suppliers.

In the first years after privatisation, corporate strategy did not feature as part of regular management activity and thus attracted less attention from company executives because they concentrated on transition from solid state regulation to a relatively independent policy. Between 1993 and 1996, the executives struggled to prevent the organisation from breaking up and to maintain production after the collapse of the Soviet market. As a result, the company formulated the strategy of boosting productivity and increasing its position on the external market. The company and its divisions had sufficient ability to maintain the long-term competitive advantages because they were effectively managed, had management controlling expenditures and the company had a strong position on the world market. The private interests of the executives were associated with keeping their position in the company and withdrawal of wealth was relatively insignificant.

From 1996, the company had been managed by the new team, which concentrated, in the first two years, on establishing full control of the company and did not give much attention to the development of company strategy. After 1998, a new vision and strategy were created and orientated to the transformation of the company into a mining and metallurgical corporation of the international rank. The board of directors established efficient administration and monitoring of the company's assets and created a corporate centre that developed a uniform strategy. The new strategy was focused on increasing the production of metals from the company's own ores, involvement of stale raw materials into the conversion processes, development of production of metals from waste products in production facilities of the Kola Peninsula, increasing direct sales to foreign producers-processors and implementation of new technologies in the mining and metallurgical areas. The company made an adjustment in the share of the physical manufacturing capacity located in more comfortable parts of Russia; arbitraging the price difference between expensive manufactories in the Taimyr Peninsula and inexpensive Russian mainland labour markets.

Additionally, the strategy included elimination of inefficient production units, acquisition of licenses for new ore deposits and essential vital energy and transport companies, and creating international alliances with companies processing non-ferrous and precious metals. In 2000, Nornickel launched an ambitious 10 year 'Development Plan', which cost $5 billion. This agenda included the modernisation of smelting lines, an upgraded copper concentrate filtration process in Norilsk plants and the establishment of technology allowing the production of refined granulated silver and nickel carbonyl powders at Severonickel (Nornickel AR 2000–1).

In 2001, the restructuring of the charter capital of the group was completed, and 96.9 per cent of Nornickel's shares were exchanged for shares of OJSC MMC Norilsk Nickel. Changing Nornickel's legal status consolidated assets and defended the company that could theoretically have been nationalised (Butrin 2004a). This share swap involved about 100,000 shareholders. As a result, the shares of individuals and of employees decreased to 9 and 4 per cent respectively, whereas two main shareholders (Potanin and Prokhorov) possessed about 55 per cent of shares. The stock market reacted accordingly – the share price of Nornickel on the RTS went up from $7 per share in January 2001 to $17 per share in December 2001 (Nornickel AR 2001).

The demand of the financial markets and new opportunities for shareholders pushed the company to the financialisation of strategy. The new strategy of Nornickel was focused on increasing shareholder value, holding leading positions on the world market in the production of its key products; improving its corporate governance to international standards and the transparency of the company.

In 2003, the largest American producer of platinum Stillwater (Montana) was acquired by Nornickel. It produced metals from raw materials obtained at the JM Reef in Montana and from recycling of automotive catalysts. Nornickel paid for the 55.4 per cent stake in Stillwater by 887 thousand ounces of palladium and just over $100 million in cash, and this deal was beneficial for Nornickel, because Stillwater had huge stocks of palladium, which had accumulated due to lower demand in the European metal market (ibid.).

In 2004–5, the nickel business of OM Group and Canadian Lion Ore were bought by Nornickel for half-annual EBITDA and 6.5 EBITDA respectively. Consequently, it received good quality mining assets in Western Australia, Finland and Africa and so the Russian share of the business declined from 98 per cent to 78 per cent (Nornickel AR 2003, 2004).

Through these acquisitions, total annual nickel production of Nornickel increased to 300 thousand tonnes. Acquiring companies in Africa had cheaper labour costs and the purchase of OM Group and Lion Ore gave new knowledge and technologies of production of nickel and could have potentially yielded savings of about $500 million a year (ibid.). This last fact reveals arbitrage of knowledge, which exploits asymmetries of knowledge because the creation of know-hows by the company itself could be more expensive than the acquisition of another company with special expertise.

After 2001, the executives began to diversify the business; the company acquired the biggest Russian gold producer, Poles, making Nornickel the leader of the Russian gold industry and the share of the gold production very quickly reached 7 per cent of total sales (Nornickel AR 2003).

For the establishment of reliable transportation of cargo passing through the North Sea Route the company bought icebreakers and an ice reinforced container ship; it acquired assets in shipping and transport companies (35.05 per cent of shares in Archangelsk Sea Port and 23.8 per cent of Enisey River Navigation). The company exploited price asymmetries between different shipping and transport companies and power suppliers. In addition, vertical integration of acquired power and transport companies reduced the share of external costs.

The critical success factor for the company was solid demand from foreign customers for non-ferrous metals and their prices. Nevertheless, commodity price volatility generated the most important challenges for the company. The company's major opportunities were beneficial facilities at Norilsk, reprocessing of tailings and international diversification.

The fundamental weaknesses of the company during that period were the political risk of state expropriation, changing taxation, geographical position, transport communication and lack of minority shareholder control. The strengths of the company that allowed it a dominant position on the global market were the reserves of ore and the weakness of national currency from 1998 to 2003. Furthermore, Nornickel was an unusually well-balanced company because it did not experience problems with energy, raw materials or markets due to the large regional gas field, ore reserves sufficient for hundreds of years and a strong demand on the global market.

Since 1998, the company strategy has been value creation and value absorption for increased capitalisation. An example of value creation is the termination of platinum group metals (PGM) law. The information on the sales of PGMs produced by Nornickel in Russia was subject to state confidentiality legislation and its exports were subject to quotas and completely depended on the Ministry of Finance and the State Treasury. However, in 2004, Potanin lobbied for the termination of this law. Because of changes in the legislation from 2005, the company was allowed to disclose the reserves, production, sales and consumption of PGMs and this rapidly increased the capitalisation of Nornickel (Nornickel AR 2004, 2005).

Management of operations

The company had five principal elements that constituted its business: mining, the tailings project, smelting, power and reserves.

Mining

Since the late 1990s, two new mines Skalisty and Gluboky with a total capacity of more than 15 million tonnes of ore were developed by the company. These mines had to compensate the reduction of higher grade ores by the main mine Oktyabrsky, which accounted for about 69 per cent of the company's copper output, 55 per cent of its nickel, 58 per cent of its PGM and 54 per cent of its cobalt (Nornickel AR 2001, 2005).

The tailings project

Between 1948 and 1975, the company accumulated enormous reserves of PGM-bearing tailings because old-fashioned technology of nickel production did not absorb PGM and they utilised it as waste materials. Consequently, the company had accumulated approximately 76 million tonnes of tailings, having a constitution of about 5.8 g/t of palladium and 2.1 g/t of platinum, and this mass contains about 19.3 million ounces of PGMs. Therefore, developing the tailings project was a key production strategy of the company and in 2001, an enrichment factory for lifting up and conversion of pyrrotine concoction was built (Nornickel AR 2001, 2005).

Smelting

According to the 2010 Development Plan, the various metallurgical operations on the Taimyr and Kola peninsulas were reorganised. As an example: the Nadezhda Metallurgical Works was the main smelter on the Taimyr Peninsula, with both hydro- and pyro-metallurgical facilities, however it had an inefficient hydrometallurgical line. For that reason, the plant was closed by 2003 and replaced with a modern nickel-cobalt refinery, which was 30 per cent larger (Nornickel AR 2000).

Power

The new Pelyatka condensed gas field was one of the most vital projects for the development of the Norilsk Industrial Region. Financing of this project was one of the investment conditions for Nornickel's privatisation. The first borehole was sunk on 15 April 1999 and the first Pelyatka gas reached Norilsk later in 2001. In order to maintain reliable energy supplies to the Norilsk industrial district and to optimise electric power costs, the company increased its share in the Russian electric power industry and controlled regional electricity suppliers (Nornickel AR 2004–6).

Pyrometallurgical gains

Metallurgically tested operations on the concentrates from the substandard grade disseminated ores and got very positive results with using pyrometallurgical processing. With a shift in the Nadezhda smelter to full pyrometallurgical processing cost efficiencies were achieved. Therefore, the company did not have significantly increased operating cost (ibid.).

Reserves

In 2005, after disclosing Nornickel reserves, its deposits hosted 6.3 million tonnes of nickel, 9.4 million tonnes of copper, 62 million ounces of palladium and 16 million ounces of platinum (Nornickel AR 2006).

Marketing

The company supplied approximately half of the world's platinoid and 20 per cent of its nickel. In addition, Nornickel was the largest Russian copper producer, and after 2004 it became the leading Russian gold producer, as well. As a part of the company's foreign market-oriented distribution policy, it created

Nornickel Europe Limited (UK), Nornickel USA and Nornickel Asia, and the new companies distributed products to the European, American and Asian markets respectively (Nornickel AR 2000–6).

The company made significant progress in long-term distribution policy, targeting sales directly to end consumers and key regional distributors. As a result, the share of long-term contracts in 2003–5 accounted for 95 per cent of nickel sales and 96 per cent of copper sales, and export sales to end consumers made up 99 per cent of nickel sales and 85 per cent of copper sales. A brokerage membership of the London Metal Exchange (LME) was made and this optimised trade operations in Western Europe, which was a dominant market. In addition, the positive situation in the metal markets helped the company to extend its sales geographically to the markets of Southeast Asia, Canada, the US and Japan (Nornickel AR 2000–6).

Financial management

After the start of the Russian reforms, Nornickel did not have the same decline in production as many Russian companies. In 1993, the company went through a year of recession when its volume of output decreased by 14 per cent. However, in 1994, it had growth of production of nickel and copper by 1 per cent and 2.6 per cent respectively and all vital plants and mines operated with a profit (net profit amounted to about $400 million). In the crisis years, relatively large investments exceeding $350–450 million were made every year; these investments maintained production on a high level (Sorokin 2000).

From 1996, the company had been managed by representatives of Unexinbank and according to the agreement with the government the bank had to raise investment amounting to $1 billion. This obligation was not fulfilled, and as a result many ecological and production projects were halted.

The new team increased accounts payable extremely quickly, from 6.3 trillion roubles ($1.1 billion) at the beginning of 1996 to 16.9 trillion roubles ($2.9 billion) in the second quarter of 1997 (Nornickel AR 1995–7). The major part of these debts was wages, tax obligations and payment for gas and electricity. For example, during that time the salary debt grew by 150 per cent and amounted to 1.2 trillion roubles that, together with massive layoffs, dramatically worsened the situation in the social sphere and generated strikes, which halted mines and metallurgical plants.

Additionally, the company sharply reduced tax payments on the budgets as illustrated in the following figures: in 1995, Nornickel transferred 653 billion roubles in the federal budget and in 1996, 234 billion roubles. As a result, in 1995, the debt to the state budget amounted to 125 billion roubles and in 1996 to 743 billion roubles ($440 million) (Nornickel AR 1995–7), which was more than double the total payment for 51 per cent of shares of the company. However, the authorities turned a blind eye to the increasing debt despite an already existing huge debt.

In the 1990s, the company needed to spend an enormous amount (about $300–$500 million) on maintaining social infrastructure of the town and the region as a part of social responsibility of the business. Since 1997, the size of the payment to the region had declined; as a result, the standard of living in the area fell dramatically. This generated mass departure of the workforce and created its deficit.

As was noted above, in 1997 Vladimir Potanin was appointed first deputy prime minister and he used his authority to lobby the special government resolution x2116 254, which permitted the company to write off about $280 million in tax debt to the region by exchanging the relatively small plant in Krasnoyarsk for the debt (Butrin 2004a). Additionally, the company was allowed to postpone payment of $145 million to the federal budget for ten years and the state pension fund of $260 million and $350 million for five and ten years respectively. Fixed costs were high at Nornickel relative to mining industry averages, partly due to the remoteness of the region and partly due to inherited inefficiencies from the Soviet era. Between 1997 and 2003, Nornickel reduced employment levels by about 3–5 per cent per annum (Nornickel AR 1997, 2003).

The complex structure of marketing divisions abroad helped to adjust the earnings capacity of the company by establishing transfer pricing between geographic subsidiaries, employing arbitrage of fiscal variations between Russia and other countries and reducing the company's customs and tax payments. For example, Table 8.1 reveals the differentiation between Nornickel's contract price of nickel and price of this metal at the LME. One can see that reduction of export income, which the company had from only one metal. This had the effect of artificially moving profit offshore, reducing taxable profit and duty as well as reducing Nornickel shareholder dividend liability.

From 1999 to 2007, Nornickel demonstrated impressive growth; the market capitalisation of the group grew by more than 25,000 per cent and reached $41 billion due to the sustained strong demand for metals produced by the company. It also developed its production capacities, and improved reliability of energy supplies, transportation links and corporate governance.

The company increased levels of transparency in terms of its colossal reserves that boosted capitalisation and regularly improved its credit rating, which reduced the cost of borrowings and improved the financial flexibility as well. The company was the first among Russian companies to obtain an

Table 8.1 Difference between contract prices of exported metal and prices at the LME

	2001	2002	2003	2004	2005	2006
Contract price nickel $/t	5561	5994	8779	12805	13422	21689
LME price nickel $/t	5945	6772	9629	13823	14744	24254
Price difference $/t (per cent)	6.45	11.45	8.83	7.36	8.96	10.57
Export nickel kt	91	160	132	122	125	99
Reduction of export income $MN	35	124	113	128	165	254

Source: Katsik *et al.* 2008.

investment grade credit rating – a long-term BBB from the international rating agency Fitch in December 2005 (Nornickel AR 2005).

Under Putin's supervision

In April 2008, Prokhorov sold 25 per cent of company shares to Deripaska, who controlled the world's largest aluminium company, UC Rusal. According to the conditions of the deal, Prokhorov received $7 billion and 14 per cent of UC Rusal shares. This was a successful outcome for Prokhorov as the shares in the company fell by 80 per cent over the next six months.

After purchasing 25 per cent of Nornickel shares Deripaska immediately announced his intention to combine Nornickel and UC Rusal. As a result of this merger, all control would be in Deripaska's hands whereas Potanin (the owner of 29.8 per cent shares in the company) would lose his share in a unified power structure. Deripaska was going to make a Russian mining giant. The idea of creating a global diversified metallurgical super giant with Nornickel as the foundation had been in discussion since he bought his shares of the company.

At the same time, Potanin agreed with Alisher Usmanov, who was the owner of 5 per cent Nornickel's shares, the football club Arsenal and sundry assets in mining and metallurgical industries, about the creation of a company, which would join Nornickel and Usmanov's Metalloinvest. The new company would be the largest mining and metallurgical company in the world. In the event of completion of this transaction, Deripaska would have lost the ability to manage the asset. These differences of view on the future of Nornickel led to one of the most significant corporate conflicts in the history of Russian business.

Considerable controversy arose around the posts of CEO, the board of Norilsk Nickel directors and its chairman of the board of directors. As a result, a protégé of UC Rusal, prime minister Putin's former chief Alexander Voloshin, was appointed as chairman of the board of directors (Rozhkova and Terentyeva 2011). An important aspect in the fight against the shareholders is the fact that by April 2011, Nornickel had bought 6.85 per cent of its own shares from the market by spending around $3.3 billion, and these treasury shares increased the voting strength of the company's management.

Vladimir Putin was interested in Nornickel and UC Rusal, and he decided that the struggle for the company between Deripaska and Potanin paralysed business and was depressing the company's market price. In August 2008, Vladimir Strzhalkovsky was appointed as CEO of Norilsk Nickel. Strzhalkovsky is a former KGB colonel from St Petersburg with experience in the tourism industry, where he progressed from being a director of a travel agency, which supplied Russian prostitutes to Finnish motels, to overseeing the country's entire tourism industry (Antonov 2003).

The appointment of Strzhalkovsky, who was far removed from the mining industry, but was Prime Minister Putin's friend, was made due to his extensive experience in state agencies. The recommendation of Strzhalkovsky as CEO together with the holding of some 41.7 per cent of Norilsk stock under repo agreements by the two largest Russian state banks, VTB and VEB, shows that Putin indirectly supervises Nornickel. Krichevsky (2009) suggests that the beneficiaries of offshore structures, which control almost all ferrous and non-ferrous metallurgy of the country, are Russian officials at the federal and regional levels.

At the time of the deal between Deripaska and Prokhorov, the value of Nornickel was estimated at more than \$52 billion. However, over eight months of conflict, the company's capitalisation declined to \$14 billion. However, this was not so much due to competition between Deripaska and Potanin, as to the global financial crisis. More information about the impact of the financial crisis on the performance of Nornickel is given in Chapter 10. In addition, between 2005 and 2010, the output of copper dropped by 14 per cent, the production of palladium dropped by 9.6 per cent and the production of platinum dropped by 7.8 per cent, despite the fact that the global demand for these metals was growing.

It has been noted that considerable conflict arose around control of the company; however, poor management became the main cause of shareholders' tension. Delyagin (2011) notes that Nornickel loses around \$500 million annually because the company sells metals via traders, relies on LME too much, and has weak cooperation with end customers. The company realised many rather dubious operations such as the sale of treasury shares to Trafigura, Norilsk Nickel's direct competitor and the termination of production of the Australian subsidiaries Black Swan and Silver Swan.

Bellona (2010) notes that the environmental situation in regions, which was affected by Nornickel, is as critical now as it was at the end of the last century. Emissions of contaminants into the atmosphere is extremely high, for example Nornickel accounts for 25 per cent of Russian industrial emissions of SO_2 in 2009 alone; the company emitted approximately 975,000 tonnes of sulphur into the atmosphere. In practice, emission levels do not depend upon reported environmental protection investment. For example, in 2009, the investment in environmental protection measures by Nornickel in the Taimyr Peninsula amounted to over \$376 million, but during this period, the reduction of emissions from all plants was only 2,000 tonnes (around 0.3 per cent). Such poor efficiency can be explained by inefficient management and that the company has been using money earmarked for environmental protection to buy equipment that is not directly used to protect the remnants of nature in the region (Delyagin 2011).

Since Strzhalkovsky was appointed as CEO, internal corruption in Nornickel has reached an unprecedented level. Some examples of which would be the company lending large funds without collateral and with low interest rates, and selling metal to offshore companies, affiliated with top managers. In addition, the management of the company operated via the 'one-day company' with a doubtful reputation as was found by the Krasnoyarsk arbitrage court (Severtsev 2012).

Nosenko (2011) notes the company increased the cost of property insurance eightfold, which in 2009 amounted to 2.265 billion roubles, or 0.7 per cent of the value of fixed assets. This cost of insurance premiums is a sufficient cause for suspicion because the average cost of premiums for property insurance, in the practice of Russian companies, is on average 0.02 per cent of the value of the insured property.

In 2008, the Third Generation Company of the Wholesale Electricity Market (WGC-3), which belongs to Nornickel, purchased 25 per cent shares of Rusia Petroleum for $576 million (OGK-3 2008) The acquisition was realised under the appearance of redeeming the interest in Potanin Interros Group's assets to salvage the company during the financial crisis. However, Interros Group is one of the largest shareholders of Nornickel, and this is another example of the pumping of assets from the company.

The purchase of assets from the shareholder controlling the company is a serious violation of corporate governance principles because it was taken without discussion with other owners. Furthermore, Rusia Petroleum is not a core asset for WGC-3 and their purchase is explained only by the desire of Interros to get access to the cash of the company (Rusal 2008b).

The development of energy networks for Nornickel was accompanied by a large-scale financial fraud, consisting of distortions of reported results and massive violations of technological standards (Vorontsov 2011).

The company has increased losses of nickel and platinum metals. For example, extraction of platinum metals in the concentrate before privatisation reached 97 per cent. Since 1998, it has declined to just 90 per cent; the share of rhodium in the standard USSR certified sample of platinum concentrate was 3.02 per cent. Currently it is around 1.5 per cent, but geological characteristics of the mines have not radically changed. As a result, the company lost metals, which could theoretically have a value of about $1 billion. Thus, supplies of rhodium from Russia on the world market fell to 2.2 tonnes (Faizulin 2011).

Delyagin (2011) tries to find an answer for the question: does the company have poor ore or poor mining skills? He supposes that the metal content in the ore is decreasing because of the long-term under-investment in the development of new mines. Nevertheless, there is another explanation. In the past two years, targets for extraction of ore have been significantly raised to a level that the mines simply could not physically manage. As a result, Russian workers do the same as they did during Soviet times. For the achievement of a given target of ore extracted, they just add waste rock that does not contain any metal and it is usually removed from the mine separately. Experts estimate that monthly each of the mines added around 6–8 tonnes of waste rock. As a result, the company lost considerable resources on the processing of waste rock (Polynko 2011).

The crumbling infrastructure in Nornickel increased the number of industrial accidents. Thus while in 2008 there were 1.7 industrial accidents per 1,000 employees at Nornickel, by 2009 this statistic has increased to 2.3, which was far above Russia's average. This was despite the fact that huge amounts of money were routinely allocated to health and safety purposes; in 2009 3.1 billion roubles was spent, which for Nornickel translates into almost 72,000 roubles per employee. Much of this money was used by the polar transport branch of Nornickel to buy four Liebherr mobile harbor cranes and a powerful river ship (Krichevsky 2009, Delyagin 2011).

In November 2010, Nornickel president Klishas proposed a cancellation of the minority shareholders' right to access full information about the activities of the company. In his opinion, the amount of information disclosed to each shareholder must depend on the number of shares held by that shareholder (Delyagin 2011).

Administrative expenses usually include salaries and bonuses of top managers, travel and executive transport expenses, office maintenance and hospitality expenditure as well as audit fees. In Nornickel, administrative expenses for executive managers are relatively similar to the wages of more than 100,000 employees. For example, in 2008 administrative expenses were $1,071 million compared to the payroll of $1,638 million.

Also in 2008, the company had an extraordinary financial policy: it declared dividends of $902 million and purchased $2.6 billion of its own shares, even though losses for that year constituted $555 million. This can be explained by the owners salvaging their assets.

Financial analysis

Since 2003, the company demonstrated impressive growth of sales, profit and capitalisation, which resulted from the sustained strong demand for metals. Between 1994 and 2002 its volume of sales fluctuated around $3 billion with a local peak in $6 billion (2000) due to a huge rise in the price of palladium as well as relatively high prices for nickel and platinum. Nornickel sales revenue growth was 800 per cent in the years 1994 to 2007 when net sales reached $17 billion (Figure 8.3). This increase was mainly explained by the boost in the average price of metals because, in physical terms, its sales were relatively consistent.

In 1996–7, and later in 2002, operating profit (Figure 8.4) was negatively affected by dramatic growth in recourses costs and a relatively low price of metals. In 1996, the operating profit dropped to a negative value because the company could not increase product prices in spite of massive withdrawal of wealth by the owners. Additionally, the relatively fast growth of the price of energy reduced operating profit more than in previous years. The Russian crisis of 1998 boosted the growth of operating profit due to a considerable reduction of external cost and labour cost.

Resource costs (see Figure 8.5), which includes external material and services purchased and employee compensation, accounted for approximately 60 per cent of total income in 1994–2007 and declined steadily to 40 per cent by 2006.

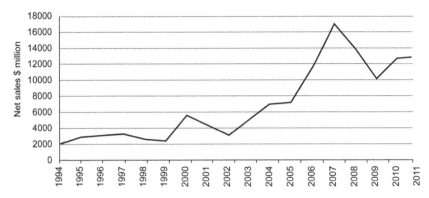

Figure 8.3 Nornickel net sales
Source: Nornickel annual reports.

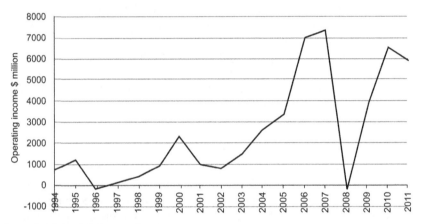

Figure 8.4 Nornickel operating incomes
Source: Nornickel annual reports.

Between 1994 and 2007, value retained in income fluctuated around 50 per cent (Figure 8.6), and the first nadir of the ratio (1996) was created by low profitability of business, high expenditure for raw materials and a substantial amount of wealth withdrawn by the owners. Since 1997, this index has had a rising trajectory, and during 1999, it reached a local zenith of 62 per cent. Later, it gradually oscillated near the 50 per cent level, and in 2006, it had a high point due to EBIDTA reaching considerable levels.

In order to establish how much of every rouble of sales revenue is value retained by the company one has to deduct all external costs. Figure 8.7 shows that there are two distinct periods 1994 to 1996 and 1997 to 2006; the first period showing a dramatic increase in external costs in income to 82 per cent and thereafter a reduction in external costs in income to 30 per cent. Both cases can be explained by considerable volatility of sales revenue.

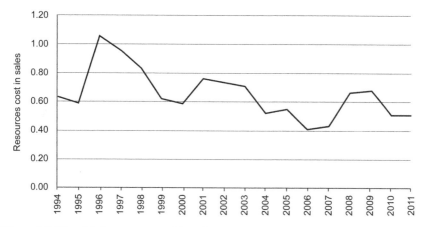

Figure 8.5 Nornickel resources cost in sales
Note: Resources cost in sales is defined as the sum of external material and services purchased and employee compensation divided by sales revenue.
Source: Author's calculation.

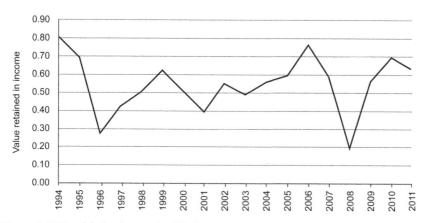

Figure 8.6 Nornickel value retained in income
Note: Value retained in income can be determined as the sum of EBITDA and labour cost divided into sales revenue.
Source: Author's calculation.

Furthermore, since 2001, the company had been increasing vertical integration by acquiring power and transport companies and this additionally has reduced the share of external costs.

One of the important financial ratios employed by the company is labour costs as a proportion of value retained (Figure 8.8). The company's share of labour costs in value retained are relatively unstable between 1994 and 2007, however, after it touches a peak of 88 per cent in 1996 it steadily declines to just over 12 per cent in the year 2006. Between 1997 and 2003, the executives managed to significantly reduce the number of employees, regulate salary and

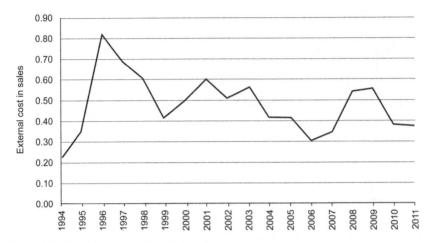

Figure 8.7 Nornickel external costs in sales
Note: External cost in sales is defined as raw materials and consumables divided by sales.
Source: Author's calculation.

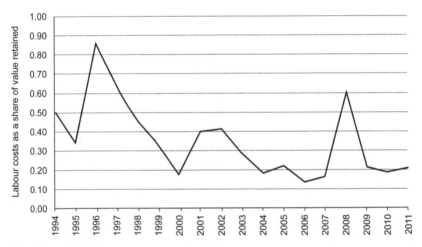

Figure 8.8 Nornickel labour as a share value retained
Note: Labour costs share of value retained is defined as personnel costs divided by operating result before depreciation and amortisation plus personnel costs.
Source: Author's calculation.

reduce the expense of maintaining social infrastructure of the town and the region. In general, the company's labour cost share of total income considerably reduced over the period. This, combined with strong sales growth, had an exceptional effect on the EBITDA, cash from operation and other results of the company.

Analysis of return on capital employed (ROCE) in Figure 8.9 shows that it has a moderately cyclical pattern and the average ROCE for Nornickel, at

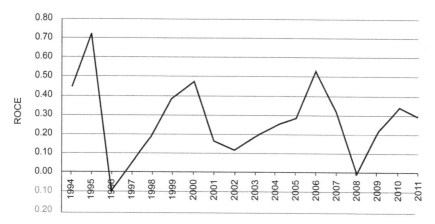

Figure 8.9 Nornickel return on capital employed
Note: ROCE is defined as an operating result before depreciation and amortisation in relation to the sum of equity and long-term debt.
Source: Author's calculation.

about 28 per cent, was more than the average level of Russian companies included in the Russian stock market index RTS. In 1996 and 2002, ROCE reached minimal levels, and afterwards rapidly recovered to a 50 per cent level (2000 and 2006) because of growth of sales revenue, which generated enormous profit margins.

Between 1996 and 1997, the company had relatively low capital employed as a share of income of about 0.5–0.6 (Figure 8.10) and a low share of profit, before interest and tax, in sales (ROS) which fell below zero (Figure 8.11).

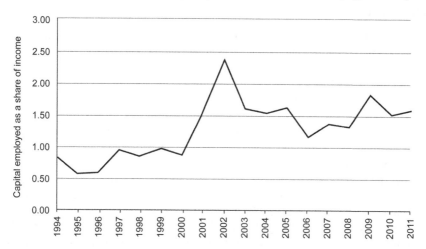

Figure 8.10 Nornickel capital employed as a share of income
Note: Capital employed as a share of income is defined as total long-term debt plus shareholders fund divided by sales.
Source: Author's calculation.

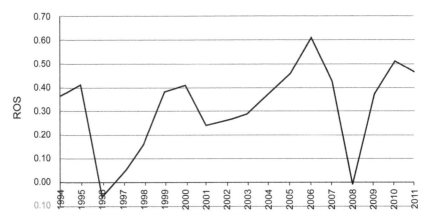

Figure 8.11 Nornickel return on sales
Note: Return on sales is defined as operating result before depreciation and amortisation divided by sales.
Source: Author's calculation.

Between 1994 and 2000, the company employed about 0.5–1.0 rouble of capital for every rouble of sales revenue, and by 2001 this had dramatically increased to 2.45 roubles of capital for one rouble of sales. In 2000, the company had a comparatively high ROS, which touched 40 per cent (Figure. 8.11) and relatively low capital employed as a share of income of 0.9 (Figure. 8.10). This combination boosted ROCE in 2004–6.

Conclusion

Nornickel was an unusually well-balanced company; it did not experience problems with energy, raw materials or markets. Despite various financial and political crises in Russia, the company maintained stable performance during the period 1989–2011.

The demand of the financial markets and a new opportunity for shareholders pushed the company to the financialisation of strategy. As a result, the new strategy was focused on increasing shareholder value. Overall, from 1993 to 2000, the company grew organically; later, it grew by the acquisition of its competitors and suppliers.

The fundamental weaknesses of the company were the political risks of state expropriation, changing taxation, geographical place, transport links and lack of minority shareholder control. By contrast, the strengths were a dominant position on the global markets, massive reserves of ore and the weakness of the national currency from 1998 to 2003. The critical success factors of the company were strong demand from foreign customers for non-ferrous metals and prices that were subject to considerable fluctuations due to the cyclical nature of these markets.

Between 1995 and 2007, Nornickel generated an average of 28 per cent return on capital employed. Sales revenue growth was 800 per cent, this increase being mainly explained by the boost in the average price of metals. In physical terms, its sales were relatively constant. After 1999, the company had a rising cash flow from operating and financing activities, which in 2007 rocketed to reach the company's record of $14 billion, and the market capitalisation of the company grew more than 25,000 per cent and reached $41 billion.

After 2008, the antagonistic conflict between Deripaska and Potanin partially paralysed Nornickel's business and depressed the market price. Considerable conflict arose around poor management and control of the company. High-level authorities were interested in Nornickel and actively regulated the tension between principal shareholders.

Reduced efficiency of business can be partially explained by a high level of internal corruption. There were serious violations of corporate governance principles, and many key decisions were taken without consideration of minor shareholders. The company had problems with corporate governance. The key task of the company is to radically improve the internal culture of the company; this means not only declaring values such as partnership, transparency, customer focus and the interests of employees and shareholders, but also following these values in every aspect of management of the company. The environmental situation was badly affected by Nornickel and contaminant emission into the atmosphere was extremely high.

9 Arkhangelsk Pulp and Paper Mill

This case study examines how Arkhangelsk Pulp and Paper Mill, which was one of the largest pulp and paper producers in Russia, carried out its operations and development between 1994 and 2011. The case shows that the company has been managed by the Titan Group, which reorganised the organisational structure and system of management. The new management established efficient administration and monitoring of the company's assets and created the corporate centre that developed a uniform corporate strategy. However, narratives disclose how APPM was employed to extract wealth for a major shareholder. This lost income weakened the company when substantial sums would be required to improve processes and increase working capital.

Privatisation

The first workshop of Arkhangelsk Pulp and Paper Mill (APPM) was built in 1940. In 1993, the company was turned into a joint-stock company. Before the start of mass privatisation, it was one of the largest pulp and paper producers in Russia. The company was organised into operating segments based on product groupings that were aggregated into three main production lines: paper, board and sulphate-bleached pulp. The paper production is the oldest one in APPM; it produced paper and school copybooks. The board production manufactured and marketed kraftliner, fluting and corrugated board products that were used for protective and transport purposes. The pulp production manufactured and marketed sulphate bleached pulp having a capacity of 285 thousand tonnes a year; this ranked the mill as the one of the largest pulp manufactories of Russia (APPM AR 2005).

All products of these productions were sold directly to manufacturers and sales agents. Besides this, APPM had its supplementary services including the power station, the mechanical repair production, the bio-scrubbing service, the electrical repair workshop and the transport division, which included motor transport, railcars, its own wharf and harbour construction.

The share distribution at the first stage of privatisation was made according to the law of privatisation, option 2, and all the members of the company were given a right to acquire common shares for vouchers, which constituted up to 51 per cent of total shares of authorised capital (APPM AR 1996). The other 49 per cent of shares were controlled by the regional authority and this ownership was reflected by the structure of the board of directors that included the executives and the representatives of the regional authority.

In the middle of 1994, the forest holdings 'North pulp' was created by the regional government and two private companies of Krupchak, Titan and Ruta. These companies invested 60 per cent of the authorised capital of 'North pulp' in warehouses and some paper equipment with actual worth of about $150,000, whereas the regional government invested in 20 per cent of the shares of APPM and shares of 14 forest manufactures and received 40 per cent of forest holdings (Butrin 2004b). Surprisingly, the 20 per cent shares of APPM were evaluated at only five times more than the face value, which was equal to about $200,000, and these shares had been substantially understated.

In 1997, North Pulp sold this 20 per cent to three companies: Jacob Jurgensen Papier, Conrad Jacobson and Wilfried Heinzel, which were the nominal shareholders of Krupchak, for €5,000,000 (Butrin 2004b). Simultaneously, these three companies bought the last 20 per cent of state shares that were offered for auction for the initial price of $5 million. In addition, approximately 3.76 per cent of shares were sold to Krupchak's companies for a near nominal price on cash and check auctions (APPM SR 1998). Between 1995 and 1997, Titan and other regional companies bought about 20 per cent of the company's shares that belonged to the company's workers.

As a result, the share distribution in 1999 was as follows: Krupchak and his companies had 65 per cent of shares, regional companies had 6 per cent and personnel had 29 per cent (APPM SR 1998). Consequently, Krupchak gained the majority of the board of directors of the company and his company Titan became the exclusive supplier of raw materials and the exclusive trader of its products.

Industrial factors

The total forested area in Russia amounts to 1.1 billion hectares; this is more than 24 per cent of the world's forest reserves (FAO 2001). Theoretically, Russia could produce up to 650 million cubic metres of timber per year without environmental damage (Butrin 2004b). However, in reality no more than 20 per cent of the allowable cut is currently being used. In 2000, the Russian forest, pulp and paper industry exceeded 2.5 per cent of Russian GDP and the industry's exports were more than $3.5 billion annually (RISI 2007), holding fourth place as a source of income after gas, oil and metals.

In the 1990s, the industry operated more than 30 pulp and paper mills with more than 1 million employed staff (including forest and services companies). However, six large companies of the North European part of Russia accounted for more than 50 per cent of the national production.

The industry manufactured relatively low-quality products and low-price pulp and paper, whereas high-tech products such as coated paper and cardboard were hardly ever produced. Additionally, the contribution of Russia to global pulp and paper output dropped from 5.2 per cent in 1980 to just 1.6 per cent in 2000 (FAO 2001).

In the main, the privatisation of large pulp and paper companies in the country occurred in 1993–4 and the adverse situation of the world paper market made them uninteresting for both foreign paper companies and frontline Russian investors, and as a result employees and managers became the first owners of the companies.

In the two first years of the Russian reforms, pulp and paper companies were not strongly affected by the industrial crisis and output of pulp and paper was declining dramatically from 8.3 billion tonnes in 1988, which was the peak year of the Soviet paper industry, to 3,028 in 1996. The reasons for this were decreasing global demand between 1991 and 1995 and the declining price of wood pulp on the world markets from $800 to $400 per tonne (see Figure 9.2) (CBK express 1996).

Additionally, the sale of Russian pulp and paper was temporary halted by foreign merchants, many round wood producers stopping their production, triggering a deficit of wood, and the economic recession of the 1990s. The Russian financial crisis of 1998 created additional opportunities for pulp producers because of adjustments in the rouble/dollar exchange rate and because more than half of the output of the Russian pulp and paper industry was being exported.

The output of cooking pulp in the Russian Federation given in Figure 9.1 shows that after the growth price of wood pulp during 1997–9 Russian pulp and paper enterprises increased their output, which raised their profitability. In addition, firms adapted to market conditions structurally reorganising both individual enterprises and the industry as a whole. The output level of major products in 1988–9 was again achieved by the Russian pulp and paper industry in 2006 excluding newsprint and offset paper. In addition, the industry became export

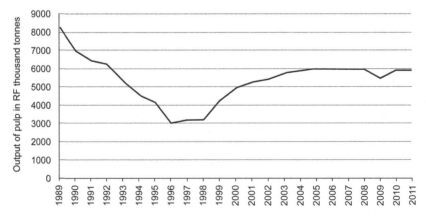

Figure 9.1 Output of pulp in Russia in 1989–2011
Source: CBK express 1996–2011.

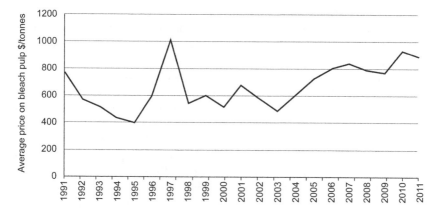

Figure 9.2 Average price on bleach pulp 1991–2011
Source: RISI (2007); CBK express 1996–2006.

oriented. For instance, between 1990 and 2000, the share of paper and board exports increased from 10.8 per cent to 45 per cent and the share of market pulp exports reached more than 80 per cent in 2000 (APPM AR 2000).

From the 1990s, logging dominated the Russian forest exports because the industry had inadequate in-depth wood processing in the immediate region of wood growth. Moreover, the round wood exports from the north-west of Russia to Finland doubled from 4–6 million cubic meters per annum in 1982–93 to 10–11 million cubic meters per annum (FAO 2002) and these exports generated a considerable deficit of raw materials for Russian paper companies and APPM in particular.

In the same period, Finland doubled its production of pulp and paper whereas the share of Russia in the world market reduced by more than two-thirds. Despite the fact that the Finnish forest companies possessed numerous pulp and paper mills worldwide with a total capacity of about 36 million tonnes per year, they did not purchase significant assets in Russia because Finland used the Russian forestry industry solely as a raw material supplier (European forest sector outlook study 2005).

Because of the deficit of raw wood, the large Russian pulp and paper companies created and developed industrial clusters, which besides processing enterprises, included logging, forest utilisation, transport and harbour companies and this process strongly impacted upon the corporate performance of Russian paper companies. In addition, substantial modernisation was performed by the companies due to the situation in the export and domestic market improving and the company receiving resources.

Market competition on the external market impacted powerfully on corporate performance. By contrast, the competition on domestic markets was weak because import duty tax increased to 20 per cent for foreign competitors. In addition, difficult technology, a deficit of highly skilled personnel and engineering infrastructure created barriers for new entrants into the business and this influenced corporate performance when companies tried to increase capacity or introduce new products. Significant increases in prices for raw materials, energy, transportation and other necessary supplies and services could adversely affect the corporation's financial results. Paper and cellulose was subject to considerable price fluctuations due to the cyclical nature of these fibre markets and, as a result, a decrease in pulp prices negatively affected the company's earnings.

From 1993 to 2002, the critical success factor of the paper industry was strong demand from foreign customers. The main opportunity facing the industry was the potential for the growth of the Russian paper market due to the low level of consumption of paper packaging and paper products. The fundamental weakness of the industry was the enormous deterioration of equipment (the average age of which was more than 25 years), low production quality, a deficit of financial and intellectual resources for development of new technology and decreasing domestic demand. Furthermore, besides the successful large pulp companies, there were about 100 smaller paper and cardboard plants in Russia that were nearly bankrupt.

In contrast, between 1993 and 2000, the strengths were enormous inventory of raw materials, relatively low cost of power, water and labour, low state standards of environmental pollution compared to Western countries and weak control of these standards. Later, from 2001, these factors were sufficiently diminished by a deficit of power and raw materials, growth expenditure and changing environmental standards.

In the period 1989–97, 80 per cent of total production costs of Russian paper companies were direct raw material costs and only 7 per cent was maintenance of equipment and amortisation whereas Scandinavian companies had 51 per cent and 37 per cent correspondingly. Because of this strategy, many Russian companies had outdated tangible assets. Later, this disproportion of production cost had been changed by the market environment, and after 2003 the major participants in the paper market had a structure of expenditure relatively similar to Scandinavian companies (Interview APPM 2010).

In most cases, between 1993 and 2007, compared with the top foreign paper companies, Russian counterparts had only two competitive advantages: cost of wood and cost of power. In 2005, round wood cost Russian mills approximately \$23 per cubic metre and the cost of electricity was \$25 per megawatt whereas Finnish and Swedish companies paid about \$50 and \$53 respectively (Ilim Pulp 2006). Additionally, since 2005, profitability of business of the industrial leaders had been declining despite the growth of production (APPM AR 2006).

All enterprises gave priority to the domestic market because it offered higher prices than the external market. However, the internal market was limited. The Russian companies were not leaders of European industry and it had shares of 1–3 per cent in different product segments. Russian companies were price takers, often required to sell products at significant discounts. For example, in 2004 Russian manufacturers shipped out two million tonnes of cellulose with the average price of $373 per tonne, however in the European market price a tonne of cellulose was about $450 (Interview APPM 2010).

The competitiveness of Russian production in the world market was further reduced by the decrease in scientific and technical potential of industry, constant increase in production costs, seasonal wood manufacture and the poor quality of forest roads.

Regional factors

The Arkhangelsk region, as the biggest region of the North-European part of Russia, has an extremely important geographical position in the country. Three arctic seas wash its coasts and the cold climate influences all aspects of life. The territory of the region is 590,000-square kilometres and forest covers 39 per cent of this area. The Arkhangelsk region is a unique area with valuable natural resources such as forestry, oil, gas and diamonds. However, the density of the population is 2.5 inhabitants per square kilometre, and outside of cities and towns infrastructure is almost non-existent (Arkhangelsk region 2007).

Economic activity of the region is concentrated in a few key sectors, and the largest share of output is produced by several large companies. In the Soviet period, economic and social development of the region was supported through additional funding from the country's budget. However, in 1992 this support was stopped due to the collapse of the national economy. As a result, the region had problems with fundraising for large unproductive enterprises, such as the Plesetsk Spaceport, the centre of nuclear shipbuilding and the Russian nuclear polygon, and outdated infrastructure.

In the first ten years of the Russian reforms, the region had a large budget deficit and could not create favourable conditions for investors in the region. Forestry, wood processing, pulp and paper were central sectors of the regional economy contributing over 40 per cent to the regional production volume; however, the tree harvest in the Archangelsk region has dropped more than 30 per cent since Soviet times.

In 2002, over 200 wood cutting enterprises operated in the region totalling eight million cubic metres, but there was potential for 23 million cubic metres (CBK express 2004, 2006; APPM AR 2003). The region could not produce this quantity because outdated logging technologies, poor road infrastructure and difficult access to forests created an impediment to increased production.

Between 1993 and 2005, about 30 per cent of Russian paper and cellulose were produced by three regional companies: Arkhangelsk, Solombala and Kotlas Pulp-and-Paper mills. About eight million cubic meters of wood were used annually by paper companies and, as a result, wood as a natural resource of the region was one of the major factors that impacted on the performance of the companies and particularly APPM.

From 1992 to 1998, regional suppliers of raw wood and the railway companies impacted strongly on rhythm and capacity of paper productions. Moreover, raw wood for paper mills was from time to time in short supply and the quality of this raw wood was not as good as desired. There was a strong battle between paper companies for raw materials. Since 1998, the paper companies of the region have bought about 40 logging companies and cut a significant proportion of their required timber themselves (APPM AR 2006).

At the end of 2000, the problem of uncertified (by international standards) timber utilisation arose among Russian timber exporters. Therefore, a number of exporters in the Archangelsk region were forced to deliver timber via new routes and operators in the Russian northwest district were forced to begin expensive certification procedures that would allow them to remain on the world market; among them was APPM.

Financial resources and consumer demand in the region were low, industrial production and infrastructure was undeveloped. Furthermore, the region did not have enough high-quality specialists and regional depopulation generated a deficit in the labour force. In addition, the region had a high level of ecological and criminal risks (Expert RA 2005).

Business strategy after privatisation

In the first years after privatisation, corporate strategy did not feature as part of regular management activity and it was paid less attention by company executives. The private interests of the executives pushed them to split the company. In 1993, the Board of Directors decided to split APPM into 11 independent subsidiaries such as 'Paper', 'Carton', 'Forest', 'Transport' and gave permission for executives of these subsidiaries to make any decisions without the control of shareholders. This also helped them to save APPM from asset confiscation, having rented out their assets to subsidiary firms.

APPM remained the owner of all fixed assets and assumed the functions of financial planning and control. After this reorganisation, only a few subsidiaries were able to conduct their work independently, make profit and pay taxes on time because of poor management, absence of the clear strategy and theft by managers.

Between 1993 and 1996, the majority of APPM was more oriented towards an attitude of 'live for today, not for tomorrow' and as a result, the company did not try to formulate any strategy, did not have a centre for making strategic decisions and did not employ strategic methods for selection, development and coordination of the portfolio of businesses. The company did not have sufficient ability to maintain long-term competitive advantage because it was poorly managed and it could not control expenditure (Interview APPM 2010).

From April 1996, the company had been managed by Krupchak's Titan Group who reorganised the organisational structure and system of management. As a result, two open joint-stock companies were formed: Arkhangelsk Pulp and Paper Mill, which was responsible for production, and Arkhbum, whose functions included supplying the mill with raw materials and selling pulp and paper (APPM AR 1998). The board of management of APPM established efficient administration and monitoring of the company's assets and created the corporate centre that developed a uniform corporate and business unit strategy.

To establish a competitive advantage over rival companies, APPM and Arkhbum used a 'focused low cost strategy'. According to this strategy, the company targeted two particular sectors of the paper industry: pulp and carton board (various types of packaging board), which provided more than 75 per cent of revenue and were highly profitable (APPM AR 2000). The first aim in the realisation of this strategy and winning a 30–35 per cent share of the Russian corrugated board market was the launching of two new corrugated board factories in Podolsk (Moscow region) and in Murmansk, which were two of the biggest and modern in Russia (APPM AR 2000, 2003).

The company's strategy was quite successful particularly in the light of strong competition on the world paper market. By the end of 2002, the mill's share in the Russian packaging board market was about 30 per cent, while in the corrugated board market it was 13.4 per cent and in the Russian pulp production it achieved 13.1 per cent (APPM AR 2004).

The changes in corporate governance in the company from 1996 to 2003 were not sufficient and it did not adopt transparency, strict corporate accountability and division of management powers. Despite the fact that APPM was a corporation, this could be considered a formality, since senior managers (Krupchak and his partners) were almost indistinguishable from the owners.

Management of operations

As stated above, APPM's manufacture had been declining dramatically since the 1990s and in 1994 reached its lowest point when 368,000 tonnes of pulp were made, almost 50 per cent less than the average volume over the previous ten years pre-reform (see Figure 8.3).

Since 1993, the production of the company had been regularly halted by the deficit of raw materials and power. Apart from these difficulties, APPM had to address problems of efficiency in operations and production; namely, they had to improve the components supply system. Selection of suppliers was irrational and taken on the spur of the moment; many raw materials and components were delivered by non reliable, often fraudulent, suppliers. Furthermore, the company frequently could not pay the suppliers on time, thus paralysing delivery of the materials.

In 1996, the new management team started reconstructing APPM. Due to the strategic reconstruction of the company, the production and financial situation at the mill improved significantly: the management structure was changed, barter was eliminated, working efficiency grew, solvency increased and relations with debtors and creditors were improved.

The management of the company released numerous projects such as putting into operation two container factories, introducing elementary chlorine-free pulp bleaching at the mill and reconstructing the paper machines.

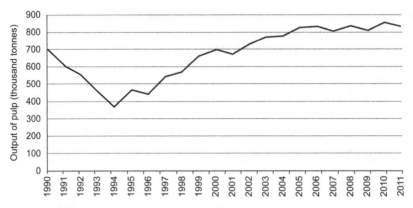

Figure 9.3 Output pulp in APPM in 1990–2011
Source: APPM AR 2000–2008.

Additionally, APPM accomplished international quality management system standards (ISO 9001) and environmental management system standards (ISO 14000); the railway park was enlarged from 150 up to 570 short log trucks and the company increased the share of wood waste instead of coal in their power balance by reconstructing its bark boiler (APPM AR 2004).

Since 1998, the company had been employing manufacturing capacity more efficiently; consequently, in 2003 pulp production at the company reached a record-breaking 770,750 tonnes, exceeding the theoretical production capacity. Conversely, APPM consumed about 175 million cubic metres of water; it was the largest air and water polluter in the region and provided for 20 per cent of total regional air emissions amounting to 52,000 tonnes. The company implemented an environmental protection program, which cost about $5 million per year (APPM AR 2002–6). Nevertheless, the environmental policy was not an important part of the company's strategy, and it did not create safe operating conditions for its personnel, protect the health of local residents in its areas of operation or preserve a healthy environment (Interview APPM 2010).

Marketing

As was noted above, in the first three years after privatisation, the company was split into 11 independent subsidiaries, which also had 11 commercial departments and sold products of APPM. Barter was a considerable type of trade between subsidiaries as well as between subsidiaries and external partners. Both of these factors generated trade disorder and the consequence was a dramatic decline in profitability of operations (Interview APPM 2010).

However, the company maintained its position on the Russian market; from 1995 to 2003, for example, about 16 per cent of cooked pulp, 35 per cent of bleached pulp and 50 per cent of kraftliner in Russia was produced by APPM (APPM AR 1996).

From 1997 to 2007, sales in the domestic and foreign markets were carried out by APPM through a subsidiary, Arbum, in which Krupchak had about 75 per cent of the shares. Arbum received a commission of about 10 to 15 per cent of sales. The advantages of sales through an intermediary were the quick payment for the products supplied and the accumulation of profit in external accounts for optimising corporate tax. Products were sold to agents, which were the European warehouses, who resold them to consumers in small batches and assumed the risks of non-payment and possible claims on quality. A significant proportion of cellulose was sold through the distributors Conrad Jacobson GmbH and Zellstoff und Papier GmbH, which were the principal shareholders of the company (APPM AR 2005).

From 1999–2007, APPM sales strategy supported the optimal balance of deliveries to the foreign markets (35 per cent) and domestic markets (65 per cent). However, priority was given to the Russian market because it was more profitable and between 1999 and 2004, the domestic market of paper and cardboard had a growth of 20 per cent annually. As a result, APPM increased its market share of the containerboard and kraftliner to 35 per cent and 50 per cent respectively (APPM AR 2005).

Financial management

From the beginning of privatisation, the company had serious problems with liquidity; therefore, the company could not meet its commitments on time either for third party contracts or wages to employees. For example, during the period of 1992–6, the company paid monthly salaries several months after the date they were due and this practice gave a start to strikes by the workforce.

From 1993 to 1996, the company's fiscal indebtedness grew at both federal and local levels and its tax liabilities had reached more than $200 million exceeding 50 per cent of sales revenue. In light of this, the tax authority proposed that the company should go into liquidation (APPM AR 1999). However, the new management team resisted liquidation.

In the first few years after privatisation, executives could not control expenditure such as direct raw materials and direct labour cost, but the considerable increase in the price of pulp and carton surpassed the inflated price of wood and chemicals. As a result, the company had a relatively stable financial position. At the end of 1995, substantial growth of raw materials and energy and the declining demand for pulp sufficiently exacerbated corporate performance.

The company had overestimated the number of employees that was required; about 10,000 employees worked in the company of which 3,500 were working for subsidiary industries, repair and services, whereas at similar capacity paper mills in Scandinavia there could be less than 1,000 workers.

Between 1994 and 1996, the company tried to reduce staff; however, it was unproductive because of robust social pressure from trade unions.

After 1996, restructuring of the organisation of the company and distribution of profit between subsidiaries were some of the main elements of cost reduction. In a period of relative stability in 1999 and 2000, APPM increased its output and raised production profitability. This may be attributed both to adjustment in the rouble/dollar exchange rate and to adaptation of the mill to market conditions (APPM AR 2004).

In the first years after privatisation, APPM had a relatively small direct labour cost as well as low power, transport and overheads in comparison to the production costs. After 2002, this situation was changed, and power and transport expenditures dramatically increased. Additionally, the company had programmes for decreasing inventory and receivables that were relatively effective (APPM AR 2004).

The company principal owners created firms whose basic function was supplying wood to APPM. Illegal income was formed by overstated invoice pricing for raw materials delivered to APPM, which were more than 15 per cent above their real price. Between 1996 and 1998, this income was used by Krupchak for buying 20 per cent of the shares of APPM and other assets.

As noted above, Arkhbum was the exclusive trader and supplier to APPM affiliated with its majority owners. It sold APPM production to friendly Western firms at prices that were at least 20 per cent lower than the market ones. This policy resulted in the non-reception of about $50 million of profit by minor shareholders. On the other hand, this policy helped the company executives to optimise taxes effectively, and one can say that the illegal wealth withdrawn did not dramatically affect corporate performance because the size of withdrawal did not exceed 20 per cent of cash flow from operating activities (Interview APPM).

Forest war

Since 2001, the attractiveness of the paper industry for strategic investors has continued to increase. As a result, APPM increased activity in the forestry segment of the industry and started to form holdings by actively buying the regional logging companies that supplied its raw materials. The company maintained its position in the pulp and paper market in conditions of intense competition.

However, at the end of 2001, the Russian tycoons Oleg Deripaska and Roman Abramovich decided to move $800 million of capital from the aluminium, oil and banking sectors to the pulp and paper industry. The plan apparently indicated a hostile takeover of APPM and other Russian paper companies (Butrin 2004b, Sologub 2004). Their company Continental Management manipulated courts, government and media and bought about 30 per cent of shares of APPM (Grishkovets 2008).

Threats of acquisition increased the share of illegal wealth withdrawn by the management and owners of APPM and decreased the transparency of business. In order to prevent hostile takeovers, Krupchak created the Pulp Mill Holding, which became a new principal owner of APPM and possessed 65 per cent of the shares of the mill (ibid.).

Despite Krupchak being elected as a member of the Russian Parliament in 2003 and having had considerable lobbying opportunities, the 'forest war' did not halt. As a result, in 2005–6 the company needed to sell its corporate bonds at a discount. Moreover, after 2007, when Krupchak's parliamentary term was finished, he needed to emigrate from Russia and had to manage his business from abroad.

Financial analysis

After privatisation, company sales (Figure 9.4) had declined to three billion roubles per annum. However, since 1998, APPM demonstrated a remarkable growth of sales that resulted from the sustained strong demand for Russian pulp and paper. Between 1998 and 2007, its sales revenue growth was 400 per cent and in 2007, net sales reached 12 billion roubles. This increase is mainly explained by the boost in the average price of pulp as well as growth in physical terms. The decisive factors that influenced the demand for the main products of APPM between 1998 and 2007 were continued growth in China and recovery of the Russian economy.

In 1996, the operating profit dropped to negative levels because the company could not increase product prices and the relatively fast growth of the price of labour and wood meant that it could not restore the operating profit to that achieved in previous years (Figure 9.6). The nadir of 2002 was created by the decreasing price of major products as well as the high price of raw materials.

After 2002, the share of total costs as a proportion of income started to fall, boosting cash earnings that were then on an upward trajectory. Resource costs held at about 80 per cent of total sales revenue and internal labour costs

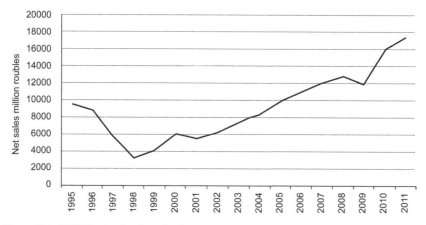

Figure 9.4 APPM net sales (nominal)

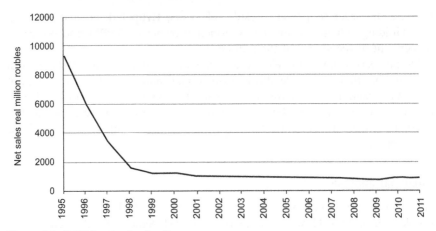

Figure 9.5 APPM net sales (real)
Note: APPM net sales in terms of purchasing power of the rouble as of 31 December 1995. Source: APPM annual and special reports. Author's calculation.

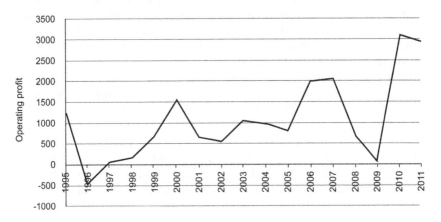

Figure 9.6 APPM operating income
Source: APPM annual and special reports.

were down to just 40 per cent of retained income (sales minus exterenal costs). The pattern of total costs follows a similar pattern to the movement in sales revenue.

Value retained in income can be determined as the sum of EBITDA and labour cost divided into sales revenue. Between 1995 and 1999, this index (Figure 9.8) fluctuated around 15 per cent, and during the cataclysm of 1996 it reached a local nadir of 7 per cent. After 1999, it rapidly improved to a new average level of 30 per cent due to the profitability of the business. In order to establish how much of every rouble of sales revenue is value retained by the company one has to deduct all external costs. Figure 9.9 shows that in 1996 external costs reach the maximum value 1.0, and between 2001 and 2011 fluctuate around 0.7.

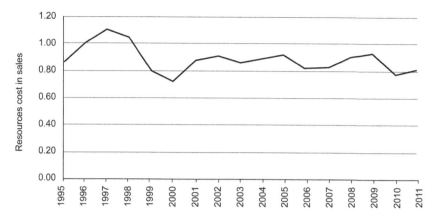

Figure 9.7 APPM resources cost in sales
Note: Resources cost in sales is defined as the sum of external material and services purchased and employee compensation divided by sales revenue.

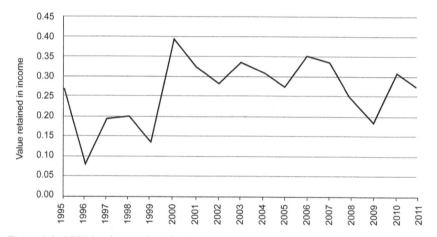

Figure 9.8 APPM value retained in income
Note: Value retained in income can be determined as the sum of EBITDA and labour cost divided by sales revenue.
Source: Author's calculation.

After privatisation, APPM had a surplus of personnel. However, in the first years after privatisation, APPM had a relatively small share of direct labour cost and overheads in total production cost. According to Figure 9.10, in 1995, the company's share of labour costs in value retained was relatively low (around 30 per cent), but in 1996 this index dramatically increased to 100 per cent due to reduced profitability of business. Later, it fluctuated considerably, and only after 2000 stabilised to approximately 40–50 per cent.

Analysis of ROCE (Figure 9.11) shows that it has a moderately cyclical pattern and the average ROCE for APPM placed at about 20 per cent. In

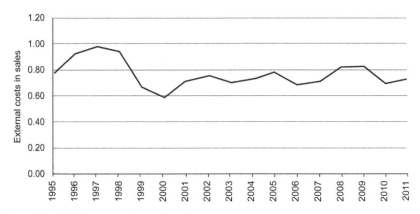

Figure 9.9 APPM external costs in sales
Note: External cost is defined as raw materials and consumable divided by sales.
Source: Author's calculation.

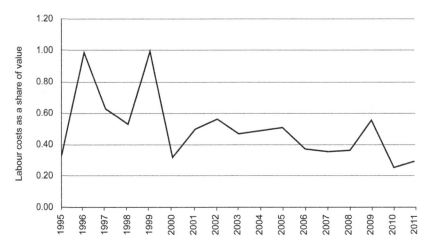

Figure 9.10 APPM labour as share value retained
Note: Labour costs as a share of value retained is defined as personnel costs divided by
operating result before depreciation and amortisation plus personnel costs.
Source: Author's calculation.

1996, ROCE reached minimal levels because in that time the company has a
low share of profit pre-interest and tax in sales (ROS) (Figure 9.12) and relatively high capital employed as a share of income (Figure 9.13), which was
about 1.2. However, ROCE after the financial crisis recovered relatively
rapidly to 50 per cent (2000) because the corporate sales generated healthy
gross profit margins.

The combination of a lower level of capital intensity (capital employed as a
share of income Figure 9.13) and increased share of cash extracted from sales
revenue boosts the cash ROCE. In the immediate post-privatisation period
this was an industry (and a company) on a knife-edge. However, after a

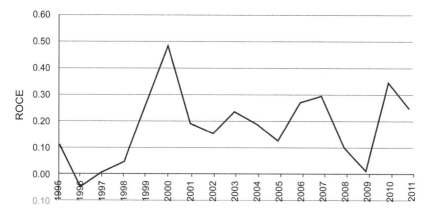

Figure 9.11 APPM return on capital employed
Note: ROCE is defined as operating result before depreciation and amortisation in relation to the sum of equity and long-term debt.
Source: Author's calculation.

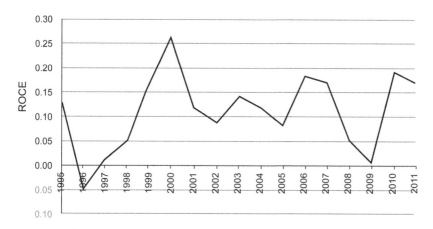

Figure 9.12 APPM return on sales
Note: Return on sales is defined as the operating result before depreciation and amortisation divided by sales.
Source: Author's calculation.

period of ten years this company had transformed its cash return on capital employed from 0–1 per cent to a steady 20–30 per cent, which is very impressive.

Although the financials of this company have been reversed there are still important risks, most notably the quality of equipment, market segment position (at the low cost/quality end) and sensitivity/exposure to exchange rates. As the company managed to improve the share of cash extracted from sales revenue it was also reducing balance sheet capitalisation (long-term debt plus equity) as a share of sales revenue. From a position where the company

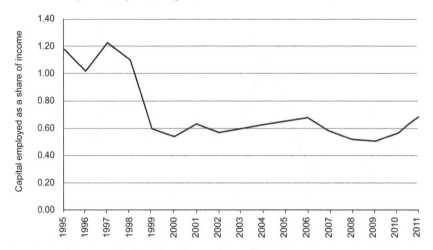

Figure 9.13 APPM capital employed as a share of income
Note: Capital employed as a share of income is defined as total long-term debt plus
shareholders fund divided by sales.
Source: Author's calculation.

had 120 roubles of capital employed for every 100 roubles of sales revenue,
this reduced to 60 roubles of capital employed for every 100 roubles of sales
(see Figure 9.13).

Conclusion

Arkhangelsk Pulp and Paper Mill before the start of mass privatisation was
one of the largest pulp and paper producers in Russia. In 1993–4, the adverse
situation on the world paper market made it uninteresting for both foreign
paper companies and frontline Russian investors. Consequently, employees
and managers became the first owners of the company.

Between 1993 and 2007, the strengths of the company were a solid demand
for Russian timber and pulp in Europe coupled with a large resource of raw
materials, relatively low cost of power, wood, water and labour, and reduced
state regulation of environmental pollution compared to Western countries. By
contrast, the fundamental weaknesses of the company were enormous deterioration of equipment, low quality of production, a deficit of financial and
intellectual resources for exploiting new technology and decreasing domestic
demand.

Since April 1996, the company has been managed by the Titan Group who
reorganised the structure and system of management. The management
established efficient administration and monitoring of the company's assets,
and created the corporate centre that developed a uniform corporate strategy.
Additionally, corporate bartering was eliminated, working efficiency grew,
solvency increased, and relations with debtors and creditors were optimised.

Debts connected with salary and taxes were paid off. However, narratives extracted from the interviews disclose how APPM was employed to extract wealth for a major shareholder who sold APPM production to friendly Western firms at prices that were at least 20 per cent lower than the market prices and extracted income out of the company.

This lost income weakened the company, when substantial sums were required to improve processes and increase working capital. In addition, operating profit was negatively affected by the dramatic growth of cost of resources and the low price of pulp.

The Russian financial crisis of 1998 created additional opportunities for the pulp producers because of the adjustment in the rouble/dollar exchange rate. After 1998, the company employed manufacturing capacity more efficiently and, as a result, 2003 pulp production of the company exceeded the theoretical capacity of production. First, this success was determined by an increase of price and recovery of the market. Second, the management of the company implemented numerous projects to increase capacity.

Between 1998 and 2007, its sales revenue growth was 400 per cent and in 2007 net sales reached 12 billion roubles; this increase was mainly explained by the boost in the average price of pulp as well as by the physical growth. Strong revenue growth translated into relatively strong profit and revenue. However, paper and cellulose were still subjected to considerable price fluctuations due to the cyclical nature of these fibre markets, and as a result operating income and cash flows in this industry were volatile and unreliable. The average company ROCE and ROE stood at 20 per cent and 10 per cent respectively, which was equivalent to Weyerhaeuser and International Paper as well as the average global industry data.

10 What can we learn about Russian firms
Success and failure

Chapter 10 presents the conclusion and the issues arising out of the cases analysed. The analysis that is undertaken suggests some key external and internal factors on corporate performance. The chapter reveals that all successful companies had similar patterns of internal factors whereas unproductive companies did not have an adequate pattern of internal factors. A comparison of the Russian companies with their international counterparts gives additional information for analysis of corporate performance.

Outcomes of privatisation

As was noted in previous chapters, it is possible to employ different methodologies and empirical techniques to examine the potential outcomes of privatisation. Therefore, to evaluate the impact of privatisation on financial and operating performance it may be useful to compare actual financial performance of divested firms with performance of the state-owned firms, and financial performance of five Russian companies with the performance of foreign companies that have relatively similar products, markets and technologies.

All of the companies described in the book were privatised in the period of 1993–6, and the last of the state shares were transferred to private shareholders in 1997. Additionally, in that time, the state had a dominant position in the board of directors of these companies and it implemented the state's policy in management decisions of the companies. APPM, Avtovaz and Nornickel received the state's main support. Therefore, for an evaluation of the impact of privatisation it is possible to assume that during 1993–6 the companies were state-owned, and during 1997–2007 they were private companies.

In the charts below, we reveal the performance of the five case study firms both before and after privatisation. We first consider the growth of sales revenue of this group of firms over the period of 1994–7, a period just before privatisation and then the period after privatisation.

We start by looking at the growth in sales where the story is mixed. Nornickel, APPM and AE improved their sales whilst the other two firms did not (Figure. 10.1).

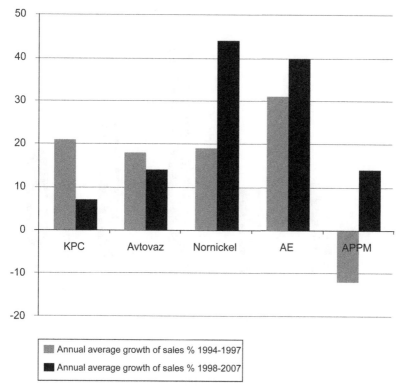

Figure 10.1 KPC, Nornickel, AE, APPM, Avtovaz: annual average growth of sales
Source: Author's calculation based on accounting data.

In terms of value retained after paying all external costs (Figure. 10.2), we find that most firms carry on as they were from one period to the next, apart from KPC, which shows a reduction in value retained and thus weakening performance. After adjusting external costs, we obtain value retained for the five firms and find that the value retained out of income follows the previous 1994–7 pattern.

Comparing the two pre- and post-privatisation periods, we find that the three companies (APPM, Nornickel and AE) improved their performance during the second period but this is not a consistent pattern for all performance measures. These three companies dramatically increased operating profit, ROCE, ROS and value retained in income.

Two other companies, KPC and Avtovaz, showed a considerably worse performance and a decline in all indexes for the period of 1998–2007 (Figure 10.1–10.4). The evaluation of the five cases above has not revealed a strong pattern of evidence that the privatised firms improved corporate performance against the state companies.

A comparison of the financial performance of the five companies against the performance of foreign firms that have relatively similar products, markets

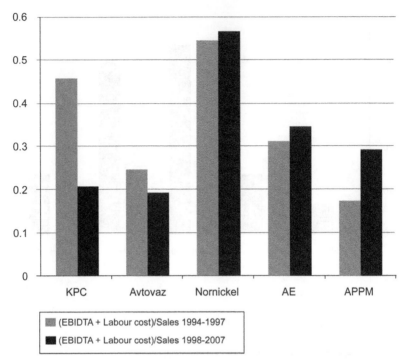

Figure 10.2 Five companies: annual average share of value retained in income
Source: Author's calculation based on accounting date.

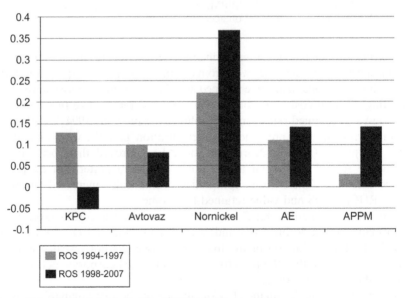

Figure 10.3 KPC, Nornickel, AE, APPM, Avtovaz: return on sales
Source: Author's calculation based on accounting date.

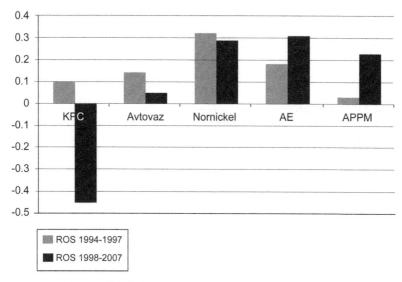

Figure 10.4 KPC, Nornickel, AE, APPM, Avtovaz: return on capital employed
Source: Author's calculation based on accounting date.

and technologies adds additional information about the outcome of privatisation.
Figure 10.5 shows the volume growth in Avtovaz, Fiat and BMW. Italian and
German car manufactories were selected because they have had a relatively
similar volume of production and similar types of cars (Figure. 10.5).

The growth of Avtovaz sales revenue was stronger than of the other two
foreign competitors, but the company's ROE was not stable and was fluctuating in the range of minus 76 per cent to 30 per cent. The overall pattern of
financial performance (both sales growth and return on equity) reveals that
Avtovaz is a relatively strong company because, after privatisation, the company was still protected from the full heat of foreign competition on its home
market and the level of average household income started to increase.

In the early post-privatisation years, Avtovaz controlled a large share of the
domestic market that was significantly protected from overseas competition.
A combination of a strong position in the market and protection and
favourable currency movements against the dollar ensured a robust sales revenue trajectory for Avtovaz.

Although the return on equity is not strong, it is relatively stable when
compared to Fiat during the last ten years but not as strong as BMW (Figure.
10.6). In addition, the ROE of Avtovaz is more volatile than that of BMW,
and relatively similar to Fiat due to wealth extraction, poor operating finances and the weak strategy of Avtovaz.

The problem, as already discussed, is that Avtovaz sales did not translate
into new investments in product and process renewal, because wealth extraction limited the rate at which the new investment levels could be maintained.

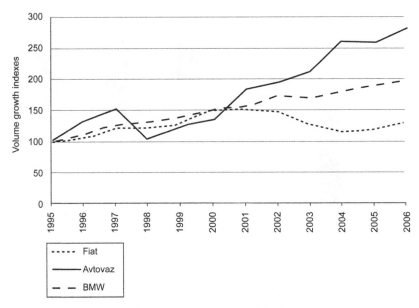

Figure 10.5 Fiat, BMW and Avtovaz: volume growth indexes
Source: Author's calculation based on accounting data retrieved from Reuters data
(2008) and Avtovaz annual reports (1995 = 100).

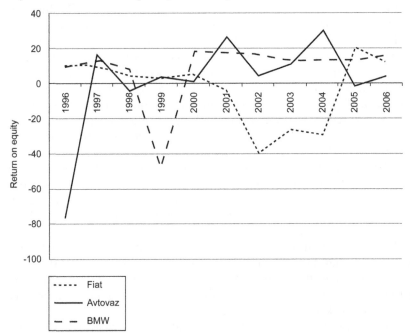

Figure 10.6 Fiat, BMW and Avtovaz: return on equity
Source: Author's calculation based on accounting data retrieved from Reuters data
(2008) and Avtovaz annual reports.

Figure 10.7 shows the volume growth in Stora Enso (Stora), UPM-Kymmene (UPM), International Paper (IP) and APPM. What is significant here is the fact that, in volume terms, all the non-Russian firms managed to maintain output volumes over the period of 1996 to 2000. Whereas output of APPM dropped by roughly a half, and this is predominantly because the company was selling low value added paper products into a depressed Russian market. However, after 1999, the company substantially increased its growth trajectory, eventually bringing it back into line with its European competitors, and this contributed to a significant improvement in the return on equity relative to APPM's European competitors (Figure 10.8).

Figure 10.9 shows the volume growth in Southern Copper Corporation (SCC), BHP Billiton Ltd (BHP), Xstrata Plc (Xstrata) and Nornickel. BHP is the biggest mining company (2007), which operated in different segments of the non-ferrous and ferrous industries, whereas Nornickel, SCC and Xstrata specialised in their own fields: SCC in copper, Nornickel in platinum and nickel and Xstrata in copper, nickel and successfully operating in different segments of the non-ferrous industry. BHP and Xstrata had mining operations in numerous countries while in the main, the other two worked in Russia and Peru.

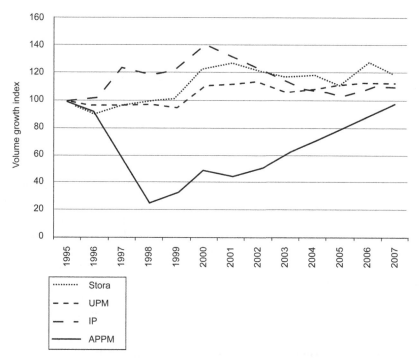

Figure 10.7 Stora, UPM, IP and APPM: volume growth indexes
Source: Author's calculation based on accounting data retrieved from Reuters data (2008) and APPM annual reports (1995 = 100).

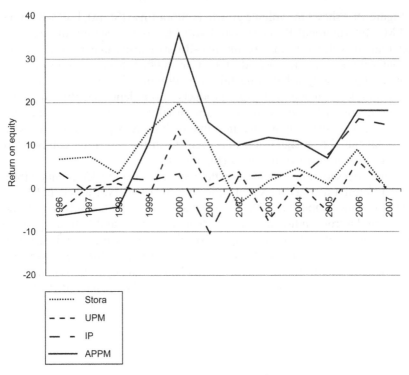

Figure 10.8 Stora, UPM, IP and APPM: return on equity
Source: Author's calculation based on accounting data retrieved from Reuters data (2008) and APPM annual reports.

As can be seen, between 1994 and 2007, despite some fluctuation of sales revenues, all companies increased their production due to growth of the global demand for commodities. In addition, the average ROE of the companies (excluding Xstrata) was around 20 per cent during this period (Figure. 10.10). According to the figures, all companies have a relatively similar pattern of growth in sales and ROE and both indexes have rising trends. In addition, there are no differences between Nornickel and other producers.

A comparison of Nornickel with the global leaders illustrates that the Russian company had a relatively similar trajectory with output falling in 1998–9 and 2002 and rising in 2003 and 2006. As well as this, the ROE of companies had similar patterns. Similarities in patterns of Nornickel and the other three companies can be more easily explained by the global tendencies of the mining industry rather than by the internal factors of Russia.

Five cases of Russian privatisation: similarities and differences

The analysis that has been undertaken using the narratives and data of the five companies suggests some key success factors of corporate performance. For

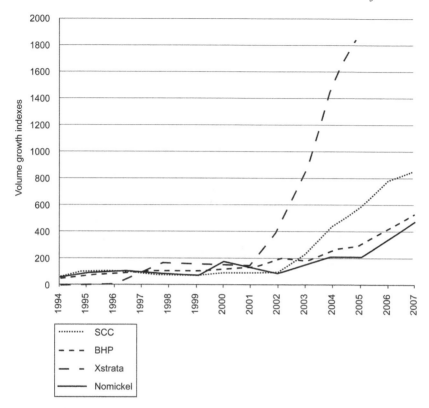

Figure 10.9 SCC, BHP, Xstrata and Nornickel: volume growth indexes
Source: Author's calculation based on accounting data retrieved from Reuters data
(2008) and Nornickel annual reports (1997 = 100). Note: Xstrata had extremely high
index in 2006 (4035) and in 2007 (6698).

KPC – a significant share of personal care, tissue and health care products in
the fast-growing domestic market. For Nornickel – strong demands from
foreign customers for non-ferrous metals and their prices. For AE – control
for expenditure and an optimal relation between price and quality. For
APPM – a strong demand from foreign customers and a large forest resource.
For Avtovaz – strong position in the Russian undeveloped car market and its
ability to struggle against the increasing amount of imported cars.

However, other factors influenced performance and these can be separated
into two groups: internal and external. The first group includes factors of an
external nature where the company management could not strongly influence
outcomes, whereas the second group of factors was to some extent under the
influence of company executives.

Figure 10.11 and 10.12 show the key external factors of corporate performance and the level of influence on the performance of the five companies.
The level of influence is measured by a scale from one to five. A score of one

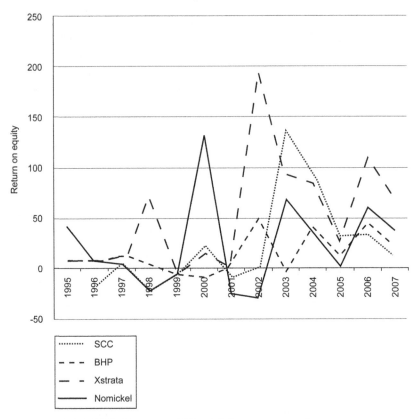

Figure 10.10 SCC, BHP, Xstrata and Nornickel: return on equity
Source: Author's calculation based on accounting data retrieved from Reuters data (2008) and Nornickel annual reports.

means that the impact of a factor is very strong, a score of two – strong, three – middling, four – weak and five – insubstantial. The scores were derived by interviewing managers of the companies (see Chapter 4).

KPC, AE and Avtovaz operated in competitive markets with a growing market trend due to the initial low level of use of consumer products in Russia. They were strongly dependent upon the introduction of modern technology and new product development, which they have been lacking. Nornickel and APPM operated during a growing global demand for commodities; they were influenced by natural resources of the regions, which supplied their raw materials. In addition, human resources and the quality of the infrastructure of the regions were crucial for the performance of the companies (Figure 10.11).

External and internal factors were grouped in different patterns that determined success or failure of the companies. In addition, these factors, such as lobbying, tax evasion and using a criminal scheme for M&A were a necessary

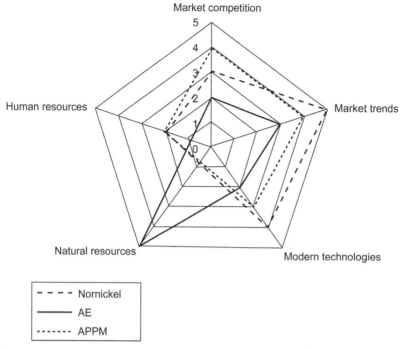

Figure 10.11 Key external factors of corporate performance Nornickel, AE, APPM
1 = Strong negative affect, 2 = Strong affect, 3 = Middling, 4 = Weak impact, 5 =
Insubstantial.
Source: Author assessment based on interviews (for a full description of the approach
to scoring see Chapter 3).

condition for the achievements of the company. Going over the main points, all
successful commodity companies (AE, APPM and Nornickel) had the comparable pattern of factors such as strong demand, growth of market, raw materials
and the ability to use them. Furthermore, they were the necessary conditions
for a positive financial and operating outcome, and they helped the managers
to take advantage of the opportunities created by the economic reform.

The more technological company AE also had an adequate pattern of factors (modern technologies and human resources of a region). Unsuccessful
companies (KPC and Avtovaz) did not have an adequate pattern of factors.
These external factors strongly determined the corporate performance of
companies between 1993 and 2011 (Figure 10.12).

Figures 10.13 and 10.14 show the key internal factors of corporate performance and the level of influence on the performance of the five companies.
Obviously, all companies tried to reduce expenditures such as production
cost, cost of sales and administration cost by decreasing the number of staff in
the company (excluding AE). As well as this, the companies had problems
with liquidity due to a substantial volume of withdrawn wealth by the

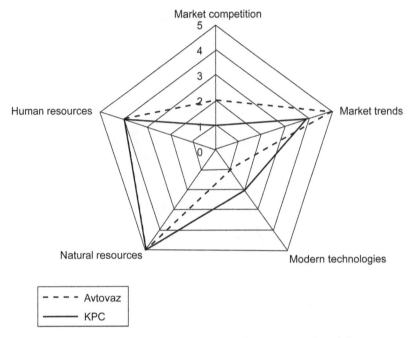

Figure 10.12 Key external factors of corporate performance KPC and Avtovaz
1 = Strong negative affect, 2 = Strong affect, 3 = Middling, 4 = Weak impact, 5 = Insubstantial.
Source: Author assessment based on interviews.

management for purchasing company shares (excluding KPC). It is important to note that in the four cases, the major shareholders used only corporate finance to purchase company shares and all companies effectively optimised taxes because of the enormous tax rates set by the Russian government.

Nevertheless, successes and failures of the companies were strongly determined by other factors such as the industry sector, in which the company competed, manufacturing capacity, the extraction of wealth by the management and effective lobbying. The last two were relatively important for owners because they helped to grab assets for a cheaper price or without any payments (Avtovaz, Nornickel and APPM), saved control for business (Avtovaz) and formed a market environment (Avtovaz and Nornickel).

Successful companies (AE, APPM and Nornickel) had similar patterns of internal factors, such as a profitable selected sector, efficient manufacturing capacity, reduced expenditures, optimised taxes, absence of a threat of acquisition and a strong lobby (Figure 10.13). Whereas the unproductive companies (KPC and Avtovaz) did not have an adequate pattern of internal factors (Figure 10.14).

As with external factors, internal factors determine corporate performance of companies and some of them were the necessary conditions for a positive financial result. However, two factors, namely lobby power and extraction of wealth, were sufficient conditions for success of the company (Nornickel and Avtovaz).

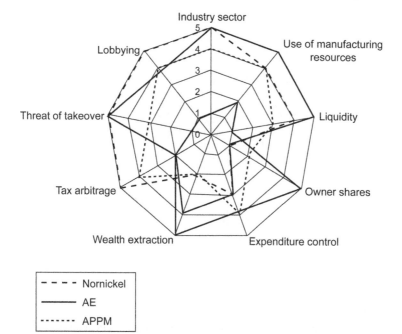

Figure 10.13 Key internal factors of corporate performance Nornickel, AE, APPM
1 = Extremely negative, 2 = Negative, 3 = Relatively positive, 4 = Positive, 5 = Extremely positive.
Source: Author assessment based on interviews.

Additionally, corporate wealth of the four companies (Avtovaz, APPM, Nornickel and KPC) became concentrated in the hands of a few business oligarchs. However, only two (APPM and Nornickel) contributed to a relatively effective management of capital. Oligarchs operating in commodity industry sectors (APPM and Nornickel), benefited from inflated commodity prices and favourable global market demand, which in turn helped to increase company cash earnings and inflate stock market valuation (Nornickel).

In the case of Avtovaz, we find that a majority of factors are negative such as availability of resources, liquidity and market conditions. However, even for strong companies like Nornickel, there are a number of negative conditions: the concentration of ownership and wealth extraction, competitive market conditions and access to appropriate technologies.

Overall, the results of the carried out analysis are mixed, and there are no clear consistent patterns. Firms that are successful financially are able to access natural resources, and they have benefited from the inflated global market demand and commodity prices. This group of Russian firms has also managed to maintain strong finances and liquidity, which helped these firms to leverage additional lending for investment in new (but at the time not the latest) technologies. It is worrying that these firms are also dominated by oligarchs, where there is a

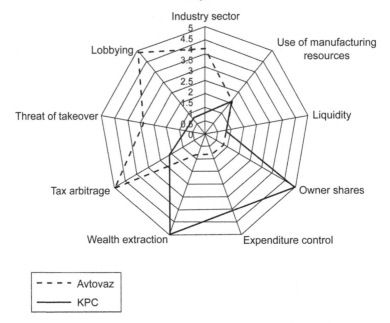

Figure 10.14 Key internal factors of corporate performance KPC and Avtovaz
The scores were derived by interviewing managers of the companies.
1 = Extremely negative, 2 = Negative, 3 = Relatively positive, 4 = Positive, 5 = Extremely positive.
Source: Author assessment based on interviews.

high level of lobbying, tax arbitrage and wealth extraction, which may damage the long-term condition of these firms.

Comparison of the value retained year index of the five companies against the growth of GDP index of Russia will be helpful, because it will add additional information about the outcome of privatisation. Furthermore, this comparison could improve the external validity as a theoretical estimate of the degree to which conclusions about the key factors of corporate performance are likely to transfer to other similar companies, other companies of similar industries, as well as other industries of the Russian economy and the economy as a whole.

Table 10.1 shows a value retained year index in terms of purchasing power of the rouble, as of 31 December 1995, in the five companies and growth of the GDP index of Russia. As can be seen between 1994 and 2007, despite some fluctuations of the value retained year index, only three companies managed to maintain a stable level of the index – AE, Avtovaz and Nornickel. Moreover, AE and Nornickel had a significant growth of the index: 9.8 and 5.4 respectively, which exceeded the growth in GDP, which rose to 1.62. According to Table 10.1, KPC had a good start position, and it managed to maintain it until 1998; later the company considerably lost its position. APPM shows an opposite history; after a tremendous fall, it improved its result and remained stable relative to GDP. The considerable growth of the Russian economy at that

Table 10.1 Value retained year index relative to Russian GDP

	1995	1996	1997	1998	1999	2000	2001	2002	2003	2004	2005	2006	2007
AE	1.0	1.4	2.4	1.9	1.9	3.7	5.0	4.2	4.6	5.2	8.9	9.8	9.8
Avtovaz	1.0	1.0	1.1	0.7	0.6	0.8	1.1	1.1	1.0	2.3	1.4	1.7	1.7
Nornickel	1.0	0.4	0.7	1.5	0.8	1.5	0.8	0.8	1.3	1.9	2.1	4.4	5.4
KPC	1.0	1.3	1.6	1.5	1.6	1.4	1.5	1.6	0.1	0.9	0.6	1.1	1.0
APPM	1.0	0.3	0.4	0.3	0.2	0.9	0.7	0.7	1.0	1.0	1.0	1.5	1.6
Russia GDP	1.0	0.94	0.95	0.9	0.94	1.03	1.09	1.14	1.24	1.32	1.4	1.46	1.62

Value retained year index (1995 = 1). Value retained in income can be determined as the sum of EBITDA and labour cost divided by sales revenue.

Source: Author's calculation based on accounting data and Russian statistics.

time was determined by the dramatic growth of commodity prices and the recovery of the national economy after the stagnation of 1990–9.

A comparison of GDP with the value retained index of the five companies illustrates that they had a relatively different trajectory and their growth or stable trajectory could be explained by the total growth of the national economy.

Conclusion

The performance analysis reveals variability in performance, where there is no single straightforward pattern. All companies had strong market competition and a growing market trend. Commodity-orientated companies were influenced by natural resources of the regions, which supplied raw materials. Human resources and the quality of the infrastructure of the region were essential for the performance of the companies due to the undeveloped infrastructure of the country and its depopulation. Some companies strongly depended on modern technologies and did not depend significantly on human resources and the quality of the infrastructure in the region.

All successful companies had similar patterns of internal factors such as the profitable selected sector, efficient employment of manufacturing capacity, reduced expenditure, optimisation of taxes, the absent risk of acquisition and a strong lobby, whereas the unproductive companies did not. It is difficult to conclude that privatisation improved financial and operating performance of divested firms. The evaluation of the five cases did not exhibit strong evidence to suggest that the privatised firms improved corporate performance relative to state-owned companies.

A comparison of the corporate performance of Avtovaz to the performance of similar foreign manufacturers shows that the performance of Avtovaz did not follow the development trajectory of Fiat and BMW over similar years as there was significantly more variation and volatility. This variation could be explained by the crisis of the national economy and the implementation and then the subsequent cancellation of export tariffs.

A comparison of APPM and Nornickel with their international counterparts illustrates that they had a relatively similar trajectory and their movements could be more easily explained by the global tendencies rather than by internal factors of Russia.

The corporate wealth of the companies was concentrated in the hands of a few business oligarchs. However, in only two cases the oligarchs contributed to effective management of capital. Businesses operating in commodity industry sectors benefited from inflated commodity prices and an encouraging international market demand that in turn helped to raise company earnings and inflate stock market valuation.

11 Can Russian oligarchs survive the global crisis

In 2008, the Russian economy met the economic crisis on a scale comparable with the default in 1998 and the recession in 1992–4. Integration of Russia into the global economy has increased the dependence of the economy upon international financial and commodities markets. When an occurrence abroad has an impact on economic growth, the value of Russian securities and corporate performance are also affected.

This chapter shows the causes and outcomes of the Russian crisis of 2008. A brief description of how the five companies survived the global crisis additionally illustrates the internal and external mechanisms of the Russian economy. It again confirms the idea about the fragility of the economic transformation.

The nature of the Russian crisis

There are different opinions of when the Russian crisis started. Former presidential advisor Illarionov (2008) assumed that the Russian stock crisis should be counted from May 2008 when the Russian stock indexes stopped growing and started falling. In the summer of 2008, the business climate drastically deteriorated because of increasing pressure of the Russian government upon domestic business. The most influential cases were the attack on the metallurgical company Mechel, conflict between TNK and BP and the war between Russia and Georgia.

On the other hand, despite real difficulties in the economy, the Russian government discouraged the use of the word 'crisis' for describing the economic situation until the end of October 2008, assuming that not using the word could help to escape the situation. Officials started to use the word crisis at the end of 2008. There was an extremely unusual situation when Russian citizens frantically withdrew bank deposits and exchanged roubles for dollars, but the authorities claimed that the economy was strong and so no panic was necessary. Simultaneously, they protected friendly oligarchs. One can say that the different perceptions of the date of the crisis are determined by how the researchers and politicians understand the foundations of the crisis and who was responsible for it.

There are many explanations of the causes of the Russian crisis. For example, the World Bank (2008) suggests four principal factors of the Russian crisis: a turnaround in capital flows, liquidity problems associated with short-term debt of the Russian banking system, a sharp drop in the price of oil and the loss of confidence in the Russian economy. However, the causes of the crisis can be split onto two groups: external and internal.

The first position considers that the troubles in the Russian financial markets are a direct consequence of overseas events such as the decline of commodity prices and decreasing foreign direct investment. Supporters of this position note that the major source of the Russian crisis is falling prices for Russian export commodities. Dominance of raw materials in the export market subjects the balance of payments to a more rigid dependence upon cyclical fluctuations than in a diversified economy. Additionally, deceleration of growth of the global economy and decline in investment activity in importing countries can have a multiplier effect causing a sharp inhibition of the commodity economy (Mau 2009). The institutional environment in a country can create a stable foundation for growth. In Russia, this was not sufficiently developed and, therefore, the institutions were unable to mitigate and correct the effects of a deteriorating economic and political situation (ibid.).

Additionally, the sufficient negative factor for Russia has been a sharp drop in oil prices from the historical peak of July 2008. In October 2008, Urals oil dropped below $70 per barrel. However, one can note that the average price of oil in 2008 was around $90 per barrel, which was significantly higher than in 2007. The relatively low price in 2009 (around $53 per barrel) was similar to an average price in the period 2005–6 when the economy grew dramatically.

Between November 2008 and March 2009, the commodity price index, which considers both fuel and non-fuel prices, fluctuated at around 100: equal to the January 2005 figure. However, the index recovered to the pre-crisis level extraordinarily quickly by the middle of 2009 (Indexmundi 2011).

The second explanation of the cause of the Russian crisis was the internal problems of the country. Former Russian Minister of Finance Kudrin (2009) writes that within the economy emerged consistently low interest rates, negative in real terms, which led to the rapid growth of lending. As a result, the economy was overheated, and it contributed to increased inflationary pressures and a fast build-up of external borrowings.

In just three years between 2005 and 2007, foreign debt of the private sector almost quadrupled. At the beginning of 2005, it amounted to $108 billion, and at the end of 2007, it was $417 billion. The rapid growth of public spending and imports were camouflaged by increasing Russian commodities prices. Additionally, before the end of the crisis year the companies had to pay foreign creditors around $56 billion (CBR 2009).

Government's struggle with the crisis

In the first few weeks of the crisis, the Russian government demonstrated strength and calmness; it naively overestimated its opportunities and tried to avoid widespread discussion of the crisis. Putin's government attributed the responsibility for the crisis to external circumstances. This was a classic example of external locus control when it is believed that it cannot control events and attributes negative results to external circumstances.

In October 2008, Russian Prime Minister Vladimir Putin laid full responsibility for the financial crisis on the government and financial system of the United States; he also declared that the credibility of the United States as the leader of the free world economy and that confidence in Wall Street is undermined forever (Putin 2008).

The anti-crisis policy of Russia was determined by the following factors. First, the rate of inflation was above 10 per cent and, together with the rapid decline of production, the economy fell into stagflation. Second, because of the high level of monopolisation of the Russian economy, the effectiveness of fiscal incentives was insufficient. The expansion of budget demand increased prices, not supply. Third, the weakness of institutions reduces the effectiveness of government initiatives. Fourth, the current global crisis has clearly demonstrated structural vulnerability of the Russian economy and its inefficiency (IET 2010).

At first sight, the actions of the government were more impulsive than systematic. Nevertheless, the actions were logical in actively helping large oligarchic groups and not panicking markets. Policy was mainly focused on supporting the financial sector and industrial companies with relatively limited support to citizens.

In 2008, the total cost of the measures was 1,089 trillion roubles (2.6 per cent of GDP), including the strengthening of the financial sector by 785 billion roubles, which in turn included subordinated loans of 450 billion roubles, together with recapitalisation and other direct support of 335 billion roubles. Supporting the real economy cost just 304 billion roubles (0.7 per cent of GDP) where the key element, fiscal stimulus aimed at firms, was 272 billion roubles (World Bank 2008).

At the end of 2008, Putin approved an 'Action Plan to improve the situation in the financial sector and some sectors of the economy' and the government published a list of 295 strategically important companies that qualified for direct state support. The list consisted of companies belonging to oligarchs or non-transparent state corporations (Government RF 2009). However, as Krichevsky (2009) notes, anti-crisis programmes of the government are not aimed at modernisation of the economy and the development of entrepreneurship, they were aimed at the preservation of the existing resource economic model in the hope of a fast recovery of commodities markets. Russian authorities constantly stated that it did not want redistribution of property or nationalisation of leading companies whereas, in Western countries, the emphasis was on increasing competition, improving the efficiency of manufacturing, technological upgrading and on the willingness of authorities to force companies into bankruptcy or change of ownership.

On 27 October 2008, the Supervisory Board of Vnesheconombank (VEB), where Putin was the chairman, distributed $10 billion to companies who were saved from the problems of a margin call. The main recipients were UC Rusal, the X5 Retail Group, VimpelCom and Russian Railways. A large part of this, $4.5 billion, was given to the company Rusal owned by Russian oligarch Deripaska (IET 2009).

The case of Deripaska is particularly interesting because of its connection with the Nornickel story. As noted in Chapter 7, in April 2008 Mikhail Prokhorov's 25 per cent stake in Nornickel was acquired by Rusal, the largest global producers of aluminium, where Deripaska is officially named as a major shareholder. Rusal took out a syndicated loan of $4.5 billion from Western banks, secured against shares of Nornickel. However, since the summer of 2008 the value of shares had fallen by more than 50 per cent. Deripaska could not repay creditors' claims by increasing the collateral of his assets and needed to ask for help from VEB. The decision was made quickly. Shares that were worth more than $14 billion six months previously were pledged to VEB for $4.5 billion (Rusal 2008a). The loan was granted to Rusal in violation of regulations regarding the granting of such loans because it was over $2.5 billion, and so was a violation of banking regulations due to high concentration risk.

Before the crisis of 2008, Deripaska acquired more than 100 companies in the six industry sectors (energy, resources, manufacturing, financial services, construction and aviation) and created Basic Element, which is one of the largest business groups of modern Russia (Basic Element 2009). Many assets of Deripaska have been easy collected because the price of acquisition or expropriation was insignificant. Deripaska's companies had an extremely aggressive policy of acquisition in different branches despite high risks. He used an ordinary scheme: he took out credit to purchase the assets and then borrowed against that asset in order to purchase additional assets. Moreover, the loan interest was paid from the cash flow of the purchased assets. However, after the financial crisis, the value of collateral dramatically fell in value and so the companies were exposed to the margin call.

One can say that under the cover of emergency anti-crisis measures it was a recovery action of a single oligarch. The state could easily acquire the Deripaska business; however, the government did not bankrupt Deripaska. Instead, it helped him to retain his assets. Subsequently, Deripaska twice received deferred repayment of $4.5 billion from VEB. In addition, he managed to negotiate a restructuring of its foreign debt by $7.4 billion (Rusal 2008a).

It is hard to imagine why Putin's government would legitimately sustain a lifeless company at enormous risk. One can suppose that, in the case of Deripaska, some members of Putin's government had a strong personal interest. It can be concluded that the government's actions during the financial crisis are carried out to protect the personal investment of members of the authorities and oligarchy.

Result for the country and business

According to the Economy Ministry of Russia, in 2009 real GDP contracted by 7.9 per cent, sufficiently less than 5.3 per cent in 1998 when Russia defaulted. This result is comparable only with 1992–3 when the Russian reforms were started (Mineconom 2009). The Russian plunge was one of the most significant in the post-Soviet area as well as more significant than other leading petroleum producing countries. Unexpectedly, simultaneously with a sharp drop in the Russian economy, the economy had a relatively high inflation rate – 9 per cent per year, whereas in the EU and the US consumer prices were stable (ibid.).

The Russian government was not able to carry out an effective anti-crisis policy and was unable to achieve growth in lending to the real sector of the economy. The official rate of the Central Bank of Russia remained at almost the pre-crisis level, and the cost of credit for business was greater than before the crisis. Because of this policy, during 2008, the MICEX index lost 67.2 per cent and the RTS index 72.4 per cent, making it one of the worst performing markets in the world.

Providing massive financial reserves to support the banking system triggered the devaluation of the rouble and a decrease in international reserves of the country. From August to January 2009, the rouble weakened by 35 per cent against the dollar and Russian reserves fell by $210 billion from their peak to $386 billion (CBR 2009).

In the next section, I would like to return to the five companies and briefly describe how they are performing in the global crisis.

Five companies and the Russian crisis

AE

The financial crisis has negatively affected the automotive market. Reduction of personal income, lack of confidence in the future, limitation of credit to dealers and customers and their reluctance to make significant investment during the crisis have become serious barriers for Russian car manufacturers.

Production of passenger cars in Russia dropped from 1,470,000 units in 2008 to 597,000 units in 2009 and truck production fell from 256,000 to 91,000 (Russia in figures 2010). Almost all car manufacturers of the country completely halted productions and had strong social tensions.

AE was badly affected by the financial crisis because its performance depends on the automotive industry in general and the major car manufacturers in particular. In the first quarter of 2009, company production and sales dramatically declined. As a result, net revenue from sales decreased by 51.6 per cent from 1.65 billion roubles in 2008 to 0.8 billion roubles in 2009. However, expenditure of the company decreased by 51.4 per cent, an almost similar reduction of net revenues, indicating insignificant decrease in the efficiency of the core business activity.

The traditional consumers of AE products dramatically reduced purchases that created the necessity for the company to develop new products and seek out new markets. High competition in the industry, increased quality control requirements of car manufacturers for automotive components and the toughening of terms of conditions dramatically increased the risk of business (AE SR 2009). The crisis has motivated the company to respond adequately to market threats, therefore, it sufficiently optimised business processes, diversified the portfolio of products and developed partnerships with foreign producers of cars in Russia.

In 2009, operating profit decreased by 90.2 per cent and the company made a loss of 93 million roubles, which was the first loss for 15 years. Nevertheless, the growing trend of the car market meant it quickly recovered, and in 2010 sales revenue of the company increased by 23 per cent; net profit was nine million roubles (AE SR 2009, 2010). ROCE of the company declined from 39 per cent in 2007 to 0 per cent and minus 37 per cent in 2008 and 2009 respectively.

Avtovaz

The financial crisis has negatively affected Avtovaz. In 2009, sales decreased by 43.8 per cent to 349,490 cars from 622,182 cars in 2008, whilst production declined by 36.8 per cent. However, the company's market share in Russia was stable at around 25 per cent. Decreases in sales and production resulted in significant losses. For 2009, the company incurred a net loss of around $1.7 billion roubles. In addition, capitalisation declined by more than 12-fold between December 2007 and December 2008 (Avtovaz AR 2010). ROCE of the company declined from 39 per cent in pre-crisis 2007 to minus 40 per cent and minus 189 per cent in 2008 and 2009 respectively.

In early 2009, the management prepared an anti-crisis programme for Avto-vaz, which included promoting an auto loan programme, reducing salaries, reducing personnel, disposing of non-core assets and outsourcing, decreasing payments for idle hours and reducing social burden (Fedorina 2009). Nearly 23,500 employees were laid off, which was one of the milestones on the way to prevent the bankruptcy of the company (Avtovaz AR 2010).

However, the major elements of the strategy were lobbied protectionist measures such as the government's rescheduling of taxes and duties and postponing of principal debt until 2017. Also, refinancing by the government at two-thirds of the refinance rate on three-year loans for purchasing of Russian cars, subsidising Russian Railways for the transport cost of cars to the Russian Far East and increasing the purchase of vehicles for state and public organisa-tions (Avtovaz AR 2010). Additionally, protectionist measures included recy-cling of old vehicles by subsidising a part of the cost of Russian new vehicles and increasing the tariffs for imported foreign cars (Government RF 2009).

At the same time, the government understood that the company actually was bankrupt because at the beginning of 2010 the debt of the plant was more than 76.3 billion roubles ($3billion) and further government support for business was impractical (Belikov 2009). As a result, the government formed a strategic alliance with Renault.

KPC

The financial crisis has not negatively affected the cheapest consumer segments of the paper industry that experienced a small rise in both demand and price. This situation was similar to the financial crisis of 1998. However, KPC could not create opportunity from the crisis because company performance had deteriorated in the previous five years.

In 2008, the results of the company's gross profit amounted to 74 million roubles. Loss of sales was 20 million roubles. The major causes of loss were permanent shortage of working capital needed to maintain stocks of raw materials, lack of qualified industrial personnel, the low level of marginal revenue due to low selling prices and incomplete capacity utilisation.

In 2009, EBITDA of the company was 7.4 million roubles, the first gain for five years. Operating profit increased to 1.1 million roubles in 2009 in comparison with a loss of 20.5 million roubles in 2008. ROCE of the company increased from minus 303 per cent in 2008 to 1 per cent in 2009. In 2009, operating profit was not negatively affected by growth in resource costs. Low quality consumer goods increased as a proportion of the total market in the crisis years due to the reduction of personal income of consumers. As a result, sales of KPC's low-cost toilet paper increased by more than 23 per cent in 2009 in comparison with 2008.

In early 2009, the management prepared an anti-crisis programme for KPC, which included reducing salaries, reduction of personnel, efficient use of energy resources and raw materials. However, the anti-crisis programme did not give positive results; in 2010–1, the company performance had deteriorated dramatically and KPC was bankrupt.

Nornickel

In the end of 2008, prices of metals produced by Nornickel fell by an average of more than 30 per cent. Demand in Europe and America, the company's main markets, declined rapidly by 23 per cent and 5 per cent respectively. The capital markets were in chaos, the management of the company was in a state of limbo and nobody knew what would happen in the near future. During the crisis, most of the company's international operations fell into the red. A number of existing production capacities worldwide were closed due to high costs and the fundamental imbalance between supply and demand in the metals market (Nornickel AR 2008, 2009).

However, demand in Asia was slightly slowed. The Asian market demonstrated greater reliability mostly due to China's purchase of metals for state reserves. As a result, sales of nickel to China in 2009 doubled in comparison with 2008. In addition, the company strengthened its position in the Indian market delivering 8,000 tonnes of nickel in 2009 (ibid.).

In the second half of 2009, growth of prices for non-ferrous and precious metals together with the introduction of measures to optimise costs, as well as the suspension of export duties on nickel and copper, helped the company to improve its financial performance (ibid.). Additionally, Nornickel's financial performance benefitted significantly from the rouble devaluation, when the rouble/$ rate moved from an average of 24 rouble/$1 in July 2008 to 35 rouble/$1 in February 2009. Low-cost production allowed the company to not reduce the production and continue the work of most enterprises in the normal form.

In the main, the drop of production was immaterial. For example, in 2009 the Group produced 283,000 tonnes of nickel, 402,000 tonnes of copper and 661,000 ounces of platinum that were relatively similar to the previous year's 300,000 tonnes, 419,000 thousand tonnes and 656 million ounces respectively (ibid.).

In 2009, the revenues of the company amounted to $10.2 billion compared with $13.9 billion a year earlier. Net profit was $2.7 billion against the net loss of $555 million, resulting in write-downs due to foreign assets and goodwill impairment. In 2009, adjusted EBITDA was $4.4 billion, and the company investment was $1.1 billion. Only in the most severe period of the crisis in 2008 did ROCE of the company decline by 1 per cent and then promptly recovered to the average figure of 20 per cent in 2009.

APPM

The financial crisis has negatively affected the global paper industry as well as Russian industry, which experienced a sharp decline in demand and prices of their products between late 2008 and April 2009. Global demand for pulp and paperboard fell by 15–25 per cent, and pulp prices dropped on the international market by 40 per cent and on the Russian market by 15 per cent (APPM AR 2009, RISI 2010). However, the global market recovered relatively quickly because of increasing demand for pulp from China, India and Brazil, which allowed suppliers to raise pulp prices at the end of 2009. Growth in world consumption of pulp and paper in 2010 was 6.7 per cent, exceeding the pre-crisis level of 2007 (ibid.).

In the paper industry of Russia, there was a severe shortage of working capital that manifested in enterprises as non-payment from buyers and rapid growth in outstanding receivables aggravating the lack of bank lending. In 2009, production of cellulose decreased by 7.5 per cent, in comparison with 2008, production of paper fell by 2 per cent and the production of cardboard fell by 3.8 per cent (Nacles 2012). However, it is essential to note that the slowdown in the Russian production of cellulose began before the global economic crisis due to lack of investment in the production capacity of the industry.

In 2009, export of major products minimised due to low world prices and the share of sales to the domestic market increased to 82 per cent of total sales. In addition, devaluation of the rouble against the dollar in 2009 increased annual sales by 426 million roubles. This moderately offset the losses from falling prices (APPM AR 2009, 2010).

Despite the crisis, APPM maintained production at a high level; capacity utilisation in 2009 was 95.6 per cent, and the output of cellulose was 810,220 tonnes, just 2.4 per cent less than in the previous year. However, a general reduction of prices for all products reduced revenue by 1.46 billion roubles and income from sales by 0.86 billion roubles. Costs of production against the previous year's expenses decreased by 3.2 per cent due to the use of cheaper raw materials, efficient use of energy and chemicals and reduction of staff by 7 per cent.

The decrease in revenue from sales exceeded the reduction in sales and production costs. This was a determining factor in reducing profits from sales, which reduced by 40.9 per cent. In 2009, EBITDA of the company was 1.3 billion roubles, but after the stabilisation of the global demand in the second part of 2009, the company's financial performance returned to the pre-crisis level. ROCE of the company declined from 10 per cent in 2008 to 1 per cent in 2009 but recovered to 34 per cent in 2010. In 2010, the average price of cardboard and cellulose increased significantly (by around 35 per cent) and reached their maximum level for the past 12 years. Therefore, the company's sales and net income increased by 37 per cent and 277 per cent respectively (ibid.).

Conclusion

Analysis of the performance of five companies shows that the impact of the financial crisis to markets of the companies was short-term and not strong. However, even the short-term decline of commodity prices and global demand dramatically damaged company earnings and stock market valuations.

In addition, one can say that fluctuations of performance were determined by internal problems of the analysed companies more than by the global situation. During the crisis, Nornickel had strong conflict between major shareholders; APPM came under strong attack by Basic Element. The Avtovaz fall sank hundreds of domestic suppliers such as AE. KPC missed excellent opportunities due to poor management.

Avtovaz was in collapse for a long time before the crisis and continued to exist only because of state donations. The inefficient and unprofitable Avtovaz received more than one billion dollars of subsidies during the peak of the crisis because the government wanted to save the largest machine-building company of the country and because the company employed a significant part of the population of the region. Again and again, the Avtovaz executives and the government created exceptional conditions that helped the firm to survive thanks to support from the state budget.

The corporate wealth of the companies was concentrated in the hands of oligarchs. Oligarchs' companies could not operate properly because the oligarchs could not contribute to effective management of capital. Oligarchs' greed has created debt default and margin calls, often followed by a panic reaction. They withdraw money from their businesses through dividends and loans to friendly offshore companies. However, it is more important that oligarchs were able to manage the government for loans and aid. The coalition between oligarchs and the government maintains their businesses.

During the crisis, the state gave support to oligarchs, transferring their losses to the state. The Russian authority did everything for the preservation and strengthening of the ownership structure. The inclusion of Russian oligarch groups in global markets and growth in the capitalisation of these companies helped the companies to obtain cheap lending. Consequently, Russia's largest financial groups are bogged down in short-term foreign debt that funded the bail-out of the price of their shares.

Putin's model of crisis management was unsustainable because it was not backed up by investment in the modernisation of production, labour productivity growth or development of small and medium-sized businesses. Putin's team faced a non-trivial institutional choice: permit the oligarchs to lose control over a significant share of Russian assets or pay for them using state funds. The choice in favour of the latter gave additional leverage to the state and redistributed assets in favour of their allies.

A close relationship existed between the government and different oligarch groups; therefore, the government mainly provided loans rather than considerable equity buyouts. The government had large financial reserves that gave an opportunity to acquire a considerable segment of the economy at knock-down prices. However, nobody wanted to redistribute already privatised assets and destroyed stability. One can say that the state realised nationalisation only when the owners are not included in their favourite group or they have inappropriate behaviour.

The crisis of 2008–9 was significantly different from the crisis of 1998. In 1998, the Russian government acted as the main cause of the crisis, being unable to service its obligations and to keep the financial system from decline. The situation changed in 2003–4 with the open ability to use resources of state security forces for the redistribution of property and the strengthening of some oligarchs at the expense of the absorption of assets and displacement of others. During this period, oligarchic business widely started to use an offshore regime and massive withdrawal of capital in order to protect it against unfriendly acquisition. The business strategy of key stakeholders of the ruling economic class began to replace long-term development strategy with short-term snatch-and-grab tactics that were focused upon extremely fast enrichment for a limited period of the commodity boom, but not in the long structural reform and modernisation of the national economy (Krichevsky 2009).

Conclusion
What will Russia do?

This conclusion presents the author's judgement about the results of the transformation of Russian business and economy for the last 20 years and the fate of Russian business. It reveals that Russia has completed its pseudo-revolution that brought down the Soviet system and adopted some elements of market economy. The author tries to evaluate the major approaches to Russian renovation and find options for the sustainable development of business in Russia.

Twenty years of Russian transformation

Privatisation was central to Russian reform and the driver of a transition process from state-owned assets to private ownership, and widespread, rapid privatisation generated oligarchs who were the major political force necessary to maintain economic reforms. Moreover, underdeveloped market institutions were transformed extremely quickly to serve the oligarchs' authority and conserve their position. Russian privatisation was a complex, chaotic and multi-dimensional endeavour where the connection between policy initiatives and outcomes remained ambiguous and often contradictory.

Privatisation thus concentrated wealth in the hands of a few owners, wealth accumulators and cash extractors, and this slowed the rate at which new technologies and productive systems were renewed to strengthen firms' positions in a competitive global market. Moreover, internal and external conditions still present a threat to these firms and act as a brake upon robust transformation. Privatisation has changed the pattern of ownership and control in those Russian firms we have surveyed, but the underlying support factors are not sufficiently robust, so privatisation may not deliver sustainable development.

The financial analysis and interview results conducted upon the five company cases in this book give mixed evidence of transformed performance with some evidence of stronger financials but an operating context not decisively improved. One should be cautious about attributing financial transformation to oligarchs who, by virtue of being both owners and managers are able to manage corporate resources more efficiently.

Overall, the results of the analysis of the cases carried out are mixed, and there are no clear consistent patterns. Firms that are successful financially are able to access natural resources and have benefited from inflated global market demand and commodity prices. This group of Russian firms has also managed to maintain strong financials and liquidity helping these firms to leverage additional lending for investment in relatively new technologies. It is worrying that these firms are also dominated by oligarchs where there is also a high level of lobbying, tax arbitrage and wealth extraction, which may damage the long-term condition of these firms.

The transition of Russian companies from state managed to private corporate capital was a fragile rather than robust arrangement. Between 1995 and 2011, the cases show that the oligarchs, by virtue of the sheer scale of their accumulated wealth, stand outside of management and control of state institutions, which represent political settlements and contribute to imposing form and consistency on human activities. The ability of Russian state institutions to regulate the behaviour of oligarchs became increasingly weaker as the financially powerful elite became stronger. Anaemic Russian institutions created an opportunity for development of oligarchy. However, it has not been a one-way process because oligarchs have also impacted upon the process of development and transformation of institutions in Russia.

Institutional reforms have practically collapsed and degenerated into either imitation or counter reforms. Putin's path toward 'centralisation' and 'stability' has almost destroyed political pluralism and competition in politics. In the current system, elections are not capable of providing change of government (INSOR 2010) and progress in implementing institutional reforms in Russia has stopped. As a result, in Russia there remains a low level of investment, many projects with a short running time, insufficient foreign direct investment and a dominance of investment in services to the local market (Gref 2009).

The system of political institutions imitates democracy and the separation of powers. In general, the mass media broadcast the government's point of view. Civil society remains extremely weak where it is trying to reach out to the authorities. Nevertheless, it retains some imitation of a dialogue. Appealing to civic awareness, this system does everything to discourage citizens' confidence in their ability to affect anything in political and social life (INSOR 2010).

Institutional transformation in Russia is a high risk. There is an extremely large dependence of the country on export of raw materials. Therefore, reducing commodity prices may create extreme scenarios such as an economic collapse, deep political problems, consumer crises, critical exacerbation of social tensions, growth of separatism, loss of important geopolitical position, catastrophic depopulation and loss of human capital (INSOR 2010).

Mau (2009) lists the main current economic challenges faced by Russia: it is difficult to maintain sustained economic growth while the population is reducing, and Russian citizens change domicile easier than change what country they are living in. In addition, he notes that the position of the country in the international market is not clear, corruption in Russia is not only a tool for unfair advantage but a method of survival and the economy depends on the price of oil, which is outside government control.

One can say that corruption is immanent within the Russian economic system, because it is one of the major regulators of economic and social life. Navalny (2011) notes that corruption in Russia is the foundation of state power and the basic idea of the elite consensus. The consensus is that all the heads of regions and districts delegate their political rights to central government. Consequently, the highest state authority delegates the economic right down to the regional authority. Any governor or district head has two responsibilities: he has to ensure that, on his territory, there are no protest rallies and that Putin or Medvedev and their political party get at least the first place of the electorate's votes. In exchange, the regional or district leader would be able to enrich himself as much as necessary without fearing any criminal prosecution, if he is doing it (enrichment) discretely and intelligently. Corruption in Russia staggers sustainable economic growth and the development of institutions.

Currently Russia has a resource-based economy where the export of crude oil, gas, ore, wood and semi-finished goods such as metals, fertiliser and grain is dominating. Russia plays a significant role as a supplier of commodities and energy in international trade.

The Russian economy is not designed to work in the modern market. Year by year, the economy loses capacity and knowledge in high-technology sectors, the structure of production becomes less diversified, and there is a trend toward deindustrialisation of the economy. As a result, Russia is doomed to exchange natural resources for expensive consumer goods, equipment and foreign technology to the extent that it cannot develop itself.

Even though many companies look attractive and operate as a typical Western company, making IPOs in London and New York, many sectors of the Russian economy remain undeveloped and incongruent with modern requirements. The economy does not have developed services and infrastructure and competitive industries based on modern technology. There is no effective mechanism for modernising the Russian economy and attracting the financial, intellectual and human resources needed to achieve this goal. The country is not a global player on the market of advanced technologies in sectors such as consumer goods, composite materials and pharmaceuticals.

One can say that investors do not have tax and customs incentives to encourage investment in innovative sectors, so private capital is not flowing into high-tech segments. As a result, Russia cannot establish technological leadership in key sectors of modern business such as high-tech chemistry, biotechnology, composite materials, information technologies and nanotechnology. Moreover, Russia cannot maintain its leadership where it was a global leader, such as the nuclear and aerospace industries.

In Putin's era, large state corporations and vertically integrated holding companies such as Russian Technologies, Rosatom, United Aircraft Corporation and United Shipbuilding Corporation have been created by the government. These conglomerates, which are mainly managed by Putin's close comrades, have consolidated enormous financial, labour and intellectual resources. Nevertheless, these corporations are ineffective, corrupt and create colossal monopolies in high-tech industries. Consequently, they cannot compete on global markets, do not have high capitalisation or expanding market niche positions. Moreover, they discourage growth in the high-tech segments of the national economy and stunt their research and production potential. In addition, they do not provide the orders for small innovation businesses or take over successful start-up companies.

There are difficulties with importing advanced technology into Russian business culture. For example, despite the fact that nearly half of the foreign cars are being assembled by Russian workers, there is no significant growth of localisation indices because the quality of the auto component products is not acceptable by the foreign car manufacturers.

Labour productivity in Russia is dramatically lower than that of developed economies and so is uncompetitive in the global economy and Russians experience a low quality of life. The reason for the low labour productivity is that many Russian jobs are outdated and unproductive. Russian labour morale is not strong; people often don't want to work or don't work hard enough.

The global crisis shows inefficiency in state management. Russia differs from many other countries in the sense that the government continues to control a relatively large share of the economy and is more heavily involved in regulation. Year by year, the government increases the degree of state regulation and it cannot replace this regimentation by market mechanisms.

The national business environment and the country's investment climate still leave a lot to be desired. Russia is losing out to rival countries in terms of its investment climate. Russia does not make the domestic market more attractive for direct investment despite regular government declarations and statements of its intentions to do so. Considerable amounts of capital are being withdrawn from Russia.

Reforms do not improve the business climate. Businesses operating in Russia often prefer to register property and transactions abroad due to the Russian tax regime, which generally is uncompetitive and lacking modern legislation. The existing legislation is inflexible and does not provide the range of instruments needed for the business community.

There is a lack of transparency in the judicial and law enforcement systems. This amounts to system-wide corruption and increased transaction costs of business. As a result, as Putin (2012) honestly notes, businessmen have to find protection and come to some sort of an agreement with authorities, rather than abiding with the law. Absence of developed institutions does not motivate Russian businessmen to facilitate effective performance; it motivates businessmen to overwhelm their competitors and establish the market position for themselves by tapping the potential of affiliated bureaucrats from the law enforcement and judicial systems (ibid.).

Putin also notes that the government has to invest more efficiently, clearly identifying the country's targets. It needs to introduce severe control over the state expenditure and to eliminate bribes in the mechanism of federal and regional public funds. By tackling this problem, the state could save between 5 and 10 per cent of the budget or approximately 1 or 2 per cent of Russian GDP annually (ibid.).

Future of the Russian economy

From the above, certain questions arise: is there an opportunity to redirect the current trends? How can Russia change this situation? The possible answers do not lie in the strategy of actual companies or the industrial operations they carry out at the macro level. Regarding these questions, there should be no hurry to submit to the temptation of setting recommendations of concrete dates and numbers. Instead, we will try to evaluate the principal approaches to Russian renovation and find options for the sustainable development of business in Russia.

Many programmes of renovation appeared at the time of perestroika as reforms required innovative scenarios and designs of development. The government and independent organisations created a few programmes that used the technical parameters and economic indicators that described a happy future for the Russian economy. In this way, the financial crisis has ignited demands for forecasting and projection of the country's strategy.

Gref (2009) notes that for the sustainable development of the Russian economy, the new paradigm of economic policy must include reforms in three main areas: spatial policy (concentration of the population to realise the effects of economies of scale and benefits of urbanisation); macroeconomic policies (supporting the policy of decreasing inflation and subsequent inflation targeting) and institutional policies (stimulating improvement in business processes, the transition to global accounting standards and disclosure information, improving corporate governance and innovation).

INSOR (2010) shows another example of economic projecting, suppose that Russia is at a crossroads, and Russian society must clearly define its goals and make a conscious decision to move past this point, down the right path and without irreversible losses. INSOR notes many external conditions that positively influence the economy. These include economic freedom, absence of corruption and bureaucratic barriers, the necessary conditions to support small business, competitive advantage, availability of venture capital, social attitudes toward commercial success, protection from criminals and bureaucratic despots and mechanisms to execute contracts. Therefore, any strategic development or plans to promote innovation should begin and end with changes in these conditions. It supposes that Russia using its competitive advantage in the production of commodities may transfer growing incomes to the development of high technology. As a result, in the global economy the country could be represented in a combined innovative sector with traditional sectors of the national economy that provide an effective technology transfer.

INSOR (2010) offers a few steps of reforms: preparation of the reorganisation of law enforcement agencies, continuation of armed forces reform, the draft of a new foreign policy doctrine, recognising that the political system, economy and social spheres must be reformed. Then, create formal and informal structures that are responsible for the legislative, organisational and staffing reforms, as well as changes in the media information policies, which depend either directly or indirectly on the state. The next step should be devoted to the launch of simultaneous and interconnected reforms in the political, economic and social spheres.

Generally, the programmes of Gref and INSOR, as well as other pro-government projects, orientate to conserve the current political situation in the country, and as a result they are unproductive and cannot be realised. As noted by Mikhailov (2011), all debates revolve around administrative modernisation, but macroeconomic stability and the non-commodity model of development are just methods and not goals. The goals of Russia could be increasing the number of native citizens and development of infrastructure.

One can say that the Russian authorities do not have any strong demand for strategic programmes because of their focus on current non-strategic problems as well as self-preservation and self-enrichment. They do not think about the place of the country in the world over the next decade, values that countries use for development and national economic priorities.

The purpose of today's political transformation can be to 'reset the trust' and to open a window for continued economic growth over the next five to ten years. If the country does not provide this 'reset' a looming political crisis may stop the progress of socio-economic reforms and sustainable development of the economy for a decade and deteriorate its position in global competition. In this context, the main tasks are restoration of public confidence in the political system, mitigation of social conflict and political confrontation in the upcoming crisis, continuation of sustainable economic development through economic reform and responsible economic policies and the formation of a viable competitive political model (Belanovsky and Dmitriev 2011).

There is a mistaken belief that modern Russia can be innovative and compete properly with the Western countries on the hi-tech market. For innovation, competitive advantage and sustainable development needs another country with different institutions and with different people.

In the last ten years, the Russian political system has existed in the form of managed democracy: authoritarianism with some decorations such as federal and regional parliaments managed by executive authorities of Russia. The flip side of authoritarianism is large income differentiation, the increase in poverty and growth of social problems because the alliance of the authority and the oligarchy has not provided substantial growth and modernisation of the economy. It has consistently demanded police regulation of public life, repression against the opposition and direct electoral fraud.

There is widespread opinion that Russia has adopted a market economy but then reverted to authoritarianism. Contrary to that position, one can say that there was not a revolution in the early 1990s but just replacement of one group of authority figures with another. The significant constituent of the Russian reforms in the last 20 years was the redistribution of assets from the state to oligarchs and the new elite. These economic and political reforms in the last two decades become more comprehensible only if we understand that Russian reforms are an instrument of redistribution of property rights. Modern Russia is a semi-feudal society, where many Russian companies have depended upon an autocratic regime and continued to employ old-fashioned models of management despite some modernisation lustre.

The bureaucracy currently holds unlimited power, making significant modernisation of the country impossible: it cannot be performed without investment, which requires protected property rights, competition and independent courts. In Russia, a reform has a chance of life if it does not affect the interests of the bureaucracy. Many important reforms, such as the administrative reform, combating corruption, judicial independence and reform of the gas industry were nipped in the bud after the first timid steps. By contrast, immediately gaining impetus were measures in which the bureaucracy was interested: transfer of control of a broad sector of the economy (state-owned corporations) without any reasonable explanation, for the monopolisation of exported gas, the closure of certain sectors to foreign investors and more (Gurvich 2011).

There is not strong demand for public institutions. The Russian middle class is composed of state bureaucrats, managers and successful entrepreneurs and differs from the structure of Western countries where professions such as engineers, doctors and teachers are dominant. As a result, the Russian middle class cannot form a strong demand for an independent judiciary and media freedom. There is no class of tax payers conscious that they maintain the state by these taxes and want to control how the government spends their money. Russian business employs a strategy of disinterest in state expenditure and consequential state disinterest in company income. It is widely supposed that this behaviour can save their business.

One can say that Russia is an interesting example of the connection between sustainable economic development and an institutional environment where undeveloped institutions limit development of the economy. In addition, unchanged authority and political elites frustrate development of institutions. Realisation of any strategy in Russia is possible only when an authority will be limited by time and will change legitimately by democratic elections. However, there is doubt that the current authority will sufficiently reform political and economic construction and that if the authority starts reforms they can finish them. Moreover, there is a serious risk of segmentation in Russia. If the country does not carry out real institutional reforms, it will maintain the current state borders only until the existence of high commodity prices because the country does not have sufficient political power and police resources to maintain control of an immense area and it will most likely face segregation.

Looking at the Russian transformation over the last 20 years, Russia has completed its pseudo-revolution, brought down the Soviet system and adopted some elements of market economy. Despite the dissolution of the Soviet Union, many political and economic elements of the Soviet system have not been eliminated. The dominant picture is insignificant development, on the one hand, and growth of authoritarianism, on the other hand. High commodity prices have preserved this situation for a long time. In addition, behind the glamorous facade of Russia there are thousands of small towns and villages with destroyed infrastructure and paralysed social lives and businesses.

Currently, the country endures because it has beneficial commodity income, as well as relatively good educational and scientific foundations in a few areas, but these last two positions are diminishing. Russia has a chance to use these advantages for its own benefit and to create the conditions for an innovation-based economy and competitive growth if it begins to build real democracy. Only democracy with competitive power, transparent and with universal procedures can provide guaranteed ownership and private property rights that can endure regardless of political conjuncture and the personal considerations of national rulers.

Afterword

On 7 May, a black limousine escorted by motorcycles moved to the Great Kremlin Palace. The cortege was moving through the desolate streets of Moscow. The boulevards and squares in the centre of Moscow were closed to the general population, and there were thousands of policemen and maximum security. All the central stations of Moscow Metro were closed; people living in houses on the Arbat area were not permitted to leave their homes. The cortege was carrying Vladimir Vladimirovich Putin to the third ceremony of the presidential inauguration. Vladimir Putin was finally back in the Kremlin. It was a surreal picture. On the same day, his political opponents were brutally beaten and arrested.

Before this day

Four years ago, Dmitry Medvedev became the president of Russia, but his four-year term did not bring any real change. Medvedev has successfully introduced a new idiom: 'Freedom is better than no freedom'. He made a sorrowful diagnosis of Russia: an archaic economy, enormous corruption and an archaic political system (Medvedev 2009). As a result, a significant share of society believed him and had faith that he could change something. In the first three years of his presidency, Medvedev formed high expectations throughout Russian society. Business and society had accumulated fatigue from Putin's management and they wanted to see a new leader who could change Russia. His amiable and sincere rhetoric inspired people and his speeches encouraged change. The president perpetuated the illusion that he led the country, but these fantasies disappeared in September 2012 when Putin said that he was coming back.

Putin and Medvedev, without public consultation and discussion, agreed to swap roles amongst themselves. This solution irritated Russian society. The December 2011 parliamentary election, which many citizens believed was unfair, had dramatically altered the political situation in Russia.

There is no ideological difference between Putin and Medvedev. Medvedev secured an extension of autocracy and made it possible for Putin to retain power indefinitely without a formal rejection of the Constitution. He could not transform Russia and could not realise any of his political projects. As a result, Medvedev did not live up to the hopes of the people. Paradoxically, he could not save Russia for Putin. Moreover, Putin took the presidency back in a new Russia.

Before December 2011, it was difficult to imagine that the political situation in Russia, which was immobile, had begun movement; many citizens finally recognised their interests and new leaders became visible on the political arena. Putin's regime is relatively young and undeveloped, but one can anticipate that Putin's regime will evolve into a strong dictatorship. However, it will be a carbon copy of the Soviet system in many aspects, such as strong propaganda, the overdevelopment of military industries and the army, limitation of movement in and out of the country, ideological education and political prisoners.

Many researchers assume that the Kremlin at the end of Medvedev's governing met serious political problems. For example, Shevtsova (2012) notes that the many factors that initially worked for Putin's powerful rule have begun to erode. Thus, the Kremlin modernisation rhetoric has made the degradation of the Russian system, which rejects any changes, more obvious. Medvedev increased the gap between slogan and reality and this gap intensified the social protest. His propaganda against corruption stood as a secret decoy towards maintaining the protection of extraordinary corruption, which is the foundation of Putin's autocracy. His repressive criminal laws and police reform have become a threat to the safety of citizens and strengthened attitudes in a considerable part of Russian society against Putin's policy. Shevtsova (2012) observes that the authority cannot control its desire; it cannot get rid of the delinquent behaviour of the ruling team's members. This team is permanently conveying powerful and economic resources to family and friends with organisations that should protect the public interest instead of being employed to maintain power. She supposes this indicates the beginning of an agony of the system where civilisation will struggle to survive with these fatal flaws.

Belanovsky and Dmitriev (2012) note that Putin and Medvedev are perceived as inept modern leaders. Citizens are requesting genuine changes in health, education, housing, personal safety as well as the efficient administration of justice. However, the current structure of power cannot provide rapid and positive changes in these areas. Current perception of these problems in the social consciousness is the result of the constant inability of authority to make institutional changes in these areas. Belanovsky and Dmitriev conclude that citizens clearly show fatigue from the ruling elite and demand a considerable change for the better within the upper stratum of central and regional authorities.

At the beginning of Putin's presidency, Russian society, which was tired from Yeltsin's reforms, was offered a relaxing Soviet-patriotic ideology, a young, energetic leader, an idea of a strong state and strengthening of order in the country. These factors were maintained by favourable external economic environment that formed the illusion of an efficient state in the public consciousness.

The economic crisis of 2008 accelerated anti-Putin attitudes because the ideological rhetoric of the authority that is usually built on unrealistic promises was almost exhausted. The middle class in large cites realised that they did live not in a country with a modern system, but in a semi-Soviet country with the 'vertical of power', strong police and authority pursuing their private interests through state-owned companies. These anti-Putin attitudes are increased in the youth stratum, whose hopes for a better life have evaporated.

High-level authorities employ the motif of protection from external threat (NATO, the US) because it is relevant to traditional expectations of Russia and it can substitute failures in domestic policy. However, the population has become more sceptical to populist rhetoric and it requires a response on the merits of the question.

One can note that protests educate the authorities, who have gained experience, realising that the traditional Russian manipulative elective technologies are not effective anymore, and it has become not so straightforward to imitate elections. The focus will be made on the prevention of proliferation of protests into the Russian provinces; therefore, it is crucial for authorities to block them in Moscow and other large cities. In addition, one can easily predict that, in the near future, the government and parliament will create an anti-revolt legislation and remove the opposition and businessmen who maintain the opposition. Pressure on the independent mass media and independent small and medium businesses will be increased (large business having for a long time been under control of the government) and the investment climate will deteriorate.

In the first days of his presidency, Putin signed orders that instructed the government to sell most state shares of companies of high technological sectors such as the United Aircraft Corporation, United Shipbuilding Corporation and the Russian Technologies State Corporation by 2016. These conglomerates, located in different parts of the country, were established by President Putin's Decrees in 2006–7 for transferring military technologies and facilities in airspace, shipbuilding, electronic and others to producing civilian products. Mostly, these corporations are led by Putin's close friends. Many of their subsidiary companies were designated as strategically important and they were nationalised and incorporated, violating the legislation. It can be assumed that, after privatisation, the best parts of these companies will be distributed between Putin's business partners for symbolic prices and the worst parts will be kept as state assets.

Putin (2012) says that the government is going to privatise a number of key assets. However, he specifies that this privatisation will be of a structural and not of a fiscal nature. This means, according to Putin's explanation, that the government will sell not only in order to obtain extra money for the budget, but primarily in order to encourage economic competition and create opportunities for private initiative. This means that the assets will be sold to people close to Putin's administration. Privatisation will be similar to the 1995 loans-for-shares scheme when unwanted bidders were cruelly cut out, and assets were distributed amongst the ruling clan. In addition, of course, the major part of privatisation income will not be transferred to the state budget.

Lack of open competition in the sale of state property will be a critical factor in shaping the destructive economic structure, low competition and high corruption. Moreover, non-transparent privatisation will create a new large wave of social tensions and could be a factor of the new Russian revolution of the twenty-first century.

Bibliography

Academic Dictionary (2009) Legal nihilism (Pravovoj nigilizm). Available from: www. dic.academic.ru, accessed 17 January 2010.

Accounting Chamber (2002) *Chamber report on the audit of Sibneft in 2002 (Otchet Schetnoi? Palaty RF O rezul'tatakh proverki Sibneft v 2002)*. Accounting Chamber of the Russian Federation, Moscow, available from: www.compromat.ru/ page_14024.htm, accessed 17 January 2011.

AE SR (1997, 1998, 1999, 2000, 2001, 2002, 2003, 2004, 2005, 2006, 2007, 2008, 2009, 2010, 2011) Avtoelektronika Special Report Code emission: 01049-A Kaluga, available from: www.ae.ru/ru/.

Andersson, T., Haslam, K. and Lee, E. (2006) Financialized accounts: Restructuring and return on capital employed in the S&P 500. *Accounting Forum*, 30: 21–41.

Andersson, T., Haslam, C., Lee, E. and Tsitsianis, N. (2008) Strategy as arbitrage. Centre for Research in Finance and Accounting (CRiFA), University of Hertfordshire.

Antonov, V. (2003) Idling volley of Neva (Kholostoĭ zalp s 'Nevy'). *Version*, 10 September, available from: www.compromat.ru/page 23154.htm, accessed 17 January 2011.

APPM AR (1996, 1999, 2000, 2001, 2002, 2003, 2004, 2005, 2006, 2007, 2010, 2011) Arkhangelsk pulp & paper mill. Annual Reports (Arhangel'skij bumazhnyj kombinat Godovyj otchety), Arkhangelsk.

APPM SR (1998) Arkhangelsk pulp and paper mill. Special reports (SR) (Arhangel'skij bumazhnyj kombinat Special'nyj otchet), Arkhangelsk.

Arkhangelsk region (2007) Arkhangelsk region (Arkhangelsk Oblast), available from: www.dvinaland.ru/region, accessed 17 January 2010.

Aron, L. (2008) 21st-Century Sultanate the American Enterprise Institute. *The Magazine*, Friday, 14 November, available from: www.american.com/archive/2008/ november-december-magazine/21st-century-sultanate/article print, accessed 17 January 2010.

Åslund, A. (1995) *How Russia Became a Market Economy*. Washington, DC: Brookings.

Åslund, A. (2007) *Russia's capitalist revolution*. Washington, DC: Peterson Institute for International Economics.

ASM (1995, 1998, 1999, 2000, 2001, 2002, 2003, 2004, 2005, 2007, 2008) Car industry of Russia Data ASM-Holding (Avtomobil'naja promyshlennost' v Rossii dannye), available from: www. asm-holding.ru. Moscow, accessed 17 January 2010.

Avtovaz AR (1995, 1998, 1999, 2000, 2001, 2002, 2003, 2004, 2005, 2007, 2008, 2010, 2011) Annual reports, Tolliatti.

Basic Element (2009) available from: http://www.basel.ru/en/about/history, accessed 17 January 2010.

Belikov, D. (2009) Avtovaz recognized disabled (Avtovaz priznali netrudosposobnym). *Kommersant*, 192 (4247), 15 October, Moscow.

Belikov, D. and Ryzhkin, S. (2005) VAZoboroneksport. *Kommersant*, 24 November, Moscow, available from: www.kommersant.ru, accessed 17 January 2010.

Belikov, D. and Semenov, N. (2005) New Chairman at AvtoVAZ. *Kommersant*, 22 November, Moscow, available from: www.kommersant.ru, accessed 17 January 2010.

Belikov, D., Emelyanova, E. and Semenov, N. (2005) Avtovaz Changed Management. *Kommersant*, 23 December, Moscow, available from: www.kommersant.ru, accessed 17 January 2010.

Belanovsky, S. and Dmitriev, M. (2011) Political crisis in Russia and the possible mechanisms of its development (Politicheskiĭ krizis v Rossii i vozmozhnye mehanizmy yego razvitiya). Moscow: Center for Strategic Research.

Belanovsky, S. and Dmitriev, M. (2012) Political crisis in russia and how it may develop (Politicheskiĭ krizis v rossii i kak eto mozhet razvivat′sya). Moscow: The Center for Strategic Research, available from: www.csr.ru/publikacii/52-2010-05-03-17-49-10/307-2011-03-28-16-38-10/, accessed 17 January 2011.

Berg, S. V. (2009) Sustainable Regulatory Systems: Laws, Resources, and Values.' *Utilities Policy*, 9(4): 159–70.

Bellona (2010) Environmental Challenges in the Arctic. Norilsk Nickel: The Soviet Legacy of Industrial Pollution. *Bellona report*, Bellona Foundation, available from: www.bellona.org/reports/norilsk-nickel-report-en, accessed 28 February 2013.

Birman, I. (1996) Gloomy prospects for the Russian economy. *Europe-Asia studies*, 48 (5): 735–750.

Black, J. A. and Champion, D. J. (1976) *Methods and issues in social research*. New York: Wiley.

Boardman, A. and Vining, A. R. (1989) Ownership and Performance in Competitive Environments: A Comparison of the Performance of Private, Mixed, and State-Owned Enterprises. *Journal of Law & Economics*, 32: 1–33.

Boldyrev, Y. (2003) *On the ointment fly in the ointment*. Moscow: Eksmo / Algorithm-book.

Boone, P. and Rodionov, D. (2002) *Rent Seeking in Russia and the CIS*. Moscow: Brunswick UBS Warburg.

Boycko, M., Shleifer, A. and Vishny, R. (1995) *Privatizing Russia*. Cambridge, MA: MIT Press.

Bromley, D. B. (1986) *The case-study method in psychology and related disciplines*. Chichester: John Wiley & Sons.

Bryan, W. (2007) Ecology Norilsk, Russia. *Time*, Wednesday, 12 September, available from: www.time.com, accessed 17 January 2010.

Butrin, D. (2004a) Non-ferrous Metallurgy. *Kommersant*, 4 March, Moscow, available from: www. kommersant.ru, accessed 17 January 2010.

Butrin, D. (2004b) Timber industry 1991–2000. *Kommersant*, 20 August, Moscow, available from: www.kommersant.ru, accessed 17 January 2010.

CBK express (1997–2011) Newsletter. Cellulosa Bumaga Karton, Moscow.

CBR (2009) Banking supervision report 2008. The Central Bank of the Russian Federation, Moscow: Novosti Press.

Chavance, B. and Magnin, E. (1997) 'Emergence of pathdependent mixed economies in Central Europe', in Amin, A. and Hausner, J. (eds), *Beyond Market and Hierarchy. Interactive Governance And Social Complexity*, Cheltenham: Edward Elgar.

Chernykh, L. (2008) Ultimate ownership and control in Russia. *Journal of Financial Economics*, 88: 169–92.

Clague, C. (1992) Introduction: The Journey to a Market Economy, in Clague, C. and Rausser, G. C. (eds) *The Emergence of Market Economies in Eastern Europe*, Cambridge, MA: Blackwell.

Coase, R. H. (1988) *The firm, the market, and the law.* Chicago, IL: University of Chicago Press.

Collected legal papers (1994) Privatisation of state and municipal enterprises in Russia (Privatizacija gosudarstvennyh i municipal'nyh predprijatij v Rossii). *Respublika – Niva Rossii*, 1–3.

Delyagin, M. (2011) Why corporate governance is once again on the agenda and do russian companies really need it? Using Norilsk Nickel as an example. 13 April, accessed from: http://delyagin.ru/articles/17133.html, accessed 28 February 2013.

Denzin, N. (2006) *Sociological Methods: A Sourcebook.* Chicago, IL: AldineTransaction.

Earle, J., Estrin, S. and Leschenko, L. (1996) Ownership Structures, Patterns of Control and Enterprise Behavior in Russia, in Commander, S., Fan, Q. and Shaffer, M. (eds) *Enterprise Restructuring and Economic Policy in Russia*, Washington, DC: the World Bank.

Enthoven, A. (1999) Russian Accountancy Adopts International Standards. *The Russian Revolution in Accounting & Auditing*, January/February: p. 22.

European forest sector outlook study. (2005) *Geneva timber and forest, study paper 20.* Main report. Geneva: United Nations.

Expert RA (1996, 2003, 2005) Regions ranking. *Expert*, available from: www.expert.ru, accessed 17 January 2010.

Faizulin, R. (2011) SCAM with precious metals in the Nickel. Series 3 (Afera s dragmetallami v nornikele. Seriya 3) *Osa Norilsk Pravda*, 16 June, www.osanor.ru/?id=407, accessed 28 February 2013.

FAO (2001) Paper and paperboard in the Russian Federation. ECE/FAO Forest Products Annual Market Review, p. 11.

FAO (2002) Gradual upturn underway in paper, paperboard and woodpulp markets. *UNECE/FAO Forest Products Annual Market Review, 2001–2002*, FAO Advisory Committee on Paper and Wood Products Forty-third session, Geneva.

Fisher, S. and Sahay, R. (2000) The Transition Economies After Ten Years. IMF Working Paper No. 00/30, Washington, DC: International Monetary Fund.

Frydman, R., Cheryl, W., Gray, H. M. and Rapaczynski, A. (1999) When Does Privatisation Work? The Impact of Private Ownership on Corporate Performance in the Transition Economies. *Quarterly Journal of Economics*, 114 (4): 1153–1191.

Gaidar, Y. (2005) *A long time Russia and world: essays on economic history* (Dolgoe vremja Rossija i mir: Ocherki jekonomicheskoj istorii). Moscow: Delo.

Ghemawat, P. (2007) *Redefining Global Strategy: Crossing Borders in a World Where Differences Still Matter.* Cambridge, MA: Harvard Business School Press.

GKI (1996) Results of privatisation in 1995 and the implementation of the RF President's Decree of 11 May 1995 (Rezul'taty privatizacii v 1995 godu i realizacii Ukaza Prezidenta RF ot 11 maja 1995) 'On measures to guarantee the federal budget revenues from privatisation income'. Moscow: GKI.

Glinkina, S. (2005) Outcomes of the Russian Model, in *Reality check: the distributional impact of privatisation in developing countries*, Washington, DC: Center for Global Development.

Goldman, M. (1997) The Pitfalls of Russian Privatisation. *Challenge*, May/June, 3: 35–50.

Government RF (2009) Anti-Crisis Measures Program of the Government of the Russian Federation for the Year 2009. Government of the Russian Federation,

Prime Minister of the Russian Federation, 19 June, available from: http://premier. gov.ru, accessed 17 January 2011.

Gref, G. (2009) Economic Crisis and Russia's Economy Perspectives (Ekonomicheskiĭ krizis i ekonomicheskie perspektivy Rossii). *Economic policy*, № 6: 20.

Grishkovets, E. (2008) War on APPM being maintained by corruption. *Kommersant*, 10 April, Moscow, available from: www.kommersant.ru, accessed 28 February 2013.

Guriev, S. and Rachinsky, A. (2003) Ownership concentration in Russian industry. Background paper for Russia CEM 2003, March 2004.

Guriev, S. and Rachinsky, A. (2005) The Role of Oligarchs in Russian Capitalism. *Journal of Economic Perspectives*, 19(1): 131–150

Guriev, S., Lazareva, O., Rachinsky, A. and Tsouhlo, S. (2003) 'Concentrated ownership, market for corporate control, and corporate governance', available from: www.nes.ru/ ~sguriev/papers/CGRussia.pdf, accessed 17 January 2010.

Gurvich, E. (2011) Upwind (Protiv vetra), *Gazeta.ru*, 06 April, Moscow, available from: www.gazeta.ru/comments/2011/04/06_x_3576209.shtml, accessed 17 January 2010.

Hardy, J., Currie, F. and Zhen, Y. (2005) Cultural and Political Embeddedness, Foreign Investment and Locality in Transforming Economies: the Case of ABB in Poland and China. *Competition and Change*, 9 (3), September: 277–297.

Haslam, C. and Glazunov, M. (2009) Oligarchs in transition: The shifting balance of ownership and control in Russia. Working paper. Centre for Research in Finance and Accounting (CRiFA), University of Hertfordshire.

History of Avtovaz (2007) (Istorija Avtovaz), available from: www.history.vaz.ru, accessed 17 January 2010.

Hodgson, G. M. (1998) The Approach of Institutional Economics. *Journal of Economic Literature*, XXXVI (March): 166–192, available from: www.geoffrey-hodgson. co.uk, accessed 17 January 2010.

Hodgson, G. M. (2006) 'What are institutions?', *Journal of Economic Issues*, 40(1): 1–25.

Human Rights Watch (2009) '*Are You Happy to Cheat Us?*' Exploitation of Migrant Construction Workers in Russia. *Human Rights Watch*, February 10, New York, available from: www.hrw.org/en/reports/2009/02/09/are-you-happy-cheat-us, accessed 17 January 2010.

Insor (2010) Russia XXI century: the image of a desired future (Rossiya XXI veka: obraz zhelaemogo zavtra). Institute of Contemporary Development, 2010 R76 – Moscow: Econ-Inform.

Intriligator, M. D. (1996) 'The Russian shock therapy', *Russian magazine*, September.

IET (1994) Russian Economy in 1993. Trends and prospects. Institute for Economy in Transition, Moscow, March, available from: www.iet.ru/en/.html, accessed 17 January 2010.

IET (1995) Russian Economy in 1994. Trends and prospects. Institute for Economy in Transition, Moscow, March, available from: www.iet.ru.html, accessed 17 January 2010.

IET (1996) Russian Economy in 1995. Trends and prospects. Institute for Economy in Transition, Moscow, available from: www.iet.ru/en/.html, accessed 17 January 2010.

IET (1997) Russian Economy in 1996. Trends and prospects. Moscow: Institute for Economy in Transition, available from: www.iet.ru/en/.html, accessed 17 January 2010.

IET (1998) Economy of transitional period; Essays of economic policy of post-communist Russia 1991–97, Moscow: Institute for Economy in Transition.

IET (2009) Russian Economy in 2008. Trends and prospects. Moscow: Institute for Economy in Transition, March, available from: www.iet.ru/en/, accessed 17 January 2011.

IET (2010) Russian Economy in 2009. Trends and prospects. Moscow: Institute for Economy in Transition, March, 31, available from: www.iet.ru/en/, accessed 17 January 2011.

Interview AE (2010) Interview Avtoelektronika, in Glazunov, M., *Accounting for Privatisation and Transformation in Russia 1990–2007*, Appendix Avtoelektronika. Unpublished Doctoral Dissertation, University of Hertfordshire.

Interview APPM (2010) Interview APPM, in Glazunov, M., *Accounting for Privatisation and Transformation in Russia 1990–2007*, Appendix APPM. Unpublished Doctoral Dissertation, University of Hertfordshire.

Interview Avtovaz (2010) Interview Avtovaz, in Glazunov, M., *Accounting for Privatisation and Transformation in Russia 1990–2007*, Appendix Avtovaz. Unpublished Doctoral Dissertation, University of Hertfordshire.

Interview KPC (2010) Interview KPC, in Glazunov, M., *Accounting for Privatisation and Transformation in Russia 1990–2007*, Appendix KPC. Unpublished Doctoral Dissertation, University of Hertfordshire.

Interview Nornickel (2010) Interview Nornickel, in Glazunov, M., *Accounting for Privatisation and Transformation in Russia 1990–2007*, Appendix Avtovaz. Unpublished Doctoral Dissertation, University of Hertfordshire.

Ilim Pulp (2006) Perspective on the forest industry of the Irkutsk region and investment projects of Ilim-Pulp, available from: www.ilimpulp.ru, accessed 17 January 2010.

Illarionov, A. (2008) Fighting Financial Fires With Blini. *The Moscow Times,* 3 October, available from: www.cato.org/pub_display.php?pub_id=9690/, accessed 17 January 2011.

Indexmundi (2011) Commodity Price Index. Indexmundi 2011, available from: www.indexm undi.com/commodities/?commodity=commodity-price-index&months/, accessed 17 January 2011.

Jensen, M. C. and Meckling, W. H. (1976) 'Theory of the Firm: Managerial Behavior, Agency Costs and Ownership Structure', *Journal of Financial Economics*, October, 3 (4): 305–360.

Joppe, M. (2000) *The Research Process*, available from: www.ryerson.ca/mjoppe, accessed 17 January 2010.

Johnson, G., Scholes, K. and Whittington, R. (2005) *Exploring Corporate Strategy: Text and Cases* (seventh edition), Upper Saddle River, NJ: Financial Times/Prentice Hall.

Katsik, D., Smirnov, A. and Panichev V. (2008) The impact finance of large companies into social and economical development of Krasnoiarsk region. Institute of Economic Forecasting of Russian Academy of Sciences (ECFOR), Krasnoiarsk, available from: www.ecfor.ru/pdf.2008/3/07, accessed 17 January 2013.

Kertzer, D. (1988) Politics and Power, New Haven, CT and London: Yale University Press.

Kim, I. and Yelkina, A. (2003) Privatisation in Russia: Its past, present, and future, SAM. *Advanced Management Journal*, 68(1), Winter: 14–21.

KPC AR (1997, 1998, 1999, 2000, 2001, 2002, 2003, 2004, 2005, 2006, 2007, 2008, 2009, 2010, 2011) Kondrovo paper company – Annual Report (Kondrovo bumazhnaja kompanija – Godovoj otchet), Kondrovo.

KPC SR (1997, 1998, 1999, 2000, 2001, 2002, 2003, 2004, 2005, 2007, 2008) Kondrovo paper company – Special Report (Kondrovo bumazhnaja kompanija – special'nyj otchet), Code emission : 00002-A Kondrovo.

Kornai, J. (1988) 'Individual Freedom and Reform of the Socialist Economy,' *European Economic Rev*ue, 32: 233–267.

Kozarzevsky, P. and Rakova, E. (1999) *Privatisation and restructuring of the enterprises in the CIS countries*. Moscow: Institute of privatisation and management.

KPMG (2005) *IFRS compared to Russian GAAP*, available from: www.kpmg.ru accessed 17 January 2010.

Krichevsky, N. (2009) *Postpikalevskaya Russian: new policy – economic reality* (Post-pikalevskaya rossiya: novaya politiko-ekonomicheskaya ryeal′nost′), Moscow, available from: www.krichevsky.ru/index.php?option=com_content&task=view&id=795/, accessed 17 January 2011.

Kudrin, A. (2009) The global financial crisis and its impact on Russia (Mirovoĭ finansovyĭ krizis i yego vliyanie na Rossiyu) *Voprosy Ekonomiki*, №1: 9–27.

Kumar, R. and Chadee, D. (2002) *International Competitiveness of Asian Firms: An Analytical Framework*. Asian Development Bank, ERD working paper series, 4.

La Porta, R., López-de-Silanes, F., Shleifer, A. and Vishny, R. (1999) The Quality of Government. *Journal of Law, Economics and Organization*, 15: 222–279.

Lazareva, O., Rachinsky, A. and Stepanov, S. (2007) A Survey of Corporate Governance in Russia. Working Papers, w0103, Moscow: Center for Economic and Financial Research (CEFIR).

Liebman, A. (2003) Methodological and information aspects of the agency problems: decision in corporate governance. (Metodologicheskie i informatsionnye aspekty resheniya agent skoĭ problemy v upravlenii korporatsiyeĭ). Doctoral dissertation. St. Petersburg.

López-De-Silanes, F. (1993) A Macro Perspective on Privatisation: The Mexican Program. John F. Kennedy School of Government, Faculty Research Working Paper, Series R96–12, Harvard University, Cambridge, MA.

Loveridge, S. (2000) Introduction to Regional Science, in: *The Web Book of Regional Science*. Morgantown, WV: Regional Research Institute, West Virginia University, available from: www.rri.wvu.edu/loveridgeintroregsci.htm, accessed 17 January 2010.

Marangos, J. (2003) *Alternative Economic Models of Transition*. Burlington, VT: Ashgate.

Marangos, J. (2004) Modelling the Privatization Process in Transition Economies, *Oxford Development Studies*, 32(4), December, Oxford: International Development Centre.

Martin, S. and Parker, D. (1997) *The Impact of Privatization: Ownership and Corporate Performance in the UK*. London: Routledge.

Mau, V. (2000) *Russian Economic Reforms as Seen by an Insider: Success or Failure?*, London: Royal Institute of International Affairs.

Mau, V. (2005) *From crisis to growth*. New Series, 21, February. Moscow: The Centre for Research into Communist Economies (CRCE).

Mau, V. (2009) The Global Crisis As Seen from Russia. *Russia in Global Affairs*, 7 (1), January–March, available from: http://eng.globalaffairs.ru/number/n12541, accessed 17 January 2013.

Medova, E. and Tischenko, L. (2006) *Lawless Privatization?* Cambridge: Centre for Financial Research, Judge Business School, University of Cambridge, available from: www.cfap.jbs.cam.ac.uk/publications/files/WP%2029.pdf, accessed 17 January 2010.

Medvedev, D. (2009) Russia, Forward! (Rossiya, vperyod!). Kremlin.ru, 10 September 10, available from: http://news.kremlin.ru/news/5413, accessed 7 June 2010.

Megginson, W. L. (2005) *The Financial Economics of Privatisation*. Oxford: Oxford University Press.

Megginson, W. L. and Netter, J. (2001) From State to Market: A Survey of Empirical Studies on Privatisation. *Journal of Economic Literature*, XXXIX June: 321–389.

Merton, R. K. (1968) *Social Theory and Social Structure*. New York: The Press.

Mikhailov, A. (2011) Give the country a chance (Daĭte strane shans). Gazeta.ru 03.30.2011, available from: www.gazeta.ru, accessed 17 January 2010.

Mineconom (2009) *About socio-economic development of the Russian Federation in 2008*. Moscow: Ministry of Economic Development of the Russian Federation, available from: www.economy.gov.ru/minec/activity/sections/macro/monitoring/doc1 233928471437/, accessed 17 January 2011.

Morozov, A. (2000) *Survey of Illegal Forest Felling Activities in Russia*. Moscow: Greenpeace Russia, available from: www.forest.ru/rus/publications/rfe/08.html, accessed 4 November 2008.

Moran, P. (2005) Structural vs. relational embeddedness: social capital and managerial performance. *Strategic Management Journal*, 26: 1129–1151.

Morrow, P. and Muchinskly, P. (1980) Middle range theory: An overview and assessment for organisational research, in Pinder, C. and Moore, L. (eds) *Middle range theory and the study of organisations*, Hingham, MA: Martinus Nijoff Publishing.

Nacles (2012) *Dynamics of production of timber products in Russia during 2005–10* (Dinamika proizvodstva lesopromyshlennoĭ produktsii v Rossii za 2005–10 gody). Moscow: The National Forestry Agency, available from: www.nacles.ru/poleznaja-informacija/statistika-lpk/rossija/, accessed 17 January 2011.

Navalny, A. (2011) When Putin will leave (Kogda uĭdet Putin), 11 April, available from: www.svobodanews.ru/content/article/3550209, accessed 17 January 2010.

Nemtsov, B. and Milov, V. (2008) *Independent expert report 'Putin. Results'* (Nezavisimyĭ ekspertnyĭ doklad 'Putin. Itogi'), Moscow: Novaya Gazeta.

Nornickel AR (1996, 1997, 1998, 1999, 2000, 2001, 2002, 2003, 2004, 2005, 2006, 2007, 2008, 2009, 2010, 2011) Norilsk Nickel. Annual Report, available from: www. nornickel.ru, accessed 17 May 2012.

North, D.C. (1992) Institutions, Institutional Change and Economic Performance, Cambridge: Cambridge University Press.

Nosenko, E. (2011) Norilsk Nickel: 'reinsurance' with the release. (Nornikel': 'perestrakhovka' s vykhodom) *Moscow Post*, available from: http://moscow-post.ru/economics/001299822033694//, accessed 17 January 2011.

Norilsk (2008) Norilsk Weather, Norilsk Russia, Norilsk, available from: www.norilskrussia.net/norilsk-weather, accessed 17 January 2010.

OGK-3 (2008) *The acquisition of OAO 'WGC-3' from the company Jarford Enterprises Inc. 25% minus 1 share of the share capital of the Company 'Rusia Petroleum'* (Sdelka po priobreteniyu OAO 'OGK-3' u kompanii Jarford Enterprises Inc. 25% minus 1 aktsiya ot ustavnogo kapitala OAO Kompaniya 'RUSIA Petrolyeum'). OGK-3, available from: www.ogk3.ru/ru-material_fact, accessed 17 January 2011.

Paliy, V. and Sokolov, I. (1988) *Theory of Accounting* (Teorija buhgalterskogo ucheta). Moscow: Finansy i statistika.

Patton, M. (1990) *Qualitative Evaluation and Research Methods* (second edition). Newbury Park, CA: Sage Publications, Inc.

Pleshanov, L. (ed.) (2001) *AvtoVAZ at the turn of the century* (AvtoVAZ na rubezhe vekov). Togliatti: Nika.

Polterovich, V. (2005) The management for reformers: some conclusions from the theory of economic reforms. *The Economic science modern Russia*, № 1(28): 7–24.

Polynko, M. (2011) Fake ore 'Norilsk Nickel' (Poddel'nye ruda 'Noril'skiĭ nikelya') *Moscow Post*, available from: http://moscow-post.ru/economics/001299662685967/, accessed 17 January 2011.

Porter, M. E. (1980) *Competitive strategy: techniques for analysing industries*. New York: Free Press.

Porter, M. E. (1985) *Competitive Advantage*. New York: Free Press.

Privatisation in figures (1994) *Rossiiskaya gazeta*, 27 January. Moscow.

PSA Peugeot Citroën (2007) *PSA Peugeot Citroën to Build Plant in Kaluga*. PSA Peugeot Citroën press release, Kaluga (Russia), 12 December, available at: www.psa-peugeot-citroen.com, accessed 17 January 2010.

Puffer, S., McCarthy, D. and Naumov, A. (2000) *The Russian capitalist experiment*. Cheltenham: Edward Elgar Publishing Limited.

Putin, V. (2008) Prime Minister Vladimir Putin held a meeting with KPRF deputies in the State Duma. The official site of the Prime Minister of the Russian Federation, 9 October, available from: http://premier.gov.ru/eng/events/news/2091//, accessed 17 January 2011.

Putin, V. (2012) Economic tasks. Government of the Russian federation. 30 January, available from: http://premier.gov.ru/eng/events/news/17888//, accessed 17 January 2011.

PWC (2006) Experience of Privatisation in the UK. Briefing Note, available from: www.pwc, accessed 17 January 2010.

Radaev, V. (2000) Return of the Crowds and Rationality of Action: A History of Russian 'Financial Bubbles' in the mid-1990s, *European Societies*, 2(3): 271–294.

Radygin, A. (1995) Privatisation in Russia: Hard Choice, First Results, New Targets. London: CRCE-The Jarvis Print Group.

Radygin, A. (1996) *Residual divestiture following mass privatisation: The case of Russia* (Ostatochnaja razgosudarstvlenija posle massovoj privatizacii: sluchaj Rossii). Moscow: RGAE F. 398.1 Д. 5546. P.104.

Rappaport, R. (1999) Ritual and Religion in the Making of Humanity. New York: Cambridge University Press.

RISI (2007) *World Pulp*. Annual Historical Data, Risi, available from: www.risiinfo.com, accessed 17 January 2010.

RISI (2010) European Pulp and Paper Outlook Conference RISI: analysis of the European pulp and paper industry. 9–11 March, Amsterdam, available from: www.iet.ru/en/, accessed 17 January 2011.

Rockart, J. F. (1979) 'Chief executives define their own data needs', *Harvard Business Review*, 57(2): 81–93.

Rosen, S. (2000), *Nihilism: A Philosophical Essay*, second edition. South Bend, IN: St. Augustine's Press.

Rozhkova, M. and Terentyeva, A. (2011) 'Do you mind that I still served in counter-intelligence'. Vladimir Strzhalkovsky, General Director of Norilsk Nickel ('Vy uchityvaĭte, chto ya vse-taki v kontrrazvedke sluzhil', Vladimir Strzhalkovskiĭ, general'nyĭ direktor Noril'skogo nikelya). *Vedomosti*, № 61(2827), 7 April, available from: www.vedomosti.ru/library/news/1467017, accessed 17 January 2013.

Rusal (2008a) UC RUSAL repays early a USD 4.5 billion loan to foreign banks. *Press releases*, 5 November, available from: http://rusal.ru/en/press-center/news_details.aspx?id=3294/, accessed 17 January 2011.

Rusal (2008b) UC RUSAL on the financial condition of MMC Norilsk Nickel (OK RUSAL o finansovom sostoyanii GMK Noril'skiĭ nikel). *Press releases*, 14 October, available from: http://rusal.ru/en/press-center/press-releases.aspx?dyncont=3630, accessed 17 January 2011.

Russia in Figures (1995) Statistical Handbook. Moscow: Goscomstat of Russia.

Russia in Figures (1997) Statistical Handbook. Moscow: Goscomstat of Russia.

Russia in Figures (1998) Statistical Handbook. Moscow: Goscomstat of Russia.

Russia in Figures (2000) Statistical Handbook. Moscow: Goscomstat of Russia.

Russia in Figures (2003) Statistical Handbook. Moscow: Goscomstat of Russia.

Russia in Figures (2007) Statistical Handbook. Moscow: Goscomstat of Russia.

Russia in Figures (2010) Basic indicators of organisations by kind of economic activity 'manufacture of transport means and equipment'. *Federal Statistics Agency*, available from: www.gks.ru/bgd/regl/b1012/IssWWW.exe/Stg/d02/14–23.htm, accessed 17 January 2012.

Rutland, P. (1995) Successes and Failures: Privatisation in the Transition Economies, available from: www.nato.int/docu/colloq/1995/95–15.htm#FN4, accessed 17 January 2010.

Samara (2007) Samara Region: Business Card (Samarskaja oblast': Vizitnaja kartochka), available from: www.adm.samara.ru, accessed 17 January 2010.

Saunders, M., Lewis, P. and Thornhill, A. (2007) *Research Method and Methodology in Finance and Accounting*, London: FT Prentice Hall.

Severtsev, N. (2012) Dioxide "Strzhalkovsky" (Dioksid Strzhalkovskogo). *Moscow Post*, available from: www.moscow-post.ru/economics/dioksid_strzhalkovskogo8957/, accessed 17 January 2011.

Shapiro, C. and Willig, R. (1990) Economic Rationales for the Scope of Privatisation. *Economy of Public Sector Reform and Privatisation*. London: Westview Press.

Shavrin, A. (1996) *VAZ: Pages of History: Memoir and Facts. Book 2. (April 1974– April 1991)* (VAZ: stranitsy istorii. vospominaniya i fakty. Kniga 2. (aprel' 1974 – aprel' 1991). Tolyatti: Avtovaz.

Shavrin, A. (1998) *VAZ: Pages of History: Memoir and Facts. Book 3. (January 1991 – October 1997)* (VAZ: stranitsy istorii. vospominaniya i fakty. Kniga 3. (yanvar' 1991 – oktyabr' 1997). Tolyatti: Avtovaz.

Sheshinski, E. and López-Calva, L. F. (1999) Privatisation and its Benefits: Theory and Evidence. HIID Development Discussion Paper 698, Cambridge, MA: Harvard University.

Shevtsova, L. (2012) Sham modernization (Pritvornaya modernizatsiya), Gazeta.ru, 3 May, available from: http://www.gazeta.ru/comments/2012/05/03/4570813.shtml/, accessed 17 January 2011.

Shleifer, A. and Vishny, R. (1996) A Theory of Privatisation. *Economic Journal*, 106: 309–319.

Shleifer, A. and Vishny, R. (1998) *The Grabbing Hand: Government Pathologies and Their Cures*. Cambridge, MA: Harvard University Press.

Soldatov, A. (2002) Gangster city on Volga (Bandograd on Volga). *Russian businessman*, no. 7, 6 September, Moscow, available from: http://www.ruspred.ru/arh/05/22rr. html, accessed 17 January 2010.

Sologub, A. (2004) Basel targeted APPM (Bazel celit ACBK), available from: www. rosbalt.ru, accessed 17 January 2010.

Sorokin, A. (2000) *Dossier of Sorokin, about mortgaging auction of 1995 and its result* (Dos'e Sorokin, o zalogovyh aukcionah 1995 goda i ego rezul'tat). FBI, available from: www.flb.ru, accessed 17 January 2010.

Stake, R. E. (2005) Qualitative case studies, in Denzin, N. and Lincoln, Y. (eds), *The Sage handbook of qualitative research*, third edition. Thousand Oaks, CA: Sage, 443–466.

Stiglitz, J. (1999) Whither reform? Ten years of the transition. A paper presented at the World Bank Annual Bank Conference on Development Economics (April 28–29), Washington, DC.

Stiglitz, J. and Ellerman, D. (2000) New Bridges Across the Chasm: Macro- and Micro-Strategies for Russia and other Transitional Economies. *Zagreb International Review of Economics and Business*, 3(1): 41–72.

Summers, L. (1992) The next decade in Central and Eastern Europe, in: Clague, C. and Rausser, G. C. (eds) *The Emergence of Market Economies in Eastern Europe*, Cambridge, MA and Oxford: Blackwell: 25–34.

Surgutneftegas (2008) Open joint stock company Surgutneftegas. Annual report 2008, Surgut, available from: www.surgutneftegas.ru/en/investors/reports, accessed 17 January 2011.

Tache, I, and Lixandroiu, D. (2006) Rent seeking behaviour in transition countries: the case of Romania. *International Advances in Economic Research*, available from: www.entrepreneur.com/tradejournals/, accessed 28 February 2013.

The Russian Legislation (1995) The Decree 1535 Basic Guidelines of the State Program of Privatisation of the State and Municipal Enterprises in the Russian Federation after July 1 1994 (Osnovnye napravlenija Gosudarstvennoj programmy privatizacii gosudarstvennyh i municipal'nyh predprijatij v Rossii posle 1 ijulja 1994 goda), Moscow: The Russian Legislation.

Tian (2000) State Shareholding and Corporate Performance: A Study of a Unique Chinese Data. Working paper, London: London Business School.

Tibar, A. (2002) Critical Success Factors and information needs in Estonian industry. *Information Research*, 7(4) July, Tallinn. Technical University Library Tallinn, Estonia, available from: http://informationr.net/ir/7-4/paper138.html, accessed 17 January 2011.

Trefil, J., Kett, J. F. and Hirsch, E. D. (2002) *The New Dictionary of Cultural Literacy: What Every American Needs to Know* (third edition). Boston, MA: Houghton Mifflin Harcourt.

Trifonov, V. (1998) How Avtovaz was shared (Kak AvtoVAZ byl razdeljon). *FLB*, available from: www.flb.ru, accessed 17 January 2010.

Uzzi, B. (1996) The sources and consequences of embeddedness for the economic performance of organisations. *American Sociological Review*, 61: 674–698.

Vickers, J. and Yarrow, G. (1988) *Privatisation: An economic analysis*. Cambridge, MA: MIT Press.

Vorontsov, S. (2011) High theft of money (Vysokovol'tnoe vorovstvo deneg) *Moscow Post*, 5 May, available from: http://moscow-post.ru/economics/000129931751443, accessed 28 February 2013.

Whibley, L. (1971) *Greek oligarchies; their character and organisation*. New York: Haskell House Publishers.

Williamson, J. (1989) What Washington Means by Policy Reform, in: Williamson, J. (ed.) *Latin American Readjustment: How Much has Happened*, Washington, DC: Institute for International Economics.

World Bank (2008) *Russian Economic Report No.17*. World Bank, November, available from: www.worldbank.org.ru/, accessed 17 January 2011.

Yin, R. (2003) *Case study research: Design and Methods*. Thousand Oaks, CA: SAGE Publications.

Index

For Product Safety Concerns and Information please contact our EU
representative GPSR@taylorandfrancis.com Taylor & Francis Verlag GmbH,
Kaufingerstraße 24, 80331 München, Germany

Printed and bound by CPI Group (UK) Ltd, Croydon, CR0 4YY
08/05/2025
01864413-0001